INNOVATION AND ITS DISCONTENTS

INNOVATION AND ITS DISCONTENTS

How Our Broken Patent System Is

Endangering Innovation and Progress,

and What to Do about It

With a new preface by the authors

Adam B. Jaffe and Josh Lerner

PRINCETON UNIVERSITY PRESS   PRINCETON AND OXFORD

Copyright © 2004 by Princeton University Press
Published by Princeton University Press, 41 William Street,
Princeton, New Jersey 08540
In the United Kingdom: Princeton University Press,
3 Market Place, Woodstock, Oxfordshire OX20 1SY
All Rights Reserved

Third printing, and first paperback printing, with a new preface
by the authors, 2007
Paperback ISBN-13: 978-0-691-12794-1
Paperback ISBN-10: 0-691-12794-8

*The Library of Congress has cataloged the cloth edition of this book
as follows*

Jaffe, Adam B.
Innovation and its discontents / how our broken patent system is
endangering innovation and progress, and what to do about it /
Adam B. Jaffe and Josh Lerner.
p. cm.
Includes bibliographical references and index.
ISBN 0-691-11725-X (cloth : alk. paper)
1. Patent practice—Economic aspects—United States. 2. Patents—
United States. 3. Technological innovations—United States.
I. Lerner, Josh. II. Title.
KF120.J34 2004
346.7304′86—dc22   2004044250

British Library Cataloging-in-Publication Data is available

This book has been composed in Galliard, News Gothic Family,
and ITC Kabel Family Display

Printed on acid-free paper. ∞

pup.princeton.edu

Printed in the United States of America

10 9 8 7 6 5 4 3

To Pam

To Frog and Jamie

Contents

Preface to the Paperback Edition

We wrote this book because patent policy in the United States has gotten seriously off the rails, in ways that endanger the long-term well-being of our citizens. The complexity and political obscurity of the subject had precluded widespread informed debate of the issues. And with the exception of fleeting controversies over a few patents on drugs or aspects of the Internet, business people and others concerned with economic policy seemed to pay little attention to patents.

Since we wrote *Innovation and Its Discontents*, there has been some modest progress in this regard. The U.S. Federal Trade Commission and the National Academy of Sciences have issued reports calling for reform of patent policy. In the summer of 2005, the Subcommittee on Courts, the Internet, and Intellectual Property of the House Judiciary Committee drafted legislation that would make major changes in how patents are awarded and litigated. And a number of major business and industry associations have gone on record as supporting various aspects of reform. Although there remain significant disagreements about what shape reform should take, the debate does appear to have become both more engaged and more substantive.

More recently, several important and high-profile patent cases drew industry and media attention and provoked wider reaction among the millions potentially affected. Patent disputes threatened to shut down first the ubiquitous BlackBerry wireless e-mail device and then the "Buy-It-Now" feature of eBay online auctions. In the first case, Research In Motion, the company that sells the Black-Berry, agreed to pay a $612 million "ransom," even though the U.S. Patent and Trademark Office had already indicated that it was likely to conclude soon that the patents BlackBerry was accused of infringing were not even valid. In the eBay case, the U.S. Supreme Court issued a ruling attempting to clarify the circumstances under which a patent holder can shut down a competitor, and sent the case back to the lower courts to resolve. (Most observers are skeptical as to whether the new rules are any clearer than the old ones.) And as of this writing, the Supreme Court, under the leadership of Chief Justice John Roberts, seems poised, over the course of the next judicial term, to rule on a number of important cases that will potentially affect the workings of the patent system. The most impactful of these is likely to be the case of *KSR International v. Teleflex*, which the Court has agreed to hear and which raises substantial questions as to whether the bar for an "obvious" invention is set too low.

We applaud the greater attention that policy makers and the general public have been giving to patent policy in the last year or so. Yet in many cases observers are still drawing the wrong conclusions about what needs to be fixed to get the system on the right track. Many have concluded that certain kinds of technology, such as Internet business methods or biotech drugs, should not be patentable. Or they have demonized certain firms for ruthlessly enforcing patents "instead of" concentrating on making and selling products.

But the problem with the patent system is neither that it doesn't fit certain technologies nor that certain kinds of firms should not be allowed to enforce patents. The problem is that the system that we use for determining who should get a patent in the first place is not sufficient. While no patent system will ever be perfect, the technology world today is awash in patents that should not have been granted in the first place, because they either are not new ideas, are overly broad, or did not sufficiently flesh out the invention at issue to deserve patent protection.

Innovation and Its Discontents provides a substantive basis for deciding how the system needs to change—for how the U.S. Patent and Trademark Office can stop granting bad patents that gum up the United States' innovation system and slow the speed of business. The book is explicitly designed to help business people, policy makers, and others who care about innovation in the economy to understand how patent policy and patent practice affect innovation and economic growth. The undesirable manifestations of current policy can be understood as the inevitable consequences of inventors, their attorneys, and competing firms' exploitation of the incentives that changes in policy and practice over the last two decades have inadvertently created. Once the book documents how we got into the current mess, it discusses ways to fix the problems. In particular, we argue for reducing the incentives to file bogus patent applications and then use them to threaten litigation, and for increasing the incentives for parties to bring information bearing on the validity of disputed patents to the patent office so that these disputes can be resolved at an earlier, less expensive, and less risky stage. Without such fundamental changes to the incentives of inventors and their representatives, efforts at reform are likely to be fruitless.

Adam Jaffe and Josh Lerner
July 2006

Preface

The origins of this book lie in our research over the past two decades. In some cases, we have used the patent system to understand other things (for example, how knowledge flows across firms); in others, we have examined the consequences of the patent system for innovation. We gradually became convinced that there was an important story that had not been adequately explored: how the patent system has changed over the past two decades, and the impact these shifts are having on innovation and growth. *Innovation and Its Discontents* tells this story.

A natural question—one we asked ourselves—is why two economists should write such a book, rather than leaving it to patent lawyers. Were this an esoteric treatise on patent law, it would certainly be inappropriate for us to be authors. But this is a very different book. Our major focus is on how the incentives provided by the patent law have affected behavior: of firms seeking patent protection, of lawyers and judges adjudicating patent cases, and of the patent officials. These types of analyses are at the heart of modern economic inquiry. Moreover, by focusing on how the incentives of the people involved can be changed to encourage more desirable behavior, we not only come to understand what has gone wrong with the patent system, but we identify how the system needs to be changed to make it support and enhance innovation.

Economic analysis of public policy is ultimately about the satisfaction of human needs and desires—for longer, healthier lives; for comfort, entertainment and education; for a healthier natural environment; and so on. The ability of our social/economic system to deliver these needs and wants is affected by many, many factors, from tax policy to our education system. But it is the overwhelming conclusion of a half-century of economic and historical research that—in the long run—the single biggest factor determining the rate at which a society improves its ability to deliver these wants and needs is technological innovation. The patent system is a crucial cog in the innovation machine. Our hope in writing this book is to stimulate informed debate on how to repair that component so that the innovation machine will be a driver of our prosperity in the years to come.

In writing this book, we have relied on help from a number of people. Adrienne Camire, Keeley Lebwohl, and Chenling Zhang helped us with researching the stories and statistics presented here. Marianne D'Amico helped us with the process in many ways. Several fellow scholars generously shared data or insights with us, especially Dominique Guellec, Bronwyn Hall, Brian Kahin, Mark Lemley, Doug Lichtman, and Kimberly Moore. Robert Benson, Jonathan Jaffe, Sonia Jaffe, Michael Jorgensen, Pam Jorgensen, Ralph Lerner, and Helen Winslow provided feedback on the draft manuscript. A number of lawyers in private practice, especially Steve Bauer of Proskauer Rose, Paul Clark of Clark & Elbing, and Sam Petuchowshi of Bromberg & Sunstein, took time out from their very hectic schedules to discuss ideas with us and to comment on our manuscript. None of these people should be held responsible for any of the ideas expressed herein; discussion sharpened the issues but did not necessarily lead to agreement. Harvard Business School's Division of Research provided financial support.

Barbara Rifkin played a vital role in helping us to take a conception of a project to completion of a book of a sort that neither of us had written before. Our editor, Peter Dougherty, was also critical in helping us turn a collection of ideas, stories, and statistics into a finished manuscript. Finally, the spirit of our mentor and teacher, Zvi Griliches, lives on in this volume. Though Zvi's untimely death deprived us of the trenchant and penetrating criticism that he no doubt would have made, we hope that his belief that rigorous analysis is the backbone of policy prescription is reflected in these pages.

They Fixed It, and Now It's Broke

ver the course of the nineteenth and twentieth centuries, the United States evolved from a colonial backwater to become the pre-eminent economic and technological power of the world. The foundation of this evolution was the systematic exploitation and application of technology to economic problems: initially agriculture, transportation, communication, and the manufacture of goods, and then later health care, information technology, and virtually every aspect of modern life.

From the beginning of the republic, the patent system has played a key role in this evolution. It provided economic rewards as an incentive to invention, creating a somewhat protected economic environment in which innovators can nurture and develop their creations into commercially viable products. Based in the Constitution itself, and codified in roughly its modern form in 1836, the patent system was an essential aspect of the legal framework in which inventions from Edison's light bulb and the Wright brothers' airplane to the cell phone and Prozac were developed.

Beginning in 1982, the U.S. Congress made two adjustments to how the patent system operates. At the time, these changes were described as administrative and procedural rather than substantive. In 1982, the process for judicial appeal of patent cases in the federal courts was changed, so that such appeals are now all heard by a single, specialized appeals court, rather than the twelve regional courts of appeal, as had previously been the case. And in the early 1990s, Congress changed the structure of fees and financing of the U.S. Patent and Trademark Office (PTO) itself, trying to turn it into a kind of service agency whose costs of operation are covered by fees paid by its clients (the patent applicants).

It is now apparent that these seemingly mundane procedural changes, taken together, have resulted in the most profound changes in U.S. patent policy and practice since 1836. The new court of appeals has interpreted patent law to make it easer to get patents, easier to enforce patents against others, easier to get large financial awards from such enforcement, and harder for those accused of infringing patents to challenge the patents' validity. At roughly the same time, the new orientation of the patent office has combined with the court's legal interpretations to make it much easier to get patents. However complex the origins and motivations of these two Congressional actions, it is clear that no one sat down and decided that what the U.S. economy needed was to transform patents into much more potent legal weapons, while simultaneously making them much easier to get.

An unforeseen outcome has been an alarming growth in legal wrangling over patents. More worrisome still, the risk of being sued, and demands by patent holders for royalty payments to avoid being sued, are seen increasingly as major costs of bringing new products and processes to market. Thus, the patent system—intended to foster and protect innovation—is generating waste and uncertainty that hinders and threatens the innovative process. In the chapters that follow, we will see many examples of these issues:

- Patents on inventions that are trivially obvious, such as the "Method for Swinging on a Swing," "invented" by a five-year-old (see chapter 1).
- Patents that have become weapons for firms to harass competitors, ranging from Rambus' efforts to exploit a semiconductor industry

standard-setting body to Smucker's steps to quash a small-time lunch caterer (see chapters 1 and 2).

- Patents that enabled companies to win huge damages awards, and even put rivals out of business, such as Polaroid's instant photography patents (see chapter 4).
- Patents in areas new to patenting, but covering purported discoveries familiar to practitioners and academics alike, such as the patents on previously well-known option pricing formulas (see chapter 5).

We will see that a tension between rewarding some innovators while potentially inhibiting the activities of others is inherent in the patent system. As we will discuss in chapter 3, there have been previous "crises," in which the patent system was seen to be dangerously out of control. But what is striking about the current situation is the clear connection between the system's pathologies and recent, seemingly innocent statutory changes. The impact of these shifts has been especially extreme in technologies that are believed to be key to current economic development, including electronics, software, and biotechnology. Approximately two decades after Congress began tinkering with the system, it is now urgent that we analyze what has gone wrong, and determine how to fix it.

It Is Not a Pretty Picture

A patent is a government-granted right to prevent other people or companies from making, selling, or using a product or process that you have invented. To get a patent, you have to file an application that explains your invention, and details how it differs from what others have done before. The government reviews the application, and (if things are working right) grants you the patent only if your invention is genuinely new. With patent in hand, you can stop others from using your invention, or you can allow others to pay you for the right to use it. If others use it without your permission, you can sue them in federal court, asking the court to make them stop, and to make them pay for the uses they have already made. The party you accused of "infringing" your patent will typically claim that what they are doing is not covered by your patent, and that your patent never should have been granted in the first place because your idea was not new. Unless you reach a voluntary settlement, a jury will decide whether the patent is indeed valid, and whether it has been infringed. As you might guess, resolving patent cases in court is an expensive proposition, often involving millions of dollars in attorneys' fees and other costs. (A more thorough and precise explanation of the patent process is presented in chapter 1.)

The previous paragraph describes the patent system today, and it describes the patent system as it was before 1982. What has changed is the likelihood that the various parties will succeed at different points in the process. Today, the applicant is much more likely to have the patent granted; the patent is much more likely to be held valid if challenged in court; and the party accused of violating the patent is more likely to be found to be an infringer and forced to pay a large monetary award.

What catalyzed these shifts? The 1980s were a time of great concern about U.S. "competitiveness," as well as a general movement to shrink government and make it more efficient and responsive. Streamlining the courts would make valid patents easier to enforce. Making the PTO run more like a business would make the process easier for inventors to use, and would also save the taxpayers money because the office would be supported by application fees rather than taxes.

These intentions may be admirable, but they have spawned some highly undesirable consequences. Many people and companies have received patents for trivial or even non-existent inventions. Moreover, many awardees have exploited the enhanced legal strength of their patents by suing (or threatening to sue) the true innovators in their industries. As a result, valuable technologies have become snarled in a web of litigation and licensing negotiations. And as young firms have found themselves unable to commercialize their ideas, economic growth has suffered. Consumers therefore have less access to new products—from lifesaving drugs to productivity-enhancing software—than would be the case if innovative companies were not distracted from innovation by litigation and fear of litigation.

How did it come to pass that these administrative and legal changes—which seemed benign when enacted—exerted such surprisingly damaging effects? Most analyses of the patent system are based on an idealized conception of that system. According to this conception, Congress establishes rules regarding which discoveries qualify for a patent, and how the rights conveyed by a patent may be enforced. The patent office and the courts simply apply and enforce these statutory rules. From this perspective, it is easy to argue that streamlining the patent process and making it easier for inventors to enforce their right to protection in the courts enhances a nation's overall innovation, creativity, and economic growth.

In practice, however, life is more complicated. Patenting rules are inherently ambiguous, and so actual patent practice depends on the decisions of the patent office. Changing the way that office is organized and funded alters its incentives; with different incentives, it produces different decisions, causing patent practice to change without any Congressional action to change the law. Similarly, the court's decisions have a tremendous effect on how the laws written by Congress are interpreted, and the composition of the court affects the kind of decisions it makes. Further, the impact of patent litigation goes far beyond the cases that are actually heard by the courts. Fear of litigation, along with threats made by patent holders, prompt some firms to sharply shift their behavior, even if these companies never appear in court. The accumulation of fees paid for the use of multiple patents makes the product development process more expensive, limiting the rate at which companies can bring new products to market. And some companies, given the choice of paying royalties or facing litigation on as-yet unproven new products, may simply drop the project altogether.

Thus, in changing administrative structures and procedures, Congress fundamentally altered the nature of substantive decisions about which patents should be granted, and which ones should be successfully enforced in court. This, in turn, has changed the behavior of inventors and firms that participate in the process. Now that it is possible to get a patent on unoriginal ideas, many more dubious applications are being filed. And with success now more likely for patent holders who sue their competitors, more such suits are filed or threatened. Increasingly, the firm with the best lawyers or the greatest capacity to withstand the risk of litigation wins the innovation wars—rather than the company with the brightest scientists or most original, valuable ideas.

Though controversies regarding particular patents have attracted the business media's attention, the fundamental changes in patent policy and their systemic implications have received little scrutiny. This book addresses that omission, systematically examining the changes in patenting since 1982 and the resulting implications for business, innovation, and society as a whole. Drawing on the experience of the past two decades, we show the changes that are needed in order to restore a healthy environment for innovation and progress.

Our approach is to analyze how the changes made by Congress have affected the incentives to all participants in the process—patent applicants, the patent office employees who review the applications, and the parties potentially involved in litigation. We show how the current system provides incentives for applicants to file frivolous patent applications, and for the patent office to grant them. It likewise encourages patent holders to sue, and those accused of patent infringement to give in and pay under threat, even if the patent at issue is of dubious validity. It does not provide good incentives for the information necessary to resolve questions about patent validity to be brought forward and analyzed appropriately. As a result, virtually all of the participants in this process, while acting in ways that make perfect sense given the incentives they face, end up collectively behaving in the pathological manner we have described.

By and large, other countries have not made the same kinds of changes in their patent systems that the United States has made. Patents in Europe and Japan remain harder to get and there is less patent litigation. But the problems that have surfaced in America are likely to be of interest far beyond the boundaries of the United States. First, dysfunction in the patent system of the world's largest economy affects innovation everywhere. Second, our basic analysis of how the rules of the patent system interact with the incentives of the people and firms involved is relevant to the improvement of patent systems everywhere, as the same pressures for stronger protection and for reduced examination costs are being felt around the world today.

Why Patents?

Governments have long recognized the broad social value generated by new technologies, and hence have sought to reward inventors of important technologies. In some cases, they have offered prizes to those who solved important problems. In other cases, kings and parliaments have offered subsidies and rewards to those who came up with unexpected discoveries that proved important for commerce and defense.

But at least since the Tyrolean leaders recognized the manufacturers of superior mining equipment in the fourteenth century, the granting of patents has been an important tool to encourage innovation, and the economic growth and improvement in living standards that new technologies provide. The holder of a patent gets the right to exclude others from making a specified product or using a specified process for some period of time. Put another way, a patent is a "negative right": the patent-holder can prevent others from using his or her discovery. A patent thereby creates a kind of monopoly for its owner, although the breadth and hence significance of this monopoly depends on the breadth or extent of the patent grant.

At first, there was little rhyme or reason behind who got patents, or how broad their patent rights were. In many instances, patents were granted to people who did not make any discoveries at all. For instance, among the fifty patents granted by Queen Elizabeth I of England during the sixteenth century were awards that gave their recipients the exclusive right to manufacture and sell such basic materials as salt, sulphur, and paper. Many of these grants of monopolies over entire important industries went to royal favorites. Not surprisingly, these awards triggered widespread popular resentment: in fact, a patent providing exclusive rights to sell wine led to rioting in the streets of London.

By the eighteenth century, however, two guiding principles emerged in Great Britain and elsewhere: that patents should be granted only for new and important discoveries, and that the breadth of the patent grant should be proportional to the size of the discovery made. Inventors were increasingly required to submit descriptions of the discoveries, in which they carefully delineated what was truly new about their inventions. Government officials would then decide whether the discoveries were novel and determine how generous a monopoly they should award. In 1769, for example, James Watt was awarded a patent for his "new method for lessening the consumption of steam and fuel in fire engines," which led over the next several decades to the first industrial applications of the steam engine, thereby initiating the industrial revolution in Great Britain.

The economic logic of granting patent protection to inventors is straightforward. If there were no incentives for those who discover and develop new technology, it is likely that fewer innovations would be developed, slowing progress and the benefits it brings. Potential inventors realize that without adequate protection rivals will rapidly copy their discoveries, and that therefore innovation is at best an uncertain route to future profits. As a result, companies would be unlikely to spend significant amounts of money on the Research and Development (R&D) that is the source of new products and processes in a modern economy. They would instead choose to spend their money pursuing other activities (for example, marketing campaigns) or just pocket it as profit.

Most scholarly analyses of the economic effects of patents assume that the system "works," meaning that the party who is the first to invent a given product or process is the party that is awarded a patent. This analytical construct is embodied in patent law within the idea that a patent cannot be granted unless the patent application is for an invention that is both "novel" and "non-obvious." In practice, these standards depend on the patent office "examiners" who must apply them. How carefully they ensure that only true innovators are awarded patents depends on the incentives they face, the rules under which they operate, and their training and ability. As we will see, an unintended consequence of the redesign of the

Patent Office has been to gravely undermine the Office's application of these standards.

The Silent Revolution

Patents have existed for many centuries. It is surprising, then, that one of the actions that triggered the new era of patent policy was an apparently benign change in U.S. judicial procedure. Almost all formal disputes involving patents are tried in the federal judicial system. The initial litigation must be undertaken in a district court. Prior to 1982, appeals of patent cases were heard in the appellate courts of the various circuits. These differed considerably in their interpretation of patent law, with some circuits being more than twice as likely to uphold patent claims as others. These differences persisted because the Supreme Court, which normally steps in to insure national legal uniformity, rarely heard patent-related cases. The justices were reluctant to devote their time to these "banal" commercial disputes.

The result was widespread "forum shopping" in patent cases. Patent applicants would crowd the hallway in the patent office where the list of patent awards was distributed at noon on each Tuesday. Upon discovering that their patent was issued, they would rush to the pay phones to instruct their lawyers to file suit against some alleged infringer of the newly minted patent, filing the lawsuit in a patent-friendly district court, such as Kansas City. Meanwhile, representatives of firms who might be accused of infringing the issued patent would be racing to the phone bank as well, ordering their lawyers to file a lawsuit seeking to have the new patent declared invalid, but filing in a district known to be skeptical of patents—for example, San Francisco. Such dueling lawsuits would usually be combined into a single action, heard in the district court in which the earliest filing was made. Often the fate of the case—and many millions of dollars in damages—would depend on which lawyer got an earlier date-time stamp on the filing documents.

In 1982, the U.S. Congress decided to address this problem, which was perceived to be undermining the effectiveness of patent protection and thereby threatening U.S. technological and economic strength. It established a centralized appellate court for patent cases, the Court of Appeals for the Federal Circuit (CAFC). The change was presented in the congressional hearings as a benign one, bringing consistency to the chaotic world of patent litigation, and predictability to the enforcement of valid patent rights. But it was clear from the beginning that advocates of stronger patent protection hoped that the new court would come down squarely on the side of patent holders.

And this is precisely what happened. Over the next decade, in case after case, the court significantly broadened and strengthened the rights of patent holders. One illustration is a comparison of the CAFC's rulings with those of the previous courts. The share of cases where a district court finding of patent infringement was upheld increased, as did the share of cases reversing an earlier finding that a patentee was not entitled to damages. Likewise, the CAFC greatly expanded patent-holders' rights along a number of other dimensions, including making it easier to shut down a rival's business even before a patent is proven valid (through a preliminary injunction) and to extract significantly greater damages from infringers.

The consequences of the CAFC's strengthening of the system for enforcing patents have been exacerbated by changes in the behavior of inventors and of the U.S. patent office, which have led to a dramatic increase in both the number of patent applications filed and in the fraction that are successful in producing granted patents. Decisions by the CAFC encouraged more patent applications, for three distinct reasons. First, the CAFC made it clear that the realm of patentable subject matter included technologies like software, business methods, and certain kinds of biotechnology that hitherto were believed by many to be unpatentable. Second, the new court issued rulings on the standards of "novelty" and "non-obviousness" that made it easier for applicants to qualify for a patent. Finally, the improved enforceability of granted patents encouraged patent applications by making the patent right more economically valuable. As a result, the rate of patent application filings in the United States began to increase shortly after the creation of the CAFC.

Just as the tide of patent applications began to rise, Congress intervened once again to modify the patent system. Beginning in the early 1990s, it converted the U.S. patent office from an agency funded by tax revenues, which collected nominal fees for patent applications, into one funded by the fees it collects. In-deed, the patent office has become a "profit center" for the government, collecting more in application fees than it costs to run the agency.

Again, this mere administrative change has had important con-sequences. Increasingly, the PTO views itself as an organization whose mission is to serve patent applicants. And, of course, what applicants want is for their applications to be granted. Furthermore, the new orientation creates strong incentives for the PTO to pro-cess applications as quickly as possible, and at the lowest possible cost. As a result, there is a widely perceived decline in the rigor with which the standards of novelty and non-obviousness are applied in reviewing patent applications. This, in turn, encourages more peo-ple to apply for dubious patents.

The Patent Explosion

Many in the patent community—patent office officials, the patent bar, and corporate patent staff—have welcomed these profound shifts in the U.S. patent system. Then again, they have much to gain from a swelling tide of patent applications.

The weakening of examination standards and the increase in pa-tent applications have led to a dramatic increase in the number of patents granted in the United States. Figure I.1 shows that the number of patents granted in the United States, which increased at less than 1 percent per year from 1930 until 1982 (the year the CAFC was created), roughly tripled between 1983 and 2002 (from 62,000 per year to 177,000 per year, an annual rate of increase of about 5.7 percent). Applications, too, have ballooned, to the point that there are now about 350,000 per year.

If this increase in patenting reflected an explosion in U.S. inven-tiveness, it would be cause for celebration. But unfortunately it is

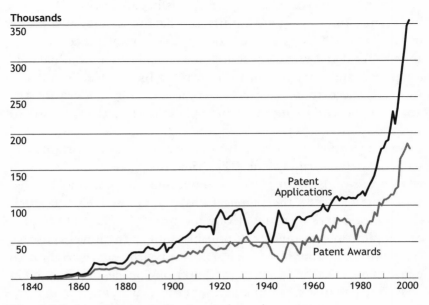

Figure I.1 Annual patent applications and awards.

clear that the rapid increase in the rate of patenting has been accompanied by a proliferation of patent awards of dubious merit. This disturbing trend is confirmed by international comparisons, which show that the number of inventions of U.S.-origin with confirmed worldwide significance grew in the 1990s at a rate less than half that of domestic U.S. patent office grants. It is also confirmed by reference to particular patents granted by the PTO for "inventions" that are not new or are trivially obvious.

Much of the problem stems from the organization of the patent office itself. Chronically strained for resources, patent office officials have struggled to find qualified examiners, particularly in the "new" areas of software, financial methods, and biotechnology where it had not previously had much expertise. As the CAFC opened the door to new kinds of patents, the limited number of examiners in these new areas were overwhelmed with applications. Examiners of financial patents, for example, often had as little as a dozen hours to assess whether a patent application was truly novel.

Moreover, retaining the few examiners skilled in the new technologies has been difficult for the office. Companies have been eager to hire these examiners, who are valuable for their knowledge of the PTO examination procedure in the new technology. Moreover, corporations and law firms can offer examiners many times over the approximately $40,000 starting salaries that the government offers. Needless to say, this federal compensation is far less than market rate, especially for the examiners of business method patent applications, who are typically required to have an engineering degree and an MBA, and often have a law degree as well.

The Patent Litigation Explosion

The proliferation of patents on previously existing technologies would sow confusion and legal uncertainty under the best of circumstances, but it has occurred just as the CAFC has been making it easier to enforce the rights they convey. The predictable result has been a parallel increase in the number of lawsuits fought over patents. Figure I.2 shows that the number of patent lawsuits was roughly constant throughout the 1960s and 1970s, began to rise with the increase in patent awards in the 1980s, and ballooned in the 1990s. As will be described in more detail in chapter 2, burgeoning patent litigation is increasingly making lawyers the key players in competitive struggles rather than entrepreneurs and researchers. As the patent system becomes a distraction from innovation rather than a source of incentive, the engine of technological progress and economic growth begins to labor.

The pernicious consequences of the evolving patent situation can be seen in two broad kinds of competitive and legal interactions. In one scenario, an established firm, frequently one whose competitive position and innovative activity are declining, realizes it has a valuable stockpile of issued patents. This firm then approaches rivals, demanding that they take out licenses to its patents. In many cases,

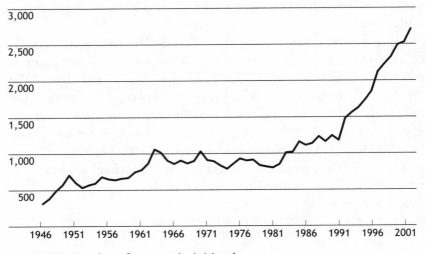

Figure I.2 Number of patent suits initiated.

they will target smaller firms, who do not have extensive financial resources to engage in protracted patent litigation.

Even if the target firm believes that it does not infringe, it may choose to settle rather than fight. The small firm may simply be unable to raise the capital needed to finance a protracted court battle or be unwilling to sacrifice investments in R&D and new facilities to finance the fight. Furthermore, there are substantial indirect costs associated with patent litigation. The pre-trial proceedings and trial are likely to require the alleged infringer to produce extensive documentation and its employees to make time-consuming depositions, and may generate unfavorable publicity. Its officers and directors may also be held individually liable, or be targeted in shareholder lawsuits if the stock price drops.

For numerous large companies—including, notoriously, Digital Equipment, IBM, Texas Instruments, and Wang Laboratories— these types of patent enforcement activities have become a line of business in their own right. These firms have established patent licensing units, which have frequently been successful in extracting license agreements and/or past royalties from smaller rivals. For instance, Texas Instruments has in recent years netted close to $1 billion annually from patent licenses and settlements resulting from its general counsel's aggressive enforcement policy. In some years, revenue from these sources has exceeded net income from product sales.

In addition to being forced to pay royalties, small firms may reduce or alter their investment in R&D. Evidence from surveys and practitioner accounts suggests that the time and expense of intellectual property litigation is a major consideration when deciding whether to pursue an innovation, especially among smaller firms. Smaller firms tend to shy away from pursuing innovations in areas where large firms have established patent portfolios. Thus, these types of enforcement activities by large firms may have the effect of suppressing innovation by younger, more vibrant concerns.

A second worrisome development has been the emergence of individual inventors who seek to "hold up" established firms in their industries. In many cases, these individuals have received a patent of dubious validity, often with overly broad claims. Yet established players have often chosen to settle such disputes, not wishing to risk the uncertainty associated with submitting a complex piece of intellectual property to trial.

Individual inventors will employ various strategies to make the battle more one-sided and drive the large firm to settle the suit. In many cases, the individual inventor will demand a jury trial, and then present himself as engaged in a "David *vs.* Goliath" dispute. He may choose a legal jurisdiction where the residents will be highly unsympathetic to the defendant. For instance, Jerome Lemelson, an individual inventor who claimed to have invented barcoding technology, filed suits against Japanese and Korean firms in the Southern District of Texas. Similarly, individual inventors frequently threaten corporations with the promise that they will obtain a preliminary injunction, which will stop the defendant from using the patented technology even before the trial begins. While an established business might be reluctant to ask for such a drastic measure, lest the other party seek a similar ban against itself, individual inventors often feel no such compunction. Given the uncertainty of the trial process, the defendant firm frequently decides to settle with an individual inventor rather than fight.

In short, the "reforms" of the patent system have created a substantial "innovation tax" that afflicts some of America's most important and creative firms.

The Scale of the Problem

Companies in the United States spend over $100 billion on R&D each year, and billions more obtaining and defending intellectual property protection for their inventions. These expenditures have been growing across almost every industry, from traditional manufacturing to services to high technology.

Indeed, in today's skeptical investment environment, intellectual property is even more important than ever. One lesson from the "dot com" debacle is that firms without a sustainable competitive advantage—such as those nine dueling on-line pet supply retailers—are unlikely to survive. Investors are looking for real yardsticks to evaluate competitive strength. Patents, trademarks, and other forms of intellectual property represent a "currency" that is used increasingly to demonstrate to financial markets, suppliers, and customers that a firm is a strong player, and can be expected to achieve a dominant position.

Though other countries have not imitated the changes made in patent procedures in the United States, they nonetheless face a number of the same issues. Proposals to issue software patents have stirred angry debates in Europe. Programmers using Linux, an "open source" program where developers must eschew intellectual property protection, and which is increasingly challenging proprietary software for servers and devices, have led the opposition. Passionate advocates argue, "software should not have owners." Over 20,000 Linux users protested when the European Community proposed to adopt patent protection for software.

These questions are important not just to the health of the economy, but also to the health of our citizens. For instance, advocates have questioned whether the broad coverage that Utah-based Myriad Genetics enjoys on its breast cancer gene patents is slowing research into curing this dreaded disease. Myriad had played a key role in identifying the two genes that can trigger breast cancer, exploiting the voluminous genealogical records of the Mormon Church to find the critical genetic markers. In recognition for its efforts, Myriad received two patents on diagnostic tests and treatments involving these genes. Myriad then entered into licenses with leading medical schools, universities, and hospitals, giving them the right to research issues related to breast cancer. But these licenses are quite limited in their scope. To cite one example, the licenses are confined to laboratory research, and do not extend to clinical settings. Yet in many earlier cases, critical insights in the treatment of disease emerged from precisely the application of new technologies to the treatment of actual patients. Since the first patent was awarded in December 1997, a number of medical school researchers have been forced to abandon their research programs due to the licensing terms.

Even the normally pro-business Bush administration has raised questions about Bayer's exploitation of its patent on the Cipro antibiotic. At the time of the October 2001 anthrax attacks, advocates pointed out that Bayer was charging the government $1.89 per pill. While this was less than the drugstore price for Cipro (more than $4.50 a tablet), Indian companies were selling generic versions of the drug for less than 20 cents each. Ultimately, the drug company cut the price it charged the government by half—but not before the government initiated plans to license the patent to generic drug manufacturers against Bayer's wishes.

More generally, the continued advancement of commercial technology is the basis for the long-term ability of our society to promote longer and healthier lives, improve living standards for all, protect and clean up the environment, and secure our safety against terrorism and other external threats. For all its warts and periodic stumbles, our capitalist free-enterprise system has demonstrated a unique ability to generate new technology: industrialized economies have increased their economic productivity more in the last two centuries than in all the millennia of previous human history. The basis for this advance is firms' pursuit of profit, which forces them to innovate. But the profit-based incentive to innovate depends fundamentally on the institutions governing ownership of the fruits of innovation. While we have not yet killed the geese that lay the golden eggs, we are increasingly hindering and distracting the people and firms that must breed, feed, and care for the geese. If we continue on this course, it is inevitable that their golden output will decline.

Patent Medicine

We find ourselves where we are today because the institutional changes of the last two decades have altered the incentives of inventors, firms, and the patent office in ways that encourage legal maneuvering and discourage innovation. The solution is to understand how these perverse incentives work, and to modify patent procedures and policy to restore the incentives for socially desirable behavior. That is the goal of this book.

Symptoms and Medical History

We begin in chapter 1, "Today's Patent System at Work," with an overview of how the patent system works, and an analysis of its effects on the incentives for innovation. Innovation in a modern economy requires large investments of time and money by private firms. But the product of this investment is not a tangible thing like a factory, and so is fraught with the risk that it will be destroyed or substantially diminished by competition. Successful innovation always calls forth imitators, making investments in innovation risky and hence potentially undesirable to investors. Patents offer a measure of protection to investments in innovation, and thereby act to foster innovation by mitigating risk. But because innovation is a competitive and cumulative process, it is frequently the case that protecting one party's innovation will threaten another's. Thus, although patent protection is crucial for the innovative process, it is not the case that making patents stronger or easier to get necessarily improves incentives for innovation. Creating good incentives for innovation requires balancing the need for patents to protect innovators, against the inherent risk that strong patents for some will prevent or hinder others from innovating.

Chapter 2, "The Dark Side of Patents," describes the extent to which the current patent system has lost this balance. Patents have become so easy to get, and are enforced so ruthlessly by the courts, that the winners of the technological competition in crucial industries are sometimes those with the best lawyers, or those simply lucky enough to have been awarded a key patent they did not really deserve, rather than those that have created the best products or services. Some firms have embarked on explicit strategies to make their money by collecting patent royalties on existing technologies rather than by developing new technologies, employing, in the words of a federal judge in one important case, "a combination of blitzkrieg and Sherman-esque tactics."

The intense pathology of the current system arises from the combination of stronger patent protection, a decline in the standards for granting patents, and the emergence of broad, apparently invalid, patents in particular industries undergoing rapid technological change. But before developing a treatment plan for the disease, it is useful to understand earlier episodes of related symptoms. Chapter 3, "The Long Debate," reviews the evolution of patent policy over the centuries. The Dutch Parliament's decision to abolish patent protection in 1859 provides a window into the ongoing discussion about these awards. Both within and without the legislature, the writings of economists and lawyers on the optimal degree of patent protection were intensely scrutinized. The arguments raged in the major newspapers, with advocates of patent protection arguing that strong property rights could stimulate investments in research, and skeptics pointing to the distorting effect that patent litigation and the exclusive rights associated with patents could have on innovation. This historical perspective provides valuable inoculation against any illusion that even the best-crafted reform can eliminate conflict and controversy in the patent system.

Diagnosis

With this background, we proceed to an analysis of how and why the changes made in the last two decades got us to where we are. Chapter 4, "The Silent Revolution," shows how the newly created

CAFC has subtly and not so subtly changed the landscape of U.S. patent law. Its decisions have expanded the realm of what can be patented, lowered the standards for receiving a patent, made it more likely that a patent once granted will stand up to legal challenge, and given patent-holders more valuable legal rewards in the form of injunctions against their competitors and juicy monetary awards. The predictable result is that patent holders are more likely to sue their competitors, and the targets of such suits are more likely to capitulate to threats of such litigation.

Chapter 5, "The Slow Starvation," analyzes the "administrative" change of the early 1990s, when Congress moved the patent office to a "pay-as-you-go" basis. Again, little thought was given to how this would affect how the patent office operated and, consequently, the quality of patent review. The office has struggled to respond to the surge of patent applications unleashed by the CAFC's rulings, especially in high-technology industries. Because its "customers" become unhappy if the backlog of unprocessed applications begins to grow, it has set performance targets for its examiners that reward them for granting patents as quickly as possible, with little regard for the care and complexity of claims in these new technologies. To make matters worse, though the idea of increased application fees was initially that users of the office should pay for its operation, Congress has been unable to resist the temptation to view patent office fees as a general source of revenue. Patent office revenues have soared with the rising tide of applications, but year after year Congress has allocated to the patent office for its operations hundreds of millions of dollars less than the fees collected. The patent office has therefore found it difficult to attract and keep highly skilled individuals to do their important work. The result has been a torrent of poorly reviewed patents, pouring out onto a legal landscape in which even trivial patents can be wielded as potent litigation threats.

We are not the first to decry the devolution of the patent system, nor the first to suggest that changes are needed to get it back on track. Chapter 6, "The Patent Reform Quagmire," discusses recent efforts to fix various aspects of the system, and analyzes why these efforts have met with such little success. The reform of patent policy has been exceedingly difficult for the U.S. Congress to address.

Powerful special interests with a stake in the present inefficient system have combined to defeat legislative and administrative attempts to reform patent policy. These challenges might seem no different from any other high-stakes policy issue today. But the complexity and apparent obscurity of these issues have made reform particularly difficult, even by Washington standards. On the rare occasions when legislation concerning the patent system has burst into the public eye, the public discourse has frequently been confused and misleading. For instance, in 1997 Congress proposed to publish patent applications in a bid to limit "submarine" patents that received overly long protection. The effort was abandoned after protests from talk radio commentators, such as G. Gordon Liddy, Oliver North, and Phyllis Schlafly, misleadingly claimed that the move would harm small inventors.

The Prescribed Treatment

Perhaps wise men would fear to tread where they have to take on the likes of Gordon Liddy and Oliver North, but in chapter 7, "Innovation and Its Discontents," we rush in to propose a revamped patent system, designed to maximize the incentives for innovation. While this venture is perhaps immodest, we accept that there cannot be a perfect system, because the conflicts among different innovators are inherent, and the decisions implementing patent rules have to be made by human beings. We therefore take as predicates of a reformed patent system that there will always be patent disputes and mistakes in granting and enforcing patents. Further, in a complex and ever-changing technological world, the information necessary to make the best possible decisions lies in many different places and is expensive to collect. The keys to a better system are therefore to create incentives to maximize the amount of information that different parties bring to the process while minimizing their incentives to use patent processes disruptively. At the same time, it is important to ensure that when mistakes are inevitably made, there is a practical and balanced process for fixing them.

Implementing this broad conception requires fundamental changes in both the patent office and the legal rules for enforcing patents. The patent office has been granting patents on old ideas because it has inadequate examination resources, and also because it is not very good at finding information about the relevant existing technologies, particularly in new, fast-moving technological fields. And when patents are granted on ideas that are not new, other firms have no practical recourse other than the risky and expensive prospect of challenging the patent in federal court. To do better, the PTO needs more resources for its examination process, and procedures revised to give outside parties having relevant information the opportunity and incentive to bring that information to the attention of the patent office. But the rules for such procedures must take into account the likelihood that outsiders will use any such process to try to erect speed bumps in the paths of competitors' valid patent applications.

The best way to conserve the PTO's resources, and bring in outside information in a way that minimizes its disruptive impact on valid applications, is to have a carefully calibrated sequence of escalating review procedures within the patent office itself. Most patents should get only a relatively cursory review, and no one will object to their issuance because they are economically unimportant. But in important cases, competitors who believe they can demonstrate that a proposed patent is not new need opportunities to make that demonstration. We propose the creation of two such opportunities, with both the intensity of scrutiny and the barriers to invoking additional review increasing at each step. This phased approach balances the need to bring in more and better information in important cases against the risk that additional layers of scrutiny will retard truly valid applications.

Procedures designed to bring in more information will reduce the number of mistakes the PTO makes. But such steps will not eliminate mistakes. The process by which such mistakes are addressed in the courts must again involve a balance. On the one hand, innovators with valid patents on truly new ideas must be able to rely on those rights to protect their investment in the new product or process. It is a principle of patent law that once the government issues a patent, the patent holder is entitled to a presumption that the patent is valid, meaning that the burden of proof lies on other parties to demonstrate its invalidity. This principle must be maintained if patents are to play their fundamental role of mitigating the risk inherent in developing new technologies. But for parties that are threatened with legal action on the basis of patents that should not have been granted, the opportunity to demonstrate that invalidity of the patent has to be sufficiently practical to provide a basis for resisting extortion.

Under the rules as interpreted by the CAFC, a finding of invalidity can only be won by convincing a jury of non-technically trained people that there is "clear and convincing evidence" that the patented idea was not really new and significant. This is a game of chance, not an orderly decision-making process, and one in which the patent holder has the status of the casino—the odds stacked in its favor. Difficult technical issues, regarding the relationship between competing inventions, should be resolved by judges and experts appointed by judges before the ultimate issue of patent validity is put to a jury. While the outcome of patent litigation would still be uncertain, the process would at least be structured with the best chance of reaching decisions on a sound technical basis.

Patent Policy Is Too Important to Leave to the Patent Lawyers

When issues of patent policy are considered by the courts, the Congress, and the Executive branch, you can be sure that the opinions of patent lawyers and patent holders will be heard. While their arguments will often be couched in terms of the public interest, at bottom their interest is in their own profits and livelihoods, not in designing a patent system that fosters the overall rate of innovation. Even the PTO itself cannot be expected to advocate necessary reform, if such reform reduces its revenues (by discouraging bogus applications) and threatens its established mode of operation. Yet the long-term well-being of everyone depends on a robust innovation system, and patents play a crucial role in that system.

Because it has been left to the special interests, patent policy seems arcane and obscure. And there are certainly many details of patent law that are mind-numbingly complex. But at its heart, the patent system is about three things. It is about technology—the endlessly curious and fascinating process by which new ideas for machines or drugs or computer programs are conceived and developed. It is about people—inventors who create and develop new ways of doing things; business people and lawyers who make decisions about investing in innovation, suing each other, and defending such suits; and government employees who must evaluate the competing claims of different parties and make decisions. And it is about how the rules and procedures established by Congress and the courts affect how the people interact with the underlying process of technological progress. That interaction ultimately affects us all, and so should concern us all.

Chapter 1

Today's Patent System at Work

In 2001, Albie's Foods, Inc., a small grocery and caterer in Gaylord, Michigan, received an unusual communication. The letter was from the law firm of giant jam and jelly maker J. M. Smucker Co. In the correspondence, Albie's—which markets pastries and sandwiches in the northern Michigan region—was accused of violating Smucker's intellectual property rights by selling crustless peanut butter and jelly sandwiches.

In particular, Smucker's claimed that Albie's had infringed Smucker's recently granted U.S. Patent No. 6,004,596 covering a "sealed crustless sandwich."[1] Indeed, as the patent abstract noted, Smucker's had been granted broad protection: "The sandwich includes a lower bread portion, an upper bread portion, an upper filling and a lower filling between the lower and upper bread portions, a center filling sealed between the upper and lower fillings, and a crimped edge along an outer perimeter of the bread portions for sealing the fillings there between. The upper and lower fillings are preferably comprised of peanut butter and the center filling is comprised of at least jelly." Probably surprising the jam magnates, Albie's decided to defend itself in federal court. In their filings,

Albie's lawyers noted that the "pasty"—a pocket sandwich with crimped edges and no crust—has been popular fare in northern Michigan since the immigration of copper and iron miners from Cornwall, England, in the nineteenth century.

A battle in federal court over peanut butter sandwiches may seem merely funny, and a little pathetic. But it is symptomatic of the larger and more profound problems with the patent system that were sketched in the Introduction. In subsequent chapters, we tell the story of how we got to the point where serious lawyers are being paid serious fees by a big company to try to shut down the PB&J operation of a grocery store. In this chapter, we lay the foundation for that story. We begin in the next section by explaining how the patent system operates. The rest of the chapter is devoted to understanding why technological innovation is so crucial to society and how patents foster it.

A Patent Primer

A patent is a legal document issued by a government agency. In the United States, patents are issued by the Patent and Trademark Office (PTO), which is part of the Department of Commerce. The PTO is headed by a Director (formerly known as the Commissioner), who is appointed by the President. The patent describes an invention, and lists one or more claims that specify what the invention does that has never been done before. The holder of a patent has the legal right to prevent anyone else from making, using, selling, or importing an object or device that incorporates any feature covered by the specified claims. This right operates within the United States, and also extends to block importation into the United States of goods whose manufacture violated the patent. Other countries have similar systems (though countries differ in the details of how they implement the patent concept). As sketched in the Introduction, U.S. patent policy and practice have changed in the last two decades in ways that undermined fundamentally the goals of the system. Other countries have, by and large, avoided these mistakes, at least to date. Nonetheless, the same fundamental principle that we apply to analysis of the U.S. system—making sure that the system creates proper incentives for patent applicants, patent examiners, potential infringers, and patent owners to use but not abuse the system—applies to the analysis of patent systems everywhere.

The Process of Patent "Examination"

To get a U.S. patent, the inventor or inventors file an application with the PTO. In order to receive a patent grant, a PTO examiner must determine that the invention meets the standards for patentability. First, the subject matter of the invention must be suitable. U.S. patent law permits the granting of a patent on the following subjects:

- A process, such as a new approach to brewing beer or to depositing circuits on silicon.
- An article of manufacture, such as a kit to identify an infectious disease or a machine, such as a new machine tool or automobile carburetor.
- A composition of matter, such as a novel type of concrete or a new molecule.
- New and useful improvements of the above.
- Any distinct and new variety of plant that is asexually reproduced.
- Any new, original, and ornamental design for an article of manufacture.[2]

As we will highlight in chapter 4, the U.S. courts have become progressively more generous in determining what subject matter is indeed patentable.

But making sure the application deals with appropriate subject matter is not the end of the story. The patent application must pass three other tests:

- Utility: Does the invention really do anything, and if so, does it solve the problem it sets out to address? In practice, the requirement that the invention be useful is not of great importance, because it is easy to make the case that almost anything is potentially useful. (For instance, Patent No. 5,023,850, covers a wrist-watch for dogs (or perhaps it is a paw-watch?) that moves at seven times the speed of an ordinary clock.)

- Novelty: Is the claimed invention really original?
- Non-Obviousness: Even if new, would the claimed invention have been obvious to one skilled in the art at the time of the invention? The "non-obviousness" requirement can be thought of as a supplement to the novelty requirement, preventing one from getting a patent on something that has not been done before, but easily could have been. Even if the invention is new, the law does not allow patenting of inventions that involve only trivial or "obvious" improvements on what has come before. Thus, if a practitioner could easily have modified some existing invention to arrive at the new invention, it is said to be obvious and hence not patentable.

The examiner's job is, in effect, to compare the invention covered by the application to what is called the "prior art." Prior art is the legal phrase for everything that was known before the time of the application. In order to get a patent, the invention must pass the tests of "novelty" and "non-obviousness" in relation to the prior art.

A patent application begins with a general description of the invention and what it does. But the legal "guts" of the patent are its "claims." The patent claims are the legal characterization of what is and is not covered by the patent, and, hence, they are worded in a very specific and legalistic way. A hypothetical patent on a mousetrap might have an abstract saying something like:

A device for catching mice or other mammalian pests not exceeding 100 grams, wherein a levered bar is attached to a spring or similar device, while being restrained by a hook, clasp or similar device, which is in turn attached to a small plate containing pâté de fois gras, wherein the connection between the pâté-containing plate and the hook or clasp is such that any disturbance of the pâté releases the levered bar, wherein the levered bar is positioned in such a way that upon release it falls where the head or neck of a rodent is likely to be located if said rodent is attempting to eat said pâté, and wherein the spring or similar device causes this movement of the bar to occur with sufficient force that said rodent is killed, incapacitated, or restrained in such a way as to prevent its escape.

Notice that this hypothetical patent abstract contains some words or phrases that make the meaning as broad as possible, such as "or other . . . pests" and "or similar device." (This language would be repeated in the "claims" that lay out the specific areas where the patent applicant seeks exclusive rights.) Such broad language is intended to make the patent cover as many different devices as possible, giving the holder of the patent maximal power to restrict competitors. But notice also that the patent contains language that limits its coverage, such as "mammalian" and "not exceeding 100 grams," and is quite specific as to the bait that is used. Such restrictions serve to distinguish the invention from earlier ones, in order to accomplish novelty and non-obviousness. If, for example, there was a previous device of similar design that was used to catch reptiles, or mammals exceeding 100 grams, the patent as drafted distinguishes the new invention from that prior art. It would still be up to the examiner, however, to determine whether adapting some previous reptile-trap to mice was obvious or not. The patent is supposed to be granted only if that jump is non-obvious. Similarly, while it is likely that no one has ever before proposed using pâté as mouse-bait, this distinction could justify a patent only if it were judged that using such high-class bait instead of cheese or peanut butter constitutes an inventive leap that would not be obvious to a skilled mousetrap designer.

If the examiner concludes that the claims in the application cannot be granted because they are not novel, or are obvious, the applicant has the opportunity to re-draft the claims, making them more restrictive, and thereby distinguishing the invention from the prior art. The process of patent examination is therefore, to a large extent, one of negotiation between the applicant (actually, it is typically the applicant's lawyers) and the examiner. The applicant generally wants claim language that is as broad as possible. The examiner may, however, insist on restrictions to distinguish the invention from the prior art. Once these parties agree on language that distinguishes the invention from the prior art, the patent is granted. If it is not possible to draft the claims in such a way as to satisfy the examiner (or if the version that satisfies the examiner is so narrow that the applicant judges it not to be worthwhile pursuing), then the patent application is denied. But because the applicant has unlimited opportunities to, in effect, amend the application to satisfy the examiner, a large fraction of all original patent applications in the United States are now ultimately granted.[3]

A key feature of this process, about which we will have much to say later, is that it involves only the applicant (and the applicant's legal representatives) and the PTO. In particular, other firms or other parties—who might in fact have information regarding the state of the prior art against which the application should be considered—are not allowed to participate. Indeed, up until recently, the entire application process was secret. No matter how long it took the PTO to resolve a given application, even the existence of that application was kept secret until a patent was granted, and was kept secret forever if a patent was not granted. Under a change made in 1999, and discussed further below, most patent applications in the United States are now published eighteen months after filing. It is still the case, however, that if you learn of an application for a patent on an invention that you think other people had already made years ago, it is difficult to prevent an invalid patent from being granted by the PTO without jeopardizing your ability to later defend yourself.[4]

So You Got Yourself a Patent

If the PTO grants a patent, the recipient of the patent (the "patentee") has a legal monopoly that lasts for twenty years from the date that the application was filed. While the inventor—and hence the patent applicant—must be a human being, the inventor can assign the patent to a company, who then has all of the legal rights associated with the patent. It is general practice for firms to require their employees to assign their patents to the employer, and it is typically the firm's lawyers who handle the application process. In this book, we will speak loosely of firms applying for and getting patents, glossing over the technicality that the inventors apply and then assign the patents to the firm.

A patent constitutes intellectual property. It can be bought and sold, left in a will, given as a wedding present, or left in the attic and forgotten, just like any other property. And, just like a house or a piece of a land, a patentee who does not want to sell the patent, can, in effect, rent it to someone else, by granting him a license to use the patented technology. The license agreement may or may not require money payments, called royalties, from the licensee to the patentee. Such royalties can be in any form the parties agree to, such as a lump sum up-front, an annual fixed amount of money, or a percentage of the revenues or profits earned by the licensee. The big difference between intellectual property and tangible property, however, is that it can be "rented" to multiple people at the same time; licenses can be granted to multiple parties, with or without restrictions as to how each of the parties may use the technology. Of course, in many cases, the patentee does not sell or license the patent, but rather uses the patented technology in its own business and relies on the patent to prevent its competitors from using its patented technology.

Now, if someone who has not been licensed undertakes activities that are covered by the claims of a patent, they are said to infringe the patent. When a patentee learns that someone is infringing its patent, it will typically write him or her a letter. This letter is likely to demand that the alleged infringing activity stop. Depending on the patentee's business strategy, the letter may offer to license the patent, in return for a royalty or other consideration. The recipient of such a letter has essentially three choices. They can agree to take a license and pay a royalty (if that option is offered); they can stop doing whatever is alleged to have created the infringement; or they can simply continue as before and wait for the patentee's next move.

In many cases, the parties will enter into negotiations to try to resolve the dispute, and such negotiations may well lead to some kind of license agreement, either with or without payment of royalties. But if such negotiations do not pan out, the patentee can try to stop the alleged infringement by initiating litigation in federal court to enforce the patent. If the patentee can prove that someone is infringing the patent, they are entitled to an injunction (an order from the court) ordering the infringing activity to cease.

They are also entitled to receive *damages*, money paid in compensation for the infringement that occurred until the resolution of the litigation.

In addition to denying that it is infringing, the defendant in an infringement suit will typically countersue, claiming that the patent itself is invalid. There are a variety of grounds for claiming invalidity, the most straightforward of which is, in effect, that the examiner made a mistake and that the invention is not novel or is obvious. Thus, to prevail in this litigation, the patentee needs the court to decide that the patent is valid and is being infringed. The alleged infringer can prevail via either a finding of non-infringement or a finding that the patent is not valid.

A Mess of Peanut Butter and Jelly

Let us now follow the PB&J patent through this process. In December 1997, Len C. Kretchman of Fergus Falls, Minnesota, and David Geske of Fargo, North Dakota, filed an application with the PTO, requesting a patent on a "Sealed Crustless Sandwich." The primary examiner was Lien Tran. Almost two years later, the patent was granted, containing ten claims. The first claim reads as follows:

A sealed crustless sandwich, comprising:

a first bread layer having a first perimeter surface coplanar to a contact surface;

at least one filling of an edible food juxtaposed to said contact surface;

a second bread layer juxtaposed to said at least one filling opposite of said first bread layer, wherein said second bread layer includes a second perimeter surface similar to said first perimeter surface;

a crimped edge directly between said first perimeter surface and said second perimeter surface for sealing said at least one filling between said first bread layer and said second bread layer;

wherein a crust portion of said first bread layer and said second bread layer has been removed.[5]

In other words, they claim to have invented putting some "filling" between two pieces of bread, and crimping the edges so as to seal the filling and remove the bread crusts. Other claims go on to elaborate on this idea, including adding what appears to be the key feature of the invention—a sandwich with three layers of filling, in which the edges of the first and third layers (e.g., the peanut butter) extend beyond the edge of the second filling (for example, the jelly) so that when the sandwich is crimped the edges of the peanut butter layers "are engaged to one another to form a reservoir for retaining said second filling in between." In simple English, the examiner's decision to allow these claims amounts to a determination that surrounding jam with peanut butter so the bread will not get soggy is a new idea, and one that was not previously obvious to skilled sandwich-makers.

In the process of examining this application, relevant prior art was identified in the form of seven previous patents issued between 1963 and 1998, and a 1994 book entitled *50 Great Sandwiches*. It is unclear how these earlier sandwich inventions differed from the Kretchman/Geske recipe. Now, it may strike the reader that one need not look to earlier patents for the evidence that cutting the crusts off of a sandwich, surrounding the jam with peanut butter, and even "crimping" the edges, were probably not new ideas. Indeed, we will see later that for some technologies, such as software, a big problem with the examination process is that the prior art exists in forms other than patents, and patent examiners are not very good at finding non-patented prior art.

In this case, however, even within the files of the PTO itself there was evidence undercutting the validity of the patent. In particular, U.S. Patent No. 2,463,439, issued in 1949, had been for a device creating very similar kinds of sandwiches. As the old patent explained: "An object of this invention is to provide . . . a means for locating said filling in the center of the sandwich and sealing the marginal edges of the pieces by heat and pressure to preclude the escape of the filling from the finished product . . . [and] a means for trimming the baked dough pieces." Not only did a family of Cincinnati restaurateurs patent this discovery, but also sold the device based on this discovery. On eBay, for instance, one occasionally sees a "Toastite" from the 1950s being offered up for sale, which would produce a "sealed crustless sandwich" akin to that described in the old (and new) patent.

But as the applicants had included neither the earlier patent nor any information about pasties or Toastites in their patent application, the patent examiner did not find this particular prior art, or else somehow judged it irrelevant. So the patent was granted, and Albie's got their "cease and desist" letter. Many small firms in their position would have simply dropped the "pasty" from their culinary portfolio, or agreed to pay a royalty if Smucker's demand was small enough. But Albie's chose to fight—at least for a while. Eventually, as in so many of these disputes, the two parties reached a private settlement.

What Has Gone Wrong?

Now one silly patent is not proof of a systemic problem. As we will see throughout the book, however, the granting of patents despite clear evidence of invalidity, in the form of prior art that makes the invention not novel and/or obvious, has become all too common. Just to stay for a moment in the bread area, there is U.S. Patent No. 6,080,436, "Bread Refreshing Method," which as the award states, is an "invention concerned with the process and apparatus for refreshing bread products, particularly open face items such as sliced rolls, buns, muffins, and the like . . . . via exposure to high heat"—what most people would call toasting. Anyone who has recently browned a slightly stale hot dog bun over a barbeque has probably infringed this award.

How could the patent office have missed these cases, where there is so much prior art and where the technology is so basic? As we will argue, such a patent—as well as peers such as "Method of Exercising a Cat" and "Method of Swinging on a Swing"[6]—are just the amusing tip of a very ominous iceberg. As a result of legal and administrative changes made between 1982 and 1990, the PTO has become so overtaxed, and its incentives have become so skewed towards granting patents, that the tests for novelty and non-obviousness that are supposed to ensure that the patent monopoly is granted only to true inventors have become largely non-operative. Simultaneously, changes in the court system have made patents much more powerful legal weapons than they used to be: a patentee is simply more likely to win an infringement suit against a broader array of possible infringers than was the case before. In other words, in the space of less than a decade, we converted the weapon that a patent represents from something like a handgun or a pocket knife into a bazooka, and then started handing out the bazookas to pretty much anyone who asked for one, despite the legal tests of novelty and non-obviousness. The result has been a dangerous and expensive arms' race, which now undermines rather than fosters the crucial process of technological innovation.

We will argue in the subsequent chapters that the key to getting this system back on track is to restructure the incentives of all of the parties—the PTO, potential applicants, other inventors, and patentees—to reduce the flow of applications, improve the rigor of examination, and reduce the incentive to use patent litigation as a competitive weapon. But before doing that we need to explore what it is that patents are supposed to accomplish, and why it is devilishly tricky to get just the right level of rigor in the patent system.

Why Do We Need a Patent System to Begin With

Let us step back a moment. Why do we grant patents? After all, even when granted for truly new inventions, and not abused, patents are still a government-sanctioned monopoly. Monopolies are bad. Why not abolish the patent system altogether?

Two Stories

Qualcomm is a communications-technology company that was founded in 1985.[7] It pioneered a technology known as CDMA (Code Division Multiple Access) that allows cell phones and other mobile communications devices to use the radio spectrum efficiently. CDMA is covered by a patent applied for by Qualcomm in 1990 and granted by the Patent Office in 1992. Qualcomm uses this technology in its own products, and has also licensed it to dozens of other companies. Qualcomm now has revenues of approximately $3 billion, with about $800 million of that coming from royalties earned on its patent licenses, and the remainder from its own sales. To get to this point, it has had to compete against large, established companies such as Motorola. It has succeeded on the strength of its technology. It is unlikely that this success could have been achieved if the CDMA technology had not been protected by patent.

Another billion-dollar company that has grown from nowhere based on patents is Biogen.[8] Founded in 1978 by a group of scientists including two who eventually won the Nobel Prize, Biogen was among the first companies to use the new techniques of genetic engineering to develop pharmaceutical products. It raised millions of dollars, first through venture capital, and then through a public stock offering in 1983, and used this money to fund the development of new products such as alpha and beta interferon and a vaccine for hepatitis B. To finance the even greater cost of clinical trials of these products, Biogen has entered into partnerships with several of the world's pharmaceutical giants. Neither its investors nor its industry partners would have been willing to invest in these products if patents had not protected them. Indeed, for the first fifteen years of its existence, Biogen never manufactured or sold any tangible "product." In effect, they "sold" the output of their research to other companies, who in turn used the Biogen technology to make products for consumers. This allowed Biogen to specialize in what it did best. Such specialization through a market for "technology" itself would not be possible without patents to protect that technology, because without patents Biogen's partners could simply go off on their own once they learned what Biogen had accomplished.

The essence of the success of companies like Qualcomm and Biogen is that they were able to use the legal protection offered by patents to document and protect their inventions. Conceptually, what patents do is convert the intangible creation of an inventor into "property" that can be bought and sold, or upon which a business can be founded. In this chapter, we provide an overview of how this works when the patent system functions as it should in support of technological progress; subsequent chapters then lay out the case that things have gone badly wrong, and show how to make things right again.

The Simple Case for Patents

The standard economic explanation of the social function of patents has three basic parts. First, the development and commercialization of new technologies—technological innovation—creates broad social benefits. Over time, it allows us collectively to live longer, healthier lives; to have growing monetary incomes; and to consume a broader array of goods and services. It is the primary reason why our lives look so different from those of our grandparents. (This begs the question as to whether we are actually any happier than our less technologically endowed forbearers, but we leave that one for others to ponder.) It is in our collective interests to create social, cultural, and legal institutions that foster technological innovation.

The next step in the argument for having patents as part of that legal environment is the recognition that the process of technological innovation is expensive. New products and services do not just spring full-grown from the creative mind of an inventor. Though an instantaneous spark of creative genius may start an innovative flame, it typically takes years of research and development to nurture that fire into a commercially viable blaze, with a lot of false alarms along the way. And that nurturing process costs money— often a lot of money.

If technological innovation is socially desirable, but expensive, then society needs to have institutions that direct time and money into the processes of research and development. One approach to this, at least hypothetically, might be to have the government use money raised through taxes to finance research and develop new technologies. In fact, the U.S. government does do a lot of R&D, particularly in areas like defense, space, and the environment that are themselves important areas of government responsibility. But in our free-enterprise system, we do not think it is a good idea to give the government the job of developing new products and processes for industry. Government is good at many things, but taking entrepreneurial initiative is not one of them.

If society wants technological innovation, but the government cannot do it, then what we need are institutions that create incentives so that private individuals and firms will invest their own money in the process. With the occasional exception of the visionary inventor who wants to see an invention to market at all cost, the incentive to invest in R&D must come, ultimately, from an expectation of making a bunch of money if the thing pans out.

To make innovation rewarding, the government must give or grant something valuable to people or firms that produce important innovations. Under a patent system, this grant takes the form of using the government's legal system to create a zone of economic exclusivity for the innovator. A more direct approach might be to simply reward the innovator with money. As will be discussed in chapter 3, in the seventeenth and eighteenth centuries the early patent system in Great Britain coexisted with the use of "prizes" to reward people who produced successful innovative solutions to particular technological problems. Some scholars of the innovation process continue to advocate the use of prizes; Michael Kremer, for example, has argued that governments or private foundations should offer a major prize as an inducement for drug companies to develop vaccines for tropical diseases (because the people and governments that need these vaccines are too poor to make this research profitable even with patent protection).[9]

While prizes may be an effective mechanism for drawing forth a specific, desired technology, they are not as effective a mechanism for bringing forth innovation in general. First, it would be expensive to hand out enough prizes to reward the gamut of industrial innovation; raising the tax money to do this would be both unpopular and economically burdensome. Further, it would be hard to figure out how big a prize to give to each innovation. In most cases, the importance of a discovery is initially uncertain. If the government tried to reward innovation in a general way with prizes, it would probably set too large a reward in some cases and not enough prizes in others. For instance, a full 50,000 pounds (several millions of today's dollars) was paid by the British government to John

Palmer, the inventor of a new way of organizing the mail. This was far more than that paid to Edward Jenner for his smallpox vaccine, which would be responsible for saving literally millions of lives in the years to come.[10] Patents, on the other hand, are by their nature proportional to the size of the discovery: the exclusive right to a modest discovery is unlikely to be worth very much, while the exclusive right to an important new technology is usually very valuable. Thus, at least in principle, patents provide an appropriately calibrated reward for different innovations.

Building a Better Mousetrap

Suppose you, or someone who works for you, gets the creative spark that is the route to a really new and better mousetrap. You spend millions of dollars putting the idea into practice, getting the kinks out of it, and testing it. Now you put it on the market; the world beats a path to your door; and everyone coming up that path pays you handsomely and gratefully for dispatching their rodents with such efficiency: the mice really love the pâté! Those profits are the very prize you hoped for when you hired the crack mousetrap engineer to begin with, and when you spent the millions developing the new idea.

So far, so good, except that all of the other mousetrap manufacturers are likely to notice that crowd on your doorstep. So what they are likely to do is to buy a couple of your new traps, and figure out how they work. If they can, they will copy your design, and sell their own version. This may be easy to do—you have already spent the money to refine the design and test it—they can simply jump in at the end and *imitate* your invention and its implementation.

While there were, in fact, thirty-four patents issued in the past twenty-five years in the United States for mousetrap-related inventions (including "rubber-band powered mousetrap," "enclosed mousetrap having improved trap mechanism," and "humane rodent trap"), it is not a particularly important economic sector. But the same economic dynamic is at work with respect to more important industrial sectors. This can be seen most clearly, perhaps, with respect to prescription pharmaceuticals. The Food and Drug

Administration (FDA) must approve drugs sold in the United States. In order to approve a drug, the FDA requires proof, in the form of expensive clinical studies, that the drug is safe and effective. This means that after a chemical compound has been discovered, and its initial use for health purposes identified, someone (usually a large drug company) must spend hundreds of millions of dollars conducting tests to prove to the FDA that the drug is safe and effective. Once the drug is on the market, however, anyone with a decent chemistry lab can figure out what it is made of, and in most cases could then manufacture and sell it.

Competition from such imitators would then drive down the price of the drug. (Indeed, this is exactly what happens when the patent expires and the drug is subject to "generic" competition.) Lower prices for drugs might seem like a good thing for society, but if competition quickly reduces the price of a new drug, the company that invented the drug would not earn significant profits from selling it. And, in a world with no patents, this scenario is exactly what drug firms would expect to unfold if they developed a truly successful new drug. Now, put yourself in the lab coat of a pharmaceutical R&D director. Every time you try to bring a drug to market, you have to ask for permission to spend a couple hundred million dollars for clinical testing. If the drug turns out to be a dud—the overwhelming majority of promising new compounds never even get approved, and many of those approved have only modest sales—you lose a couple hundred million. If it turns out to be successful, you can sell a bunch of it. However, in this hypothetical patent-free world, all your competitors would then jump in and sell it too, so you would not really make much money selling it. Maybe you would make back part of what you spent developing it, but probably not all of it. So the game you are playing is "heads you lose big, tails you lose only a little." This is not a game that your board of directors is going to let you play for very long. And if no one plays this game, no new drugs get developed.

Thus, patents make new drugs expensive, which is bad. But if they were not expensive, the revenue from selling them would not justify the large cost of developing them. So nobody would undertake such development. And expensive new drugs are better than no new drugs. This is the tradeoff at the heart of the patent system. We grant monopolies, knowing that this will make the patented products more expensive, and allow some holders of patent monopolies to earn "obscene" profits. We do this because the prospect of those obscene profits is what drives firms to develop new products and processes in the first place, and the flow of revenues from one generation of successful products provides a reliable means of financing the research necessary to develop the next generation.

Controlling the Risks Inherent in Innovation

This risk of imitation hangs over all investments in R&D. And the nature of the innovation game is such that the profits or returns from innovation are extremely skewed. Most investments in new products and processes fail, meaning that their investors lose money. A very small fraction of investments in new products or processes succeed. For the overall "game" of investing in new technology to be worthwhile, the successes must earn enough profit to cover not only their own costs and reasonable return, but also the costs and a reasonable return on those costs for all of the failures. Otherwise, the overall investment strategy will be a loser. Suppose you (or other investors) can put their money in the bank or in Treasury bills and earn a safe $5 per year for every $100 you invest. Now suppose you have the option of investing in a series of research investments. You expect that nine out of ten will fail, meaning that you will earn no money on those investments: you will only get back the amount you invested. About one out of ten will "succeed."

Success, of course, comes in different magnitudes. Suppose that "success" in this case was likely to mean that you earned $20 for each $100 invested. That seems like quite a healthy return, four times as great as the safe return of Treasury bills. But the problem is that you cannot know in advance which of the ten projects will succeed, and which will fail. On average, you have to expect that you are going to end up with nine duds for every success. This means that on an investment of $1,000 ($100 in each of ten projects), you would expect to earn only $20 (zero on nine of them, $20 on the one success). This gives you an average return of only

$2 on each $100 invested, much worse than just leaving the money in the bank. In order to consider playing this risky "game," you have to expect that the "successful" project will in fact earn more than $50 on each $100 invested, a very high return indeed. Looked at in isolation, you might even say that this project was earning "obscene" profits. But that "obscene" level of profit is what is needed to make the overall portfolio worthy of investment.

This example actually understates the risk in many R&D investments, because it assumes that the "failures" earn a return of zero, meaning that if you invest $100, you end up with "only" $100. But many R&D investments produce large negative returns. That is, you may invest $100 and simply lose it all. It is easy to see that this likelihood increases even further the profit that must be earned on the "successes," if the overall return on a portfolio of investments is to be adequate. Consider, again, the pharmaceutical industry. Studies of pharmaceutical R&D estimate that if you screen 5,000 to 10,000 compounds for possible clinical use, on average 250 of these will show enough promise to be put into pre-clinical testing. Of these 250, five will show sufficient promise to enter clinical testing; the rest are simply abandoned. Clinical testing is where the really big bucks get spent, typically in excess of half a billion dollars per drug.[11] Of these five drugs subjected to expensive clinical testing, on average only one will be approved by the FDA. And, of course, FDA approval does not ensure large profits. Many approved products have small markets. If we combine the risks of failure at the clinical trial and market stages, 80 percent of these expensive testing efforts are complete losers, never leading to an FDA-approved product. About 14 percent lead to an FDA-approved product, but do not earn sufficient profits to recoup their own development costs. Only 6 percent earn sufficient profits to recoup their own investment costs, and, of course, this 6 percent must also earn sufficient profits to pay for all of the losses on the other 94 percent of compounds tested.[12]

Generally speaking, neither the managers of firms nor investors like risk. Investments that are risky are less likely to be undertaken, all else being equal. So the high risk associated with R&D tends to discourage firms from undertaking it, even if the rewards are reasonably high. Investment in new technology is therefore handicapped by its riskiness, when compared with other forms of spending (for instance, expenditures on heavier marketing of an existing brand). Furthermore, when a business builds a new factory or buys some new equipment, it does not normally worry that its competitors will simply come and steal the equipment. When a business invests in R&D, it is "building" an asset that it hopes to profit from, just as it does when it builds a factory. But the asset that you build with research is intangible. Being intangible, it is much easier for other firms to steal.

This is where the patent system comes in. Your ability to patent your better mousetrap allows you to build a security fence around your idea, analogous to the security fence that you might build around your factory. Like any fence, it will not necessarily prevent all theft, but it will make theft harder and hence make the property more secure. And the knowledge that this fence will be available if you "build" your intangible property through R&D makes you more willing to take the risk of building it to begin with.

The U.S. Constitution authorizes the Congress to establish a patent system, with the stated purpose being "[t]o promote the Progress of Science and useful Arts." This is often interpreted in terms of creating incentives for inventors. And incentives for inventors are important. As illustrated by the example of drug development, however, it is at least as important to provide incentives for the investments that must be made after the initial spark of invention has ignited. Patents protect an individual's or firm's investment in the development of an idea, as much as they protect the invention itself. In this, as in so many other ways, the Founding Fathers showed amazing foresight. While the United States was a largely agrarian and craft-based economy in the eighteenth century, the patent system that was built on the Constitutional foundation provided the basis for technological progress that propelled the United States into a position of global technological superiority in the nineteenth and twentieth centuries.

In summary: we want investments to be made in technological innovation. We do not think it will work well to have all or most such investments made using public funds, so we need to provide incentives for private individuals and firms to make the investments. The likelihood of imitation if new products are successful makes such investments very risky, and, hence, in the absence of a way to protect against imitation, we worry that not enough would be spent on R&D in the private sector. Patents provide such a mechanism, although we will soon see that even the best-functioning patent system is not costless.

Patents have played a role in many of the most important inventions of the last two centuries. Thomas Edison was issued thousands of patents, and the patents that he held played important roles in the commercialization of many of the inventions for which he is most famous. In many cases, of course, it is hard to know how things would have worked out if the invention could not have been patented. One case where it is clear that without patent protection the invention never would have made it to market is the photocopier, better known to many as the "Xerox" machine.[13] There are actually two distinct ways in which the patent system was responsible for this invention. Chester Carlson worked in the patent division of P. R. Mallory & Company, a small electrical components maker during the Great Depression. Part of his job was meticulously copying the text and images in patent documents—which he found exceedingly tedious. This tedium induced Carlson to try to develop a machine to do it.

There were cameras, of course, but photography was messy and expensive. Carlson set about trying to develop a dry reproduction technique, working in the kitchen of his New York apartment. In 1937 he patented the key technological idea that still underlies many copiers (and computer printers) today: using patterns of static electricity to stick tiny particles of dry ink onto a surface, and then running paper over that surface to produce an image. (The word "toner," which we use today for this powdered ink, was invented by the Xerox company—but we are getting ahead of the story.)

Our older readers no doubt recall that in the late 1930s—and throughout the 1940s and 1950s—office workers were still gossiping around the water cooler, not the Xerox machine. Indeed, it was not until 1960 that the Haloid Xerox 914, the first commercially successful office copy machine, was introduced. The reason for this two-decade delay was that it turned out that coming up with the key technological insight into the concept of dry copying was not the really hard part of building a workable dry copier. The hard part was designing and building a reasonably priced, reasonably sized machine that would feed sheets of paper onto and off of the copy surface, and do it in a way that did not generate so much random static electricity that it destroyed the process. Carlson himself spent about ten years on this. (When his wife threw him out of the kitchen, he worked in the back of his mother-in-law's beauty shop.) But the problems were not successfully solved until the project was taken over by a small photographic supplies company located in Rochester, New York, then called the Haloid Company. Haloid saw inadequate growth potential in their traditional businesses. Searching around for something new, they stumbled on Carlson's work, and bet the company on it. They licensed Carlson's early patents in 1946, and began spending a quarter of the company's annual net income on developing a workable office product based on Carlson's "electrophotography."

Though it took a decade and a half, this bet eventually paid off, and Haloid eventually changed its name to "Xerox" Corporation, a name coined from the Greek *xeros* ("dry") and *graphos* ("writing"). The Carlson patent had, of course, expired before success of the 914 Model allowed Xerox to make any money on the idea. Along the way, however, Haloid/Xerox had managed to patent many of the subsidiary technologies that allowed the system to function. Even with the basic patent on electrophotography long gone, Xerox had such a strong patent position in dry copying technology that it was sued in the early 1970s by the Federal Trade Commission for monopolizing the photocopier market (which it had created), and settled the suit by agreeing to license some of its patents.[14]

You do not bet the company on a purchase that you cannot "own" if it is successful. While vision, persistence, know-how and luck were all important ingredients in the long struggle to make a practical photocopier, the patents were also essential. The image of Chester Carlson toiling in the kitchen and beauty salon fits our mythology of invention. But the fifteen-year slog by Haloid/Xerox to get the thing to work is paradigmatic of the time and money it takes to commercialize inventors' brilliant flashes. And that simply would not have occurred without patent protection.

The Simple Case Is Too Simple

The above explanation of the desirability of patents contains a lot of truth, but it also leaves a lot out. The things that it leaves out can be grouped into three categories of issues:

1. Companies have other methods for preventing imitation, so patents are but one of many tools in a toolkit that firms have available to protect their profits from innovation.
2. Inventions do not occur in isolation. Inventions from different firms overlap and build on each other. This means that if one firm gets a patent, it can retard or stifle inventions that other firms might otherwise undertake, thereby clouding patents' overall effect on technological progress.
3. Some firms and individuals use patents more like grenades than like security fences, threatening others' property rather than just defending their own.

Other Means of Protecting New Products and Processes

In some cases, imitation can be prevented or at least inhibited through secrecy. For instance, there is a safe somewhere in Atlanta in which it is said that the formula for Coca-Cola resides. This formula is not patented, but others supposedly cannot exactly duplicate Coke. Because the drink is a mixture of complex natural substances, it is not possible to duplicate it simply by analyzing the stuff. Similarly, Microsoft does not publish the source code for its Windows operating system. Even if there were not patents on components of Windows, it would be virtually impossible for a would-be imitator to create an exact duplicate of the system.[15] As a legal matter, "trade secrecy" is a distinct form of protection for intellectual property. If a company makes appropriate efforts to prevent the disclosure of secret information that is valuable to its business, then employees or competitors, who somehow get access to such a trade secret, can be sued if they attempt to use it commercially. This protection is completely separate from any protection provided by patents. Secrecy can be particularly valuable in protecting new processes rather than new products.

Another way that firms can protect innovations even without patents is through a first mover advantage. Notice that in the mousetrap imitation story told above, once the competitors notice your success and come in with their copies, they are able to take away many of your customers. But because you were the one who had the innovation, you were in the market first. Sometimes, simply being first is enough to confer a lasting advantage over others. Such an advantage can come about because consumers are reluctant to switch brands once they have purchased one variety of a product and come to rely on it. Such reluctance is partly just human nature, captured in numerous clichés such as "if it ain't broke don't fix it" and "don't change horses in midstream." It also has a straightforward economic basis in those cases where it is difficult or impossible to verify the quality of a good before you purchase and use it. Having made the investment to try one brand, and learned that it works well for you, it is costly to try another, unknown brand, and take the risk that it will disappoint. Once you have found a mousetrap that really works, why fool around with an imitator, even if, in the store package, it looks like it is equivalent?[16]

First-mover advantages are often augmented by brand loyalty. The introduction of the new mousetrap is likely to be accompanied by an advertising campaign with animated rodents cringing in fear of the new MouseStomper®. The company's goal is to get consumers to routinely associate that name with the new technology. If the product really works, if there is a period of time in which nobody else can match the new technology, and if the ad campaign is appropriately catchy, then a significant number of consumers will develop loyalty and not defect when the imitators come along.

The ability of firms to use secrecy, a first-mover advantage, brand loyalty, and other strategies to protect their innovations means that innovation would not grind to a total halt without the protection of patents. Indeed, numerous important innovations are never patented, or are patented but the patent protection is not really important to their commercial success. This does not mean that patents are unimportant, but it does mean that their importance in maintaining the flow of new technologies varies across different industries and different kinds of firms.

Cumulative and Overlapping Innovation

Imagine that you have purchased one of those new MouseStomper mousetraps and put it to work in your kitchen. It does much better than any mousetrap you have used before, but, once in a while, the culprit still manages to escape with the pâté. You want to know why, so you spend weeks hiding in your broom closet, where you can watch the MouseStomper at work without scaring away the mice. After a while you figure out an improvement in the Mouse-Stomper that makes it even more effective.

We do not particularly want to encourage people to spend large amounts of time in their broom closets, but we do generally want to encourage improvements in existing technologies. And, just as the case with "original" inventions, inventing and developing improvements is time-consuming and costly. So we need to have good incentives.

Obviously, the firm that is making and selling a given technology has an incentive to improve it. But in many cases, they may not be the ones in the best position to make such improvements. As in the broom closet example, it is often customers who have good ideas about product improvements. More generally, one of Mouse-Stomper's competitors might not just imitate the new technology; they might actually figure out a way to do it even better. So how do we create broad incentives for people to invest in improvements?

The obvious answer is to grant patents on improvements, and such patents are indeed allowed, *if the improvement embodies some idea that was not covered by the patent on the underlying technology.* This seems fair. But in practice it is tricky to implement. To make the patent on the original invention useful, its owner must be given some latitude to modify the invention and still have it be covered by the original patent. But if such latitude is too wide, then many improvements are likely to fall under the original patent. So there is a tradeoff: granting broad patent protection gives the maximum incentive for "original" inventions, but it may actually discourage improvements.

A classic example of the tradeoff between rewarding pioneering inventions and allowing improvements is the Edison electric light bulb. Edison was granted the basic patent on incandescent lighting in 1880. For the next dozen years or so, there was much dispute about the validity and breadth of this patent. Many companies offered competing products. A number of these contained important improvements in the design of the filament and the bulb itself, and the cost of the bulb trended steadily downward. Then, in 1891, Edison General Electric Company won an infringement suit against its competitor United States Electric Lighting,[17] and subsequently won injunctions against a number of competitors. The flow of improvements then slowed, until the expiration of the patent allowed competitors to re-enter and resume their efforts to improve Edison's design.[18] Now, surely Edison's invention was about as novel as they get. And Edison and his assistants put a lot of time and money into testing different materials until they succeeded with the carbon filament, justifying a patent to allow significant profits to be earned on the invention. But acknowledging the legitimacy of Edison's patent and his efforts to enforce it is not inconsistent with recognizing that the monopoly thereby created temporarily inhibited the subsequent improvement of the invention and the development of the industry more broadly.

In principle, subsequent inventors with good ideas about improving an important invention ought to be able to negotiate an agreement with the owner of the original patent that allows the improvement to be implemented. This could be done by granting the improver a license to use the original patent, or by selling or licensing the improvement back to the holder of the original invention. After all, if the improvement is really a good one, both the original inventor and the improver have an incentive to see it implemented. In practice, however, such agreements often are difficult to work out. After the Wright brothers patented their basic design for an aircraft stabilization and steering system, there were many others who wanted to work on a wide variety of different ideas for aircraft. But the Wright brothers refused to license anyone, and engaged in protracted litigation with a number of designers.[19] With the entry of the United States into World War I, the U.S. government in fact pushed the major aircraft manufacturers, including the Wrights' firm, to license their patents as a package, in order to ensure the rapid manufacture of planes and the development of new designs. The rapid development of numerous different aircraft concepts in the years after the establishment of this "patent pool" suggests that the pioneering patent—combined with the unwillingness or inability of the inventors to cooperate with their technological followers—temporarily retarded the development of technology.

Thus, there is an inherent tension between providing strong patent rights to encourage break-through innovations, and the inhibition that those strong protections may create for the development of subsequent improvements.[20] A related problem is created by the reality that firms are often working more or less in parallel on related research. Multiple firms may each apply for patents on what are, in effect, different versions of the same idea or set of ideas. In principle, what should happen is that each should be entitled to a patent only on those aspects (if any) of their creation that are unique and truly new. In practice, this is very hard to do. What is likely is that each will be granted a patent that describes its invention in a way that leaves considerable ambiguity as to whether or not the inventions of the other firms are or are not covered. As a result, all may suffer uncertainty about what products they can or cannot legally sell. In the face of potentially overlapping patent grants, the risks associated with bringing new products to market are augmented rather than reduced, because expensive litigation with uncertain outcomes is added to other worries.[21] Thus, the patent system in such cases may well inhibit rather than encourage innovation.

Sometimes parallel development leads to a situation where the problem is not so much uncertainty about patent rights, but patent rights that interfere with each other. In the early history of radio, the British inventor Marconi was granted a basic patent on radio transmission, and also acquired another patent on the two-element vacuum tube, or diode. (Some of us are old enough to remember when radios and TVs had "tubes.") The diode was a crucial and fundamental invention, but it was improved upon by the three-element tube or "triode" invented by Lee De Forest. AT&T held the patent on the triode. The courts ruled that the triode was an improvement on the diode, and as such AT&T and De Forest could not use the triode without a license to the diode patent controlled by Marconi. Marconi refused to grant such a license, but of course he could not, himself, make triodes without a license from AT&T, which was not granted. As a result, the triode, which was widely seen as a major improvement, was simply not used for some time.[22] So again we see a situation where patent rights retard the improvement of technology, and do so despite the incentive faced by the parties to use license agreements to solve the problem. Apparently, inventors are a stubborn lot.

So It Is Hard to Get It Right

In summary, much is at stake in creating institutions that create incentives for innovation. Because of the inherent riskiness of the innovation process, patents are crucial in many cases to provide enough protection that investors are willing to put up the money to develop new technology. But patents are blunt instruments. Because of the complexity of the evolution of technology, the monopoly that they create will sometimes retard rather than encourage competition. This means that, in the best of worlds, a patent system is a compromise among competing objectives.

But the perfect need not be the enemy of the good. It is possible to make a patent system that does a better job of separating the wheat from the chaff, and which reduces the incentives to engage in litigation. Before turning to a more detailed diagnosis of the disease, and proposing some medicine, we conclude this chapter with an example that re-emphasizes how valuable patents can be when the system works properly.

The Way Things Are Supposed to Work

Howard Dananberg is perhaps an unlikely hero for a book on innovation policy in the New Economy of the 21st Century.[23] Dr. Dananberg is a podiatrist in Bedford, New Hampshire. His mission in life is to make people's feet hurt less. To that end, Dr. Dananberg has patented a number of inventions that relate to the design of shoes. In July 1998, he was issued U.S. Patent No. 5,782,015 for the "Comfortable High-Heel Shoe." The authors of this book do not have any personal experience on this, but we are told that many people consider the phrase "comfortable high-heel shoe" oxymoronic. Dr. Dananberg, however, likes a challenge, and undertook a scientific analysis of the manner in which high-heeled shoes cause the body's weight to be supported by the different bones in the human foot. Based on this analysis, he developed a set of formulas describing the design of the shoe insole, depending on the height of the heel, in order to distribute the wearer's weight as evenly as possible. These formulas are, in effect, the subject of Patent No. 5,782,015.

If this really works, it is hard to imagine a better example of the metaphorical "better mousetrap." The world has not yet beaten a path to Dr. Dananberg's door. But the story of how Dr. Dananberg and his associates have gone about trying to build that path is instructive of the crucial role that a patent can play in the commercialization of a new technology.

If Dr. Dananberg can really make Comfortable High-Heel Shoes, then he ought to be able to sell a lot of them, and thereby make a lot of money. (Interestingly, Dr. Dananberg actually cares about making people's feet hurt less, not just making money, but that is somewhat besides the point of the story.) So in 1997, Dr. Dananberg founded a company called HBN Shoe in order to commercialize his technology. But in order to sell shoes, there are a lot of things that you need to be able to do besides design their insoles to be comfortable. You have to be able to design shoes that are fashionable, you have to be able to manufacture the shoes, and you have to get the shoes into stores so women can buy them.

Not surprisingly, as a start-up company, HBN Shoe is not in a very good position to do any of these things. Naively, it tried initially to just make a bunch of really comfortable shoes and offer them to shoe stores. But the founders had no knowledge of shoe fashion or of the nature of the relationships through which shoe manufacturers get their shoes into shoe stores. So after failing to make and sell shoes itself, HBN is licensing its shoe design technology to companies that are already in the shoe business. It is negotiating agreements with companies that make shoes and shoe components, to make shoes using Dr. Dananberg's design, and with retailers like Nordstrom to sell them. Under these agreements, HBN will collect a small royalty payment on each pair of shoes sold. By licensing the technology rather than trying to sell shoes itself, HBN greatly increases the potential market for the new technology. The retail shoe market is highly fragmented: in a global market of hundreds of millions of shoes sold every year, fewer than ten U.S. women shoe brands sell more than a million pairs annually. Thus, if HBN entered the market itself, it is exceedingly unlikely that it could ever have gotten its shoes on more than a tiny fraction of women's feet. By licensing, however, HBN can work with—not against—multiple otherwise competing shoe brands, so there is no fundamental limit to the extent of its market penetration.

The fact that HBN holds a patent on this technology is crucial to this process. Getting these shoes into the market is not just a matter of showing Nordstrom the formulas and signing a contract. HBN has had to spend millions of dollars finding a way to implement the invention so that it would be compatible with current shoe production methods. Then it had to make sample shoes, purchase molds, and work with the manufacturers to make sure that the technology was properly implemented. Under its most optimistic projections, it will be years between the time when this money is spent and any profits can be made from the licensing agreements. To get the cash it needed to make the technology commercially workable, and get it into the market, HBN had to convince potential investors that once the product was established in the marketplace, HBN would earn sufficient royalties to pay out an attractive return on the invested capital.

What would be the prospects for getting a return on this investment if there were no patent? Let us consider the other mechanisms, described above, for protecting the profits from a new product. Obviously, secrecy would not work: to license the technology, HBN has to teach other companies exactly how it works. (Indeed, because of the way the technology is actually incorporated into the shoes, HBN has separate licenses with makers of shoe components, makers of the shoes themselves, and the shoe retailers.) And even before it is in a licensing agreement, it has to show potential licensees enough about the technology to convince them it is worth licensing. So there is no way that HBN could get this product into the marketplace with the formula locked up in a safe like that for Coke.

HBN might have some first-mover advantage, but it would be severely limited by the fact that women get to try shoes on in the store before they buy them. If someone else stole their technology, and advertised their high-heeled shoes as comfortable, women who loved HBN shoes could try the imitation in the store and get a pretty good idea whether it really worked as well. HBN *is* trying to establish brand loyalty. They have dubbed the technology Insolia™ and have created a logo in which the word "Insolia" is drawn in script in the shape of a shoe: their licensing agreements require that this symbol be stamped on all the shoes. Their hope is that this symbol will become widely known, and women will look for it when buying shoes. But that will take time: at best it might suffice to protect HBN's market position after the patent expires. In the absence of patent protection, it is hard to imagine that loyalty to such a new and unknown brand would prevent early imitation. And given HBN's start-up position, it is unlikely that it could raise the money necessary to get the product to market if the patent could not counter the threat of easy, early imitation.

In summary, Dr. Dananberg's invention, licensed widely to the established makers and retailers of high-heeled shoes, offers the possibility of a boon to womankind (not to mention the occasional drag queen). Maybe the good doctor would have had sufficient incentive to make his original invention, even if he could not have patented it, because he is actually motivated to stamp out sore feet. But, as is typical, getting the idea from paper onto women's feet requires significant investment. This investment would simply not be made in the absence of a mechanism to protect the product's market position in such a way as to provide a reasonable prospect for profits. In cases like this, where the technology cannot be commercialized while keeping it secret, and where the fact that the firm with the great idea is a start-up precludes relying on a pre-existing market position, patent protection is likely to be key to raising investment funds to commercialize that great idea.

Hoping for Happy Endings

It remains to be seen whether the future will see millions of fashionable female feet comfortably shod in Insolia shoes. What matters for our purpose is that the protection offered by the patent system has allowed HBN to try. Of course, for every Qualcomm or Biogen, there are dozens of other start-ups that also raised money on the strength of their patents, spent that money trying to commercialize their product, and failed. But the dynamic process of many young technological fish trying to swim upstream to spawn in the market, with only a few actually making it, is the essence of our modern economy. And, in many cases, it is patent protection that allows them to try.

So whether or not our inventive heroes manage to conquer all of the obstacles put before them, their patents serve the honorable and socially desirable function of allowing them to try. One can quite literally look around any modern home, office, or factory and see myriad products that we take for granted, that would not have made it to market if their developers had not had patent protection to make feasible the investment necessary to commercialize new technology. Unfortunately, weapons that do good in the hands of heroes can be very destructive in the hands of others. We turn now to consideration of the darker side of patent protection.

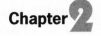

Chapter 2

The Dark Side of Patents

Situations in which there is considerable ambiguity about exactly what is covered by related patents held by different firms are not uncommon. Often, the firms holding these patents manage to get along peaceably, like two neighbors who do not know exactly where the line is that divides their lawns, but do not worry about it too much because they each have sufficient room to enjoy their backyards. And yet, just as some people cannot seem to get along with their neighbors, some firms seem increasingly to want to do battle over patent rights. Even more worrisome, some firms have clearly ceased to see patents as defensive weapons (to be used to protect the firms' innovations from imitation by others) and wield them instead as offensive weapons (to be used to threaten and disrupt the ongoing and future business plans of competitors).

The escalation of patent litigation that has occurred over the last two decades may be due in part to a general trend toward a more litigious society. It is also partly due to the escalation in patenting; the more patents there are, the more there are to fight over. But there is also a less natural set of forces at work. With the creation of the CAFC and its rulings that make it easier for a patentee to prevail, the incentive to sue has been ratcheted upward. And the disastrous deterioration in the examination standards of the over-worked PTO has planted the seeds for thousands of noxious patent weeds, which are now fighting with each other—as well as with the valuable flowers and vegetables—to take over the garden. In this chapter, we describe the costly and disruptive consequences of this nasty landscape.

"Rembrandts in the Attic"

Shortly after the CAFC's creation in 1982, firms came to under-stand that patentees' likelihood of success in court was improving. Partly as a result, a number of firms began to assert their cases for royalties on patents that they had held for some time but had not previously actively enforced. In particular, the semiconductor firm Texas Instruments (TI) successfully asserted its patents for several inventions pertaining to the design and manufacture of integrated circuits. Prior to the 1980s, the semiconductor industry had never been one in which patent protection was considered a significant aspect of competition. Firms did take out patents on aspects of their research, but the conventional wisdom was that it was too difficult to tie a patent to a particular product and the products changed too quickly for patents to be used effectively to garner economic returns from innovation. Such returns, it was thought, were better protected by strong first-mover advantages. Reflecting this reality, Texas Instruments had virtually no licensing revenues when it de-cided to assert a number of the patents in its portfolio against its competitors in the mid 1980s. This strategy was so successful that by 1999, the firm was estimated to be earning about $800 million from patent licensing revenues, which represented more than 55 percent of TI's total net income.[24]

Noticing TI's success, other companies began to systematically explore their portfolio of existing patents to find hidden gems that they could pull out and assert against competitors. By 1999, a widely discussed book urged companies to look for "Rembrandts in the Attic" to gain competitive advantage.[25] While this strategy has been profitable for many companies, it is less clear that it fosters innovation. If these masterpieces were stashed in the attic when they were originally painted, it is hard to argue that their patent protection was an important aspect of the company's original incentive to create them. Profits earned from such ignored or disused patents much more resemble a windfall to the company than a research incentive. Worse, the emergence of such dormant patents disrupts the ongoing process of innovation, as firms that thought they had control of their technology find out that they owe royalties to someone else. And, as discussed further below, it has led to a kind of patent arms' race in the semiconductor industry.

The ultimate attempt to dust off some attic material and try to make a bundle out of it was British Telecom's (BT) claim that a 1989 patent covered the execution of a "hyperlink" on the World Wide Web. Hyperlinks are those highlighted or underlined bits of text that you click on, and are magically transported to another Web site. The hyperlink is at the heart of how the Web operates, and if BT could claim a royalty from everyone who uses hyperlinks, it would be able to buy a whole collection of Rembrandts.

BT's 1989 patent was for a "videotex" technology developed in the age of central computers and remote terminals connected to those terminals by telephone lines.[26] It was applied for in 1980, based on research done over the decade of the 1970s. It described a way for a user at such a terminal to identify on screen a bit of text that related to a block of data sitting at the remote central computer, and, by marking that text, have the data transferred from the remote computer to the user's terminal. In December 2000, BT filed suit against Prodigy, an Internet Service Provider, claiming infringement. If BT had won this case, it would have been in a position to demand royalties from all users of the web. Fortunately, the judge in the case construed the relevant claims of the 1989 patent to cover a single central computer connected to dedicated remote terminals, and then granted Prodigy's request for a ruling that this description does not cover the Internet and hence that there was no infringement.[27] Thus, in the end the courts seem to have squelched this particular power grab. But what is scary about this case is that BT's assessment of the current state of the patent landscape gave it sufficient hope of prevailing so as to make this case worth bringing. And, as we shall see, this is not an isolated case.

When the Patent Landscape Becomes a Thicket

Texas Instruments' aggressive exploitation of its existing patent portfolio changed fundamentally the way patents are used in the semiconductor industry. The problem with patents in this industry is that there is so much overlap among the technologies developed by different companies that it is difficult to bring any product to market without potentially infringing patents held by other companies. A single product—a particular semiconductor "chip"—may incorporate technology covered by dozens of patents, and for each of these patents there could be conflicts with related patents held by other companies. If there were litigation over each of these patents, the industry would screech to a halt. Even negotiating licensing agreements for each of these patents would be complex and time-consuming. Thus, when TI changed the culture of the industry by successfully demanding royalties for several of its patents, the whole innovation process in this sector was threatened.

Cross-licensing as a Means to Avoid Litigation

But innovation does proceed. It is facilitated by the widespread practice of broad "cross-licensing" agreements among the major companies.[28] In a cross-licensing agreement, each company lists a large number of patents that it owns. Under the agreement, both companies are typically allowed to use any of the patents on the list. Each company grants to the other company a broad license to use its patented technology. If the two companies' portfolios are of comparable size and quality, the agreement may not involve any money changing hands. In effect, each company simply trades the right to use its patents for the right to use the other party's patents. If one company's portfolio is judged inferior, then sometimes some form of payment will be made to compensate for the difference. A large semiconductor company will typically have such cross-licensing agreements with many other companies. This means that the company can design its products without having to worry about infringement suits with respect to the large number of patents covered by the agreements.

Widespread reliance on cross-licensing of patents is especially important with respect to technologies related to technological "standards." Standards are important with respect to many electronic technologies, because components made by different manufacturers need to communicate and interact with each other. Different cell phones need to be able to communicate; different memory cards need to work in different computers. Typically, an industry association or other standard-setting body establishes the technological parameters by which technologies complying with the standard will function. Now, by definition, different products that comply with a given standard are going to have certain technological elements in common. To the extent that these common technological elements are covered by patents, those patents have to be licensed broadly, or the whole point of having a standard would be undermined. While there have been some prominent cases of companies trying to capture a standard by patenting some key element of the standard and then suing for infringement or holding out for large royalties, the standard-setting bodies try to make sure that the patented elements of an agreed-upon standard are licensed on reasonable terms.[29]

Cross-licensing Restricts Competition

While the widespread practice of broad cross-licensing permits innovation in semiconductor and related industries to proceed, it raises the question of whether the patents are actually serving any useful function. If everyone licenses everyone else to use their patents, why bother to take out patents on new technology? The answer seems partly to be that the companies are like countries in an arms race: since the terms of the cross-licensing agreement are driven by the size and quality of each company's patent portfolio, every company wants to have the best portfolio, in order to be in the strongest position in cross-licensing negotiations.

Of course, if everyone patents in a frenzy, then no company's portfolio will get ahead of the others, so no one really gains. But if any one company decided not to patent, it would have little or nothing to "trade" in licensing negotiations, and it would either have to pay significant royalties to secure access to others' technology or it might be left out of the game entirely. Collectively, the companies might all be better off if they just stopped patenting, but there is no way to bring about such a simultaneous change in behavior. (The analogue of an "arms control agreement" by which they formally agree not to pursue patents would probably violate the antitrust laws.)

The previous discussion suggests that widespread intensive patenting, accompanied by widespread cross-licensing, is a waste of time. Under some circumstances it can be worse than a waste—it can stifle competition by eliminating the incentive to compete through new technology. If we can be confident that we will have access to a wide pool of new technology from many cross-licensing partners, we may not feel as intense pressure to develop new technology of our own. At its worst, firms can use cross-licensing agreements to join forces in control of markets.

An egregious example of using patent cross-licensing to suppress competition was the patent-pooling agreement made by Summit Technology and VISX, pioneers in the development of equipment for photorefractive keratectomy, better known as laser eye surgery.[30] Summit and VISX each had patents on this technology, and believed that each was in danger of being accused of infringing the other's patents. But rather than enter a simple cross-license agreement of the sort described above, they instead created a jointly owned partnership. Each firm gave control of most of its patents to the partnership. Further, they agreed that only the partnership could license the technology to third parties, and that both parent companies would have to approve any such license. In effect, this gave each company a veto over any attempt by the other to license technology to third parties, effectively eliminating competition between them to offer such licenses. Finally, each company had to make a minimum payment to the partnership of $250 for each surgery using its equipment, thereby effectively placing a price floor under the royalty agreements that either might negotiate with doctors wanting to use the equipment. The Federal Trade Commission (FTC) challenged this arrangement in 1998, as being anticompetitive and therefore in violation of Section 5 of the Federal Trade Commission Act.[31] The companies settled with the Commission by dissolving the patent partnership, and replacing it with a simple cross-licensing agreement.

Cross-licensing is not the whole story of patenting in the semiconductor industry. What makes cross-licensing work is symmetry or near symmetry between the two companies. Large, established firms are roughly symmetric in both their exposure to being sued, and their ability to threaten to sue. Exposure to being sued comes from having products on the market, and, importantly, having large capital investments tied up in those products and thereby at risk of loss if the product is threatened. But an important component of the semiconductor industry is small firms that design new semiconductor chips but do not manufacture any. Such a firm has no risk of being sued, and hence nothing to gain from a cross-licensing agreement. For them, patents serve the more traditional function, as in the Comfortable High-Heel Shoe. Since the design firm is not going to manufacture its new chip itself, it can recover the cost of having designed it only by securing a royalty from some other firm that is going to make and sell the chip. Thus, for such small design firms, patent protection is crucial in order to allow investment in product innovation.

A more problematic asymmetry arises when a small firm—typically a start-up new entrant—does bring a new product to market. Since such a start-up has a product on the market, it does face risk of infringement suits from established firms. But because it may have a relatively narrow technology base, it is at a disadvantage in negotiating cross-licenses. Established firms may refuse to cross-license, or demand large royalties for doing so. A small start-up may not be able to afford large royalties—even with backing from venture capitalists with the deepest pockets. Or an entrant with an important new technology may be forced to forfeit its technological edge if it has to cross-license that new technology in order to avoid infringement suits related to older technology that it builds upon or uses to achieve compatibility with existing systems.

The difficulties a small firm faces in playing the cross-licensing game are illustrated by the case of Lexar Media, Inc., one of the pioneers of compact flash memory cards for digital photography.[32] The technology of "flash" memory—small, removable memory cards that can be used with PCs, Palm Pilots, or digital cameras—was developed over the course of the 1990s. Sandisk Corporation applied for a patent in 1993 that was granted in 1997, covering a removable memory device in which the memory controller resides on the removable card. Many major semiconductor companies signed cross-license agreements with Sandisk, allowing them to make compact flash memory products without fear of infringing Sandisk's patents. But Lexar was unable to come to terms with Sandisk. Since such negotiations are confidential, there is no way to know why. But it is likely that Lexar's small portfolio gave it much less bargaining power than Intel or other large semiconductor manufacturers, while at the same time it was reluctant to license its digital photography patents to Sandisk and thereby lose its edge in that market segment.

Sandisk sued Lexar for patent infringement in 1998. Lexar countersued, claiming that Sandisk was infringing one of Lexar's patents. In March 2000, the judge in the case ruled that Lexar was guilty of "contributory infringement," because its digital photography products caused the consumer to infringe Sandisk's 1997 patent every time the consumer used the Lexar card. The judge refused, however, to rule on the validity of the Sandisk patent, leaving that issue for a jury at trial. Under heavy pressure from the judge to settle the case, Sandisk and Lexar finally reached a cross-licensing agreement in the fall of 2000. In the settlement, Lexar agreed that Sandisk's patent is valid and was infringed by Lexar's flash memory products then on the market, paid $8 million in royalties for such infringement through March 2001, and agreed to a 4 percent royalty beyond that date for certain products that continue to use the Sandisk technology. Sandisk agreed that Lexar's newly designed products do not infringe on Sandisk's patent, and paid $2 million to Lexar to license one of Lexar's patents.

The resolution of this case illustrates a continuing difficulty with the uncertainty of patent litigation. While Lexar can now get on with its business, the validity of the Sandisk patent has still not been established. If it had been invalidated at trial, Lexar would have avoided paying royalties and would also have saved everyone else from having to do so. Its decision to settle rather than "roll the dice" on a trial is an understandable one. And the judge's pressuring the parties to settle rather than bear the costs of a trial is also understandable, from the narrow perspective of the specific case. But, as is often the case, resolution of the conflict through settlement leaves in place the uncertainty of other parties, meaning that they continue to face the difficult choice of paying to license a patent of uncertain validity, or bearing the cost and risk of proving it invalid.

Biotechnology and Patented Research Tools

Another sector characterized by cumulative and overlapping innovation is biotechnology. Many of the patents in this area are for extracting or manipulating genetic material. This means that the development and commercialization of a new genetically engineered product may utilize a number of patented techniques. In principle, licenses could be negotiated to secure all of the needed rights, but as the number of needed licenses gets large this becomes problematic, both in terms of time and money.[33] In some cases, the owners of patents on tools for genetic manipulation insist on "reach through" licensing, whereby someone using the tool would not only need to pay a fee, but also pay royalties derived from the revenues of any product developed using the tool. The royalties on such licenses are typically small—1 percent or less of product revenues—but if a product development effort uses several such tools, the overall profitability of such a development effort can be seriously undermined. In effect, the need to secure multiple reach-through licenses can impose a large tax on the innovation process, and thereby significantly retard innovation.

One might expect this industry to develop the practice of broad cross-licensing that has evolved in the semiconductor industry. This does not seem to have emerged. It is hard to tell whether this is due to intrinsic differences between biotechnology and semiconductors, to differences in the institutional structure of the sectors, or only to the lack of experience with agreements of this kind among biotech firms.

The potential conflict between rights of "initial" inventors and the process of cumulative innovation is made particularly acute by the close connections in biotechnology between commercial development and fundamental academic research. Historically, universities and others engaged in academic research have not typically been targets of patent infringement suits. This is partly because there is a doctrine in patent law of an "experimental use exception," whereby otherwise infringing activity cannot be prevented if it occurs "for amusement, to satisfy idle curiosity, or for strictly philosophical inquiry." But it has never been clear that this narrow exception covers much of what universities do; the fact that they have rarely been sued in the past may have been due to a lack of concern or focus by patent holders as much as a belief that universities were truly exempt.

As universities have increasingly sought to enforce their patents in recent years, this may be changing. A recent CAFC decision has sent ripples of fear through the general counsel's offices at universities. In a case between Duke University and a former faculty member named John Madey, the experimental use exception was construed so narrowly that whatever fig leaf it may previously have provided university activities may have shriveled to the point of irrelevance.

Madey is a physicist who was wooed away from Stanford by Duke in 1988. While at Stanford, Madey had received two patents on "free electron lasers" (FEL). Duke built an FEL lab for Madey, including equipment covered by Madey's patents, and Madey headed this lab for almost a decade. Madey and Duke then had a falling out, and Madey was removed as head of the FEL lab and left the university. Duke continued to operate the FEL lab, and Madey sued, claiming infringement of the patents that he held from his Stanford days.

The district court judge framed the experimental use exception as covering activities "solely for research, academic or experimental purposes." Relying in part on Duke's established patent policy that states that Duke is "dedicated to teaching, research, and the expansion of knowledge . . . [and] does not undertake research or development work principally for the purpose of developing patents and commercial applications," he found that the Duke FEL was covered by the experimental use exception, and granted Duke's request for a ruling in its favor.[34]

Madey appealed, and the CAFC overruled the district judge's finding with regard to the experimental use exception and did so with language that seems, ironically, to say that universities, by their very nature, are not eligible for the experimental use exception. The court begins by considering whether the experimental use exception should be discarded entirely. It concludes that the exception should continue, "albeit in [a] very narrow form."

What is this form? The CAFC rejected the district court language of "solely for research, academic or experimental purposes," saying that this was impermissibly broader than the earlier test of uses "for amusement, to satisfy idle curiosity, or for strictly philosophical inquiry." It then went on to consider whether the FEL could come under this rubric. It concluded:

> . . . major research universities, such as Duke, often sanction and fund research projects with arguably no commercial application whatsoever. However, *these projects unmistakably further the institution's legitimate business objectives, including educating and enlightening students and faculty participating in these projects.* . . . In short, regardless of whether a particular institution or entity is engaged in an endeavor for commercial gain, so long as the act is in furtherance of the alleged infringer's legitimate business and is not solely for amusement, to satisfy idle curiosity, or for strictly philosophical inquiry, the act does not qualify for the very narrow and strictly limited experimental use defense. (emphasis added)

In other words, because the "business" of universities is, in fact, teaching and research, when students and faculty conduct research in university facilities they are pursuing the university's "business" objectives and, hence, are not eligible for the experimental use exception. Although the court technically sent the case back to the district court to determine whether the FEL could qualify under its articulated standard for experimental use, it is hard to imagine how any university research could qualify, given the CAFC's rejection of experimental use that "is in furtherance of the alleged infringer's legitimate business" and its definition of "educating and enlightening students and faculty" as "business" objectives. The Supreme Court refused to hear an appeal of the CAFC's *Madey* decision in June 2003.[35]

It remains unclear what the practical impact of this decision will be. It could be limited, because when a faculty member produces a patentable invention, the patent is normally assigned to the university. The Madey case is unusual because Madey owned the patents himself. The more common situation would have been that Duke could fire Madey and still use his patents, because Duke itself would own those patents. Even with a scientist like Madey who moves from one institution to another, the typical situation would have been for his earlier patents to be held by Stanford, and it seems unlikely that Stanford would have sued Duke over a research facility. In the biotechnology area, however, it is increasingly common for academic researchers to be working on projects very similar to research being conducted by commercial firms. As discussed above, this research could arguably require licensing or cross-licensing of many patents. Cross-licensing works best where institutions are in fairly symmetric positions, but firms and universities are inherently different from one another, making this situation problematic at best. Indeed, the major role played by universities in this area could inhibit the emergence of broad cross-licensing, precisely because universities' culture and incentives are so different from those of firms.

This is not to say that universities should always be protected by an experimental use exception. This would make it unprofitable, for example, to develop a new device whose market is largely academic research labs; if they could copy it with impunity there would be no market. But the CAFC's reasoning that being in the "business" of experimentation makes you ineligible for the experimental use exception merely avoids the hard issue of balancing an inventor's right against society's interest to foster additional research and experimentation.

When Things Get Downright Nasty

The previous section illustrates a number of ways in which the patent system, even when functioning as intended, can sometimes inhibit—rather than stimulate—innovation. Returning to the metaphor of patents as fences around the property that techno-logical developments represent, Robert Frost said, "good fences make good neighbors." Patents are, inherently, somewhat vague and ambiguous fences, and this ambiguity will always produce some level of dispute.

As patents have been strengthened in the last two decades, how-ever, some firms have gone beyond pushing the arguably ambigu-ous borders of their technological property, to making dramatic claims to ownership of seemingly distant parcels. By suing or threatening to sue competitors or would-be competitors, these companies have sought to achieve royalties or scare away competi-tion. As noted in the Introduction, the number of patent suits filed more than doubled over the decade of the 1990s.

Defending a patent infringement suit is expensive. Based on a survey of intellectual property lawyers in 2000, the cost of de-fending a large (more than $25 million at risk) patent infringement suit is about $2 million to $4.5 million.[36] For cases with less than $1 million at risk, the cost was $300,000 to $750,000 or about half the amount in dispute.[37] Given these large costs, and the realization that cases seem to have increasingly favored patent holders, even targets that think they are not infringing have a strong economic incentive to give in rather than fight. This means there are probably many cases of stifled competition that we do not even know about.

Sometimes people do stand and fight. One such case is that of Rambus and Infineon.[38] Rambus is a small company that designs—but does not manufacture—computer memory systems. It makes money by licensing its patented designs to other companies, who manufacture computer memory and sell it to computer makers.

Over the course of the 1990s, however, Rambus engaged in an extended campaign to abuse the patent system and essentially extort licensing royalties from memory manufacturers. The basis of this campaign—which a trial judge eventually described as "employing a combination of blitzkrieg and Sherman-esque tactics"[39]—was Patent Application No. 07/510,898 filed in 1990. The PTO and Rambus concluded that this application covered a multitude of different inventions. As is increasingly common, the PTO permitted Rambus to file many "continuations" derived from this original 1990 application, in which aspects of the original application were put forward as inventions in their own right. Over the course of the next decade, the PTO granted at least fifteen separate patents based on this 1990 application.

This process of filing divisional applications is intended to shape the patents and claims that are ultimately granted so as to fit the invention or inventions that have been made into the appropriate legal form. In many cases, a patent application may describe a technology with many potential implementations or "embodiments," only some of which are delineated in the specific claims in the award. Such a failure to claim all embodiments may arise because some embodiments were not foreseen at the time of original application, or it may arise simply from a desire not to over-complicate an application with too many claims. Since it is the claims that determine the scope of exclusion that the patentee can enforce, embodiments that are not covered by the claims may be difficult for the patent holder to protect. A divisional application allows a patentee to gain protection for embodiments of the discovery that were not included in the claims of the initial award, and thereby is an important aspect of allowing the inventor to claim what was truly invented in an orderly and efficient way. But the opportunity to file divisional applications is also used strategically by patent applicants, because it allows the applicant to shape its patents to evolving circumstances while retaining the priority date associated with the original application.[40] In Rambus's case, as late as 1999 it was modifying its patent claims to try to ensure that they covered new generations of memory chips. But the 1990 priority date, retained from the original application, meant that the novelty of these claims was evaluated relative to the "prior art" of a decade earlier. In a rapidly evolving field such as semiconductors, this gave Rambus a huge advantage.

The 1990 application relates to the design of DRAM (Dynamic Random Access Memory) chips, which are used for, among other things, the memory of PCs, servers, and other computers. In the early 1990s, Rambus offered a license to memory manufacturers for a DRAM design called a "Rambus DRAM" or RDRAM, based on patents derived from the 1990 applications. Many memory manufacturers used this technology, paying royalties to Rambus under licensing agreements. But semiconductor technology evolves rapidly, and the RDRAM was soon made obsolete by the development of the SDRAM and then the DDR SDRAM. Unwilling to lose its licensing royalty stream, Rambus tried to expand the reach of its patent portfolio to cover these newly developed chips.

Two important features of the computer memory industry are that many different companies manufacture both memory and computers, and that computer makers and consumers benefit greatly if memory made by different companies is interchangeable. This requires that memory chips be designed consistent with industry "standards," which are technical specifications that ensure that memory made by any company, so long as it meets the standard, will work as expected in any computer design. To this end, the Electronic Industries Association established a Joint Electron Devices Engineering Council (JEDEC), a voluntary association of memory and computer companies to establish such standards for semiconductor devices.

Because interchangeability is so important, most memory products are made to be consistent with the relevant standard. This means that any company that has a patent that covers technology required by such a standard is in a very strong position; it can insist on royalties from the entire industry. For this reason, standard-setting groups like JEDEC are very sensitive to the existence of patents that might cover technology incorporated into a standard. Further, they would like to know about patent applications that cover technology that might be incorporated in the standard, because otherwise they might establish a standard, move the entire industry toward using that design, and then find that a patent is granted that allows someone to hold the entire industry hostage.

For this reason, JEDEC, like many such associations, require their members to (1) disclose any pending patent applications that bear on the elements of standards under discussion, and (2) license any patents that end up covering the standard to everyone in the industry at "reasonable" royalty rates. Of course, defining what constitutes a "reasonable" royalty, and enforcing a reasonable royalty policy, are tricky undertakings. This difficulty makes the disclosure obligation all the more important, so that the people working on drafting standards have a clear understanding of the extent to which products designed to conform to the standard are going to be subject to royalty claims.

In the early 1990s, when the standards for SDRAM chips were being discussed at JEDEC, Rambus was a member of the organization. The JEDEC committee working on standards for DRAM knew that one patent from the 1990 application had been issued. But Rambus did not disclose to the committee that it had additional divisional applications pending. Worse, unbeknownst to the other members of JEDEC, Rambus was crafting yet more applications (still retaining the 1990 priority date) in which it attempted to cover the features of the JEDEC SDRAM standard as that standard was being discussed at committee meetings attended by Rambus representatives.[41]

Rambus eventually withdrew its membership in JEDEC, but it continued to file additional divisional applications derived from the original 1990 application. In 2000, Rambus filed suit against Infineon, a memory manufacturer, claiming that its products made under the JEDEC SDRAM standard (as well as additional products made under the subsequent DDR SDRAM standard) infringed four Rambus patents. These four patents were applied for between 1997 and 1999—an eternity in the memory chip sector after the original application whose priority date they retained. After being slapped with Rambus's infringement suit, Infineon counter-sued, claiming that Rambus's abuse of the JEDEC standard-setting process constituted fraud under Virginia law. As recompense for this fraud, Infineon demanded damages, and an injunction against Rambus's attempting to enforce the relevant patents.

In the spring of 2001, the judge in the case threw out Rambus's infringement case, after interpreting the claims in Rambus's patents in such a way that he ruled that the jury could not possibly conclude that Infineon had infringed.[42] To use again the words of the trial judge, Rambus' attempt to construe its patents to cover Infineon's products "was completely untethered to the language of the patent claims or the written description, and, in many cases, flatly contradicted the written description . . . [T]he clear and convincing evidence shows that Rambus knew, or should have known, that its patent infringement suit was baseless, unjustified, and frivolous."

This "baseless, unjustified and frivolous" lawsuit cost Infineon over $8 million to defend.[43] Infineon got a (temporary) reward, however, when the jury decided in favor of Infineon on the fraud claim, and awarded damages of $3.5 million, which was reduced by the judge to $350,000. In addition, the judge found that the baseless nature of Rambus suit, Rambus' fraudulent behavior and its misconduct during the litigation justified an order that Rambus reimburse $7.1 million of Infineon's attorneys' fees.

Unfortunately for Infineon, and, we believe, the establishment of good policy relating to patents and standards, the CAFC subsequently overturned the jury's fraud finding.[44] Essentially, the CAFC concluded that JEDEC's policy regarding the obligation to disclose pending patent applications was very narrow—basically limited to applications for patents that a party wishing to comply with the standard would necessarily infringe in order to comply. Since Rambus documents, and testimony of its employees, established clearly that Rambus explicitly modified the language of its patent claims to try to cover devices with features that were revealed to Rambus in JEDEC meetings, there can be no doubt that Rambus violated the intent and spirit of the JEDEC policy—to prevent individual companies from gaining an advantage over their rivals by patenting aspects of the standards being discussed. In effect, the appeals court did not dispute (because the trial record is very clear on this) that Rambus tried to commit fraud, but ruled that they did not succeed: despite Rambus's best efforts to craft their patent claims around the elements of the standard, it was, in the court's judgment, possible to comply with the standard without infringing any of the Rambus patents. And the court ruled that, as a legal matter, there could be no fraud in this case because the JEDEC policy only required disclosure of patent applications on inventions necessary for the standard.

In a dissenting opinion, CAFC Judge Prost pointed out Rambus's clear efforts to abuse the JEDEC process, as well as testimony at trial that this kind of abuse was prohibited by JEDEC. He argued that the question of whether the JEDEC rules prohibited the kind of behavior Rambus engaged in was a factual question, on which an appeals court is not supposed to second-guess the jury. Because of this close decision, Infineon took the somewhat unusual step of asking the entire CAFC court to review the panel decision and then appealed the CAFC's decision to the Supreme Court. A number of standard-setting organizations filed "friend of the court" briefs supporting Infineon's request for review, arguing, naturally enough, that if Rambus was allowed to get away with its chicanery, the entire standard-setting process would be undermined.[45] However, both the full CAFC and the Supreme Court refused to intervene, thereby upholding the CAFC's two to one decision sending the case back to the district court for another trial on the infringement claim.

Thus, by a two to one vote, the CAFC threw out the jury's fraud finding against Rambus. Since the district court judge's awarding of attorneys' fees to Infineon had been based in part on fraud (as well as misconduct during the trial itself), it remanded that issue to the lower court, to determine whether, in the absence of a fraud finding, Infineon was still entitled to have its fees reimbursed. Finally, the CAFC unanimously overruled the lower court's interpretation of the patent claims and its finding of non-infringement based on that claim interpretation. Rumbus is moving forward to retry the case, but Infineon still has the right to press its fraud claim under a parallel California statute and the Federal Trade Commission is investigating Rambus's behavior.

Whether or not justice is ultimately done in this case, it tells a disturbing story about a patent system that seems to have broken loose from its moorings and the proper role of encouraging invention and facilitating the commercial development of new products. Whatever one concludes about whether Rambus managed to stay on the right side of JEDEC's disclosure policies, this much is clear. Invention and innovation are hardly encouraged by a system that permits a patentee, in an industry in which technology advances dramatically every few years, to create new claims, based on what they learned at meetings of a standard-setting body, and then have those claims evaluated for novelty relative to the prior art of nine years earlier. In a way that is ultimately far more serious than PB&J sandwiches, this case calls into profound question whether the PTO is doing its job when reviewing applications. And the willingness of the CAFC to overrule a jury's finding about the fraudulent nature of that behavior makes it hard to avoid a sense that the judicial deck is also stacked in favor of patentees.

Patented PB&J Sandwiches

As the experience of the late 1980s and 1990s showed that firms could gain significant competitive advantage by aggressive patent enforcement, companies naturally tried ever harder to get patents locking up important aspects of the technology in their industries. It is the job of the patent office to ensure that patents are only awarded for truly new ideas. But when the patent office falls down on the job, then the "quality" of the patents issued deteriorates, and patent litigation becomes a free-for-all in which companies try to get patent-based property rights on existing technologies, and then use these rights to wage war against each other.

Be Sure to Make Them Click Twice

While the PB&J patent discussed in chapter 1 is amusing, these low-quality patents have real consequences when their owners sue to enforce them. Amazon.com was granted Patent No. 5,960,411 in 1999 for a "Method and System for Placing a Purchase Order Via a Communications Network."[46] This patent claims a method by which a Web site, having previously stored information about a customer, can allow the customer to make a purchase with a single "click" of a mouse. Amazon quickly sued barnesandnoble.com, claiming that B&N's "Express Lane" purchasing method infringed the patent. Within three months, Amazon had secured a preliminary injunction against B&N, on the grounds that it was likely to eventually prevail at trial and would suffer irremediable harm in the meantime from competition with B&N. As a result, B&N's Express Lane service offering had to be shut down, before B&N even had an opportunity to try to prove that the Amazon patent was invalid. One could almost feel the Internet shudder.

Many observers believe that the Amazon patent should never have been granted, either because others had already implemented similar systems, meaning that Amazon's was not novel, or, if no one had done exactly what Amazon did, they easily could have, meaning that the invention fails the test of non-obviousness. If "one click" could be patented, then virtually any approach to the Internet and the Web could be patented. Coming as it did at the height of the dot-com boom, Amazon's bombshell led to a flood of patent filings, and a lot of nervous hand-wringing by Web companies who suspected that there was someone, somewhere with a patent or a patent application that could be claimed to cover what they were doing.

It took over a year, but the CAFC overturned the preliminary injunction that Amazon had won. While the appeals court did not address directly whether or not B&N infringed the Amazon patent, they ruled that there was sufficient doubt about the validity of the patent that Amazon should not have been granted a preliminary injunction.[47] (As discussed in chapter 4, patentees are only supposed to get the benefit of a preliminary injunction if there is a high likelihood that the patentee will prevail at trial.) In the end, Amazon and B&N settled the case, so that the legal status of the Amazon patent remains uncertain.

In the aftermath of the one-click imbroglio, applications for patents on so-called "business methods" have continued to swell; even the crash of the dot-com boom in 2000 and 2001 has not caused the tide to ebb.[48] Many observers remain highly skeptical about the validity of these patents, and great uncertainty surrounds whether ongoing e-commerce activities are in danger of generating infringement suits. In short, there is grave doubt whether the patent system is encouraging or retarding innovation in this area.

The Battlefield Assessment

The last fifteen years have seen litigation over patents with a frequency and scale that was previously unusual. While every case has its own specific facts and consequences, a number of general observations emerge:

- Enforcement of patents has changed long-established patterns of technology development in a number of key industries. Maintenance of a strong patent position is essential for competitive success in semiconductors, computers, software, biotechnology and many other industries.
- Patent litigation is expensive and risky. Even the threat of being forced to defend against patent infringement will, in many cases, compel companies to pay royalties or abandon particular products.
- The cumulative nature of innovation in several important industries puts multiple innovative firms in constant conflict with each other. The patent system seems increasingly to be a source of uncertainty and costs, rather than a mechanism for managing and minimizing conflict.
- The unnecessary costs and risks associated with patent litigation have been gravely exacerbated by the deterioration of examination standards at the patent office. We have gone from a system that before 1980 gave out rifles and handguns, after some amount of background checking, to one that today hands out grenades and bazookas to anyone who asks for one.

Firms have always been eager to make money, and are always willing to exploit the legal system when it presents opportunity for commercial advantage. The granting of patents on important inventions has frequently involved controversy, and the exclusivity patents create has always been a source of concern and unease. But the developments described in this chapter were not the inevitable evolution of modern capitalism. They can be traced to specific changes that Congress made in how the patent system operates. The next chapter looks at the long history of political controversies surrounding patent policies, and then the subsequent two chapters look in detail at the changes made in the United States in 1982 and 1990.

Chapter 3

The Long Debate

T he legislators gathered to consider the national patent system. Angry industrialists complained of many flaws in the current system. Foremost among these was the scanty review that patent applications often received and the frequency with which manufacturers were surprised by new patents granted for established technologies, endangering ongoing commercial activities with the threat of baseless litigation over patent claims. The critics noted that an observation about the British patent system was equally applicable here: "the present machinery gives the minimum advantage to the inventor and inflicts the maximum disadvantage to the public."[49] Others took a more extreme view, and argued that patents were utterly unnecessary: one popular maxim was that "geniuses, just as the stars, must shine without pay."[50] The newspapers of the day were full of arguments by lawyers and economists about the merits and drawbacks of patents, and the extent to which these awards spurred innovation and economic growth.

Despite its similarity to recent events in the United States, this drama transpired over 130 years ago, as the Dutch States General met to consider the fate of its patent system. Reflecting both the flaws of the Dutch patent award process and the European-wide skepticism about the value of these awards, the legislators took a dramatic and unprecedented step: they abolished the Dutch patent system.

This historical episode highlights the fact that the issues being discussed today in the United States are not new ones. The basic questions being debated in Internet chat groups and Washington policy salons—for instance, about the virtues of weak versus strong patent rights and comprehensive versus more cursory examinations of patent applications—have long been argued. So too, the worries expressed today about patent quality and its impact on the economy have echoed across the centuries.

The history of patents around the globe could also easily fill many volumes the size of this one. Thus, our goal in this chapter will not be to deliver a comprehensive history of the patent systems of the world. Rather, we will simply present the stories of three oft-forgotten dramas, where debates over the nature and quality of patent awards led to dramatic and heated discussions that shed light on the complexity and durability of the issues we face today.

Our motivation in presenting these is not to instill in our readers an appreciation for musty archives. Rather, these illustrations help establish three key lessons:

- Worries about detrimental economic effects of granting patents are not new. Rather these debates are almost as old as the institution of the patent grant itself.
- There are no easy solutions to the problems of running a patent system. There is an inherent trade-off in this system, between rewarding innovators and burdening commerce, competition, and other inventors. Numerous approaches have been attempted over the years, and none has satisfied everyone.
- The process of change in the patent system resembles a pendulum. Festering problems often lead to a dramatic shift in patent administration, which often goes too far in the other direction, generating a new set of problems of its own.

With the benefit of this historical context, we will then turn in chapters 4 and 5 to understanding the two key changes that have occurred in the U.S. patent system over the past two decades. As before, we will see that these changes occurred at least in part to redress a perceived historical drift toward weakening patents. Consistent with the historical pattern, they produced a dramatic swing of the patent pendulum that now cries out for adjustment in the other direction.

Scene 1: Shuffling the Deck

Rulers—whether kings, princes, or presidents—have long granted exclusive privileges to their subjects. In some cases, the subjects have gained the exclusive right to ply a trade; in others, to use a new product and process. Given the prevalence of these practices, it is hard to discern precisely when the first real patent system emerged.

Some have argued that the Alpine mining law promulgated by King Wenceslaus II in 1300 constituted the world's first patent law; others point to the Venetian Republic's legislation of 1474.[51] What distinguished these early codes from previous grants of exclusive royal privileges was the linkage between the granting of the privilege and the undertaking of an invention. For instance, when Galileo applied to the Doge of Venice for a patent on a new water irrigation device, he highlighted the lengthy research process in which he had engaged.

It took several centuries, however, for the principle to be firmly established that patents should only be granted for significant new inventions. The evolution of patent law to incorporate this principle was especially dramatic in England.[52] There, as elsewhere, patents initially emerged as just another special privilege that was granted by the heads of government. Some rulers made a genuine effort to insure that patents were granted only for significant discoveries, though some might quibble whether Edward III's grant of a patent on manufacture of the philosopher's stone would qualify. Other leaders were less scrupulous. Most notoriously, Queen Elizabeth I granted patents for many of the daily necessities of life, such as salt, vinegar, and starch, even though they had been widely employed for many centuries.

These patents stirred widespread resentment. Many of the awards went to royal favorites as rewards for their loyalty. In the case of the starch patent, for instance, the courtiers who received the award owed the Queen an extensive sum: by this grant, she hoped that they would raise enough funds to repay her.

The pernicious effects of these unjustified grants of exclusivity were exacerbated by the one-sided nature of the litigation process. Patent-holders had broad privileges to search the property of potential infringers, and seize potentially infringing goods. In many cases, patentees would visit factories and warehouses not because infringements were likely there, but because they expected that the owner would be willing to make a payment to avoid the trouble and damage that a search would entail.

But the targets of the patent-holders, the alleged infringers, had no way to challenge these awards. Because patents were considered a personal grant from the Queen (an exercise of her "Royal Prerogative"), those who challenged these patents could be found by the Queen's Court to be showing contempt of the Queen—with dire consequences.

These conditions triggered a Parliamentary rebellion in 1601. While earlier efforts by parliamentarians to raise questions about these grants had been met with royal scorn or censure, now a critical mass of legislators spoke out. A torrent of resentment spewed forth in the House of Commons. Case after case of monopolists abusing their privileges was brought to light, including the nearly twenty-fold increase in the price of sea salt after the Queen had granted a patent. Legislation was drawn up to curtail these rights. After four days of feverish debate, the Queen herself appeared at Parliament and announced that she would reform the system if the bill were withdrawn. Among the steps that she took were curtailing some of the most objectionable patents, such as those on salt, vinegar, pots, and brushes, and submitting the others to the test of the courts.

This edict led immediately to a test case. The Queen had granted a patent in 1598 to Edward Darcy, one of her grooms, for the manufacture and importation of playing cards over the next twenty-one years. Darcy was far from the inventor of the playing card. In fact, Elizabeth had previously granted patents on playing cards to other courtiers in 1576 and again in 1588. Soon after the Queen's proclamation, Darcy challenged a would-be competitor in the Privy Chamber. The two parties' lawyers debated vigorously whether the patent was a valid one, and whether the Queen had the right to grant such monopolies at all.

In 1603—perhaps not coincidentally, only a few months after the Queen's death—the courts ruled that patents are only legal when they benefit the public as a whole. In the words of the summation of the alleged infringer's counsel, the case laid out the principle that would guide patent offices around the world: "Where any man by his own charge and industry or by his own wit or invention doth bring any new trade into the realm or any engine tending to the furtherance of a trade that was never used before and that for the good of the Realm; that in such cases the King may grant to him a monopoly patent for some reasonable time . . . otherwise not."[53] This finding was codified in Great Britain some twenty years later, when the Statute of Monopolies established the principle that patents should only be granted to "true and first inventor and inventors."[54] Even in these cases, the act imposed some important curbs, such as restricting patents on inventions that were "contrary to the law, mischievous to the state, [that led to] raising prices of commodities at home, or hurt at trade, or generally inconvenient."[55]

These curbs were not the final solution to this problem. Even after the passage of the Statute, there remained a strong temptation to enhance the Crown's revenues by granting exclusive rights in exchange for a share of the profits. But this act established the ground rules for a new era. By the mid-seventeenth century, the granting of patents as royal patronage, not associated with an invention, was greatly reduced. Equally important, the principle that someone accused of infringing a patent had the right to challenge the validity of the patent itself was embedded in the law.

Scene 2: Reducing the Barriers

By the end of the eighteenth century, the patent system was again sparking controversy in England. But now the shoe was on the other foot: leading industrialists argued that the patent system was one in which awards were far too difficult to obtain.[56]

The object of the wrath of the inventors—which included such luminaries as James Watt, who greatly improved the steam engine—was a very old piece of legislation, the Clerk's Act of 1535, enacted in the reign of Henry VIII. This law dictated a multi-step process before any official grant could be made. Patent applicants had to contact as many as ten distinct offices, with new sets of forms often prepared for each. Even the sovereign's signature needed to be obtained, not just once, but twice.

While these review steps were ostensibly to ensure that no inappropriate patents were issued, they also had another motive. The preamble to the Clerk's Act stated quite brazenly that a purpose of the act was to finance underpaid government clerks. Applicants had to apply for separate awards to cover England, Ireland, Scotland, and Wales, each of which entailed separate forms and fees. The cost of a patent for the United Kingdom during this period was £400, more than 50,000 of today's dollars. As Charles Dickens related in his "Poor Man's Tale of a Patent": "Look at the Home Secretary, the Attorney-General, the Patent Office, the Engrossing Clerk, the Lord Chancellor, the Privy Seal, the Clerk of the Patents, the Lord Chancellor's Purse-bearer, the Clerk of the Hanaper, the Deputy Clerk of the Hanaper, the Deputy Sealer, and the Deputy Chaff-wax. No man in England could get a Patent for an Indian-rubber band, or an iron-hoop, without feeing all of them. Some of them, over and over again." These requirements may not have posed a forbidding barrier to the wealthiest inventors, such as the gentleman-farmer who wanted a patent for a pen in which to grow exceptionally fat hogs. But for the average middle-class inventor, the delay and cost were formidable challenges. Inventors wryly pointed out that it was perhaps not an accident that the Great Seal Patent Office was located in the same building as the Bankruptcy and Lunacy Offices.

Moreover, the patent application process allowed opponents ample opportunities to stymie the patent through the use of "caveats." These essentially allowed other firms to describe existing approaches or discoveries that might be relevant as the government officials considered the patent application. Frequently, these caveats were very vague, and consequently difficult for the inventors to effectively rebut. Some established firms would make a practice of simply opposing all patent applications in their field, in the hope of ensuring that they remained unchallenged by new manufacturers. In a number of instances, the established firms used the opportunity to review their new rivals' patent applications—putatively undertaken to help prepare a caveat filing—as a convenient mechanism for conducting industrial espionage.

The efforts to reform this system, however, moved only slowly. From 1785, when the first meeting of inventors was held to discuss patent policy, the reform effort proceeded by fits-and-starts. Periodically, some action would emerge—legislation was introduced in 1795 and 1820, a parliamentary inquiry was launched in 1829, and so forth—but the initiative would soon peter out and be abandoned.

Three reasons account for the sluggish response. First, this inaction reflected the entrenched power of established actors. Not surprisingly, patent office officials, and the solicitors who worked closely with them, questioned the need for dramatic changes in a system that was proving so highly lucrative for themselves.

Second, the sluggish response reflected the lack of unity on the part of the inventors. Being highly entrepreneurial and individualistic characters, they had little aptitude for working together in a concerted manner. Often locked in bitter battles over particular inventions, they found it hard to establish a united front.

Finally, the slow response also reflected real concerns about the possibility that the changes might have undesirable consequences. For instance, reservations were frequently expressed about reformers' calls for patents to be examined by a single examiner, who would decide whether the patent should issue. Some feared that it would be impossible to retain sufficiently expert patent examiners; others worried that these would be partial to certain applicants. Similarly, the proposal to cut the costs of patents triggered much concern: would not the patent office and the courts be flooded by trivial patent applications? Given that few members of parliament had the time or inclination to develop an expertise in patent policy, these uncertainties and misgivings deterred bold action.

The lack of consensus at this time about desirable policies to encourage invention is evident in the ongoing argument for abandoning the system of patents altogether in favor of the use of prizes. As noted in chapter 1, in these years Parliament established several prizes to encourage specific desired inventions. Backers of the prize approach hoped to make even greater use of this mechanism, but many others were skeptical of this approach. Fueling the skeptics was the possibility that the government would not honor its commitment to pay the prize money once the inventions were made. To cite but one famous example, the British government had set up a £20,000 prize in 1714 for a navigational device that would allow sailors to determine their longitude at sea. (While it was relatively straightforward to determine latitude—the distance between the North Pole and Equator—by observing the stars, the determination of how far a ship was east or west of London was much harder. Captains needed to rely on guesswork, and numerous tragic shipwrecks resulted.) A lone inventor, John Harrison, went to London in 1730, hoping to claim this prize, but the Board responsible for paying out the prize resisted doing so for a full thirty-three years, demanding additional proofs of the accuracy of his device. Ultimately, the intervention of both Parliament and the King was required before he received (close to) the full amount promised.[57]

Meanwhile, the debate over patents waxed and waned across the decades. Over the course of the 1840s, petitions from inventors flowed into parliament. These highlighted the concerns that had been articulated many decades earlier by James Watt and his peers, illustrated with dramatic tales of inventors who had been unable to garner patents and financial rewards. By 1851, there were at least eleven inventor's committees seeking to reform the patent system. The groundswell of protests reached the point in 1851 where Parliament announced the establishment of yet another commission to examine the issues with the patent system.

After extensive investigations, the commission concluded that many of the concerns expressed by inventors did indeed have to be addressed. This recommendation was largely put into effect with the passage of the Patent Law Amendment Act of 1852. Parliament established a single patent office, with a streamlined administrative process. Moreover, the costs of a patent filing were reduced considerably: an initial patent grant could now be obtained for £25, rather than the £300 up-front fees previously required. (There were, however, additional fees, that had to be paid as the patent matured.)

This bill was, to be sure, not the end of the patent reform process. It was not until 1883 that an office resembling a modern one, with a formal process for ascertaining whether the invention was a reasonable one, was established. Thus, the broad historical trend in nineteenth century England (paralleled, as we will see in the next chapter, by the evolution of the U.S. patent system) was for the needs and demands of the increasingly vocal and powerful inventor and industrial communities to carry the day over those who worried about the downside of a powerful patent system. The result was to codify and institutionalize a system that made patents less expensive and more reliable, while increasingly formalizing the process for trying to ensure that grants were made only to true inventors. In this way, the patent system gradually took its place at the heart of the process of technological innovation that propelled the industrial revolution. But as we will see, the controversies over the costs and benefits of this approach did not end with these reforms.

Scene 3: The Dutch Rebellion

At roughly the same time that the patent system was being solidified in England and the United States, there was also a broad anti-patent movement in many parts of Europe.[58] While this was partially motivated by abstract considerations, concerns about the ability of the patent system to ensure high-quality rewards were a critical ingredient in the debate.

The motivations for this rebellion were several. Some critics posed philosophic arguments, for instance, questioning whether intellectual ideas should have owners. Others were more sympathetic to patents in principle, accepting the argument that society would find it in its best interest to encourage discoveries by rewarding innovation. These critics argued, however, that it would prove too difficult to devise a system that would reward true inno-

vators fairly. The editors of *The Economist* expressed this view suc-
cinctly: "The community requires . . . that skillful men who con-
tribute to the progress of society be well paid for their exertions.
The Patent Laws are supported because it is erroneously supposed
that they are a means to this end."[59]

Once again, many alternatives were discussed in the major European journals of the day. Some felt, for instance, a national or international body (whether comprised of government officials or industry leaders) could do a far better job of spurring innovation by
apportioning rewards rather than granting patents. These officials
could, like the British efforts discussed above, designate prizes in
advance for certain critical discoveries, or else apportion rewards
after significant-but-unexpected innovations had been made.

These alternatives, however, were also bitterly criticized. The
British economist John Stuart Mill expressed skepticism that government officials could determine the proper value of a discovery.[60]
After all, in many cases the value of an invention was only revealed
after many years. Far more natural, he suggested, was the principal
of exclusivity that a patent award provided. Others, noting the arbi-
trariness and corruption that an award system could induce,
reached an alternative conclusion. The German politician Bismarck,
for instance, stated that "instead of making again hopeless efforts
to revise the Patent Laws,"[61] rewards for intellectual property
should be abolished entirely.

Nowhere was this debate fiercer than in the Netherlands.[62] The
Netherlands had been one of the early champions of the patent system: in fact, it and Great Britain were the two European countries
that had most consistently granted patents from the sixteenth century to the mid-nineteenth century.

Yet by the mid-1800s, Dutch enthusiasm for the system was
wearing thin. In part, the growing Dutch opposition to the patent
system was a reflection of the general anti-patent mood that was
sweeping Europe at the time. But much of the Dutch patent unease
seems to have been the consequence of the distinct features of the
existing Dutch patent law, which had been enacted in 1817. As was
the case in other countries at this time, this legislation did not require that patents be examined. For instance, applicants simply had

to declare they had invented a discovery: the honesty of the individual making the declaration was often simply taken for granted. When the King and one of his ministers examined the application, in many cases it appears the scrutiny was none too exhaustive. As a result, patents often issued for inventions that were neither novel nor practical. An instance of the second category that especially incensed critics was Patent No. 945, which proposed to employ a steam engine to cut diamonds automatically.

In principle, the Dutch could have addressed this problem by instituting systematic examination of patent applications, as did the United States in 1836 and Britain in 1883. But there were other objections to the patent system as it operated in the Netherlands. Perhaps most objectionable, patents were not published until the expiration of the award, which occurred fifteen years after the award (and in some cases even later). This approach—unique to the Dutch system at the time—was justified on the grounds that discoveries might otherwise be imitated too easily, presumably because patent-holders would not have the resources to track down all infringers. But the consequences of such secrecy were frequently dire. A manufacturer could never be sure of his position when a patentee would appear, claiming to own a patent granted many years before, that covered a new product that the firm had just introduced, or even worse, a product the firm had relied upon for many years. Because of this danger, observers claimed, Dutch firms were less willing to innovate than their peers in London or Hamburg.

These discontents gradually bubbled up among Dutch manufacturers. After a long discussion of their grievances, the Netherlands Society for the Promotion of Industry decided in 1864 to send the King a petition calling for the abolition of the patent system. While many of the complaints might have been addressed by more modest alterations, the conversation became progressively more heated as the debate progressed. No great inventions were due to patents, the abolitionists declared: after all, is not the head start, or "first-mover advantage," that an innovator gets a sufficient spur to innovation? Furthermore, by abolishing its patent system, the Dutch could set an example that would be followed all through Europe.

While some industrialists followed suit in demanding the abolition of the patent system, others remained more cautious. Many of the grievances could be addressed by more modest modifications to the patent code, following the lead of Belgium, which had just rewritten theirs. Moreover, many industrialists expressed skepticism as to how sustained the anti-patent movement would be: they anticipated, rather, the Netherlands could find itself isolated, with angry neighbors resenting their cavalier infringement of discoveries patented elsewhere.

It was only a matter of months, however, before the issue reached the States General, the Dutch parliament. The advocates of the patent system tried futilely to poke holes in the abolitionists' arguments. For instance, J. L. de Bruyn Kops, who also served as an economics professor at Delft, pointed to the 126 patent applications on "velocipedes" (bicycles) filed in the previous year in England. Even if but "2 or 3 which perhaps would prove to be useful," granting patents on these inventions might still make sense, because the benefits to society from a more efficient personal transport device would be great. But with skepticism about the patent system swaying industrialists and citizens alike, the momentum was overwhelming. In July 1869, the Second Chamber of the States General voted forty-nine to eight to abolish the patent system, and the Dutch ceased to grant patents.

This proved to be the peak of the European anti-patent movement. Some have attributed the waning of this movement to the recession of 1873 and the protectionist spirit that emerged across Europe. Many of the most vehement advocates for abolishing patents were in favor of free trade as well, and the eclipse of this one cause hurt the other. But the Dutch would stubbornly stick to their no-patent system until 1910, even though the parliamentarians' predictions that they were in the vanguard of a new movement were not borne out. The impact of the absence of patent protection during this period remains controversial: while certainly the country underwent extensive industrialization during these years, local inventors complained bitterly that their ideas were being too readily copied by competitors and that they were thereby impeded in innovating.[63] Eventually, the relentless pressure from trading partners in Germany and elsewhere led to the abandonment of this position.

Some More General Patterns

We began this chapter with a simple proposition: that the debates about the patent system seen today are far from unique. Rather, these discussions have been heard in other times and places.

The more skeptical reader may still question whether the examples are representative, or are just three oddities over the course of history. To address this possibility, we present some more systematic worldwide evidence. For this purpose, we focus on the sixty largest countries (by total economic activity) in 2000. These nations include the historical winners that have experienced very rapid growth, such as the United States and Japan, and those who have encountered economic reversals, such as Argentina and South Africa. We look at the changes in their patent systems over time, gleaning this information from the many guidebooks to patent policy that have been published over the past century-and-a-half.

Figure 3.1 simply shows the number of policy changes each decade in a number of substantive areas of patent policy.[64] Because the number of countries in the sample changes over time (for instance, countries such as Algeria and India did not exist as independent entities before World War II), we present in each year the ratio of the number of patent reforms undertaken to the number of independent nations in the sample at the beginning of the relevant decade. The chart highlights the fact that changes in patent protection have been commonplace. In fact, there have been five visible waves of patent policy changes. One can see, for example, the "Patent Controversy" of the 1850s and 1860s discussed in the third vignette above. The most recent wave, in the 1990s, is associated with changes that have been implemented around the world in response to the attempted harmonization of worldwide patent policy that was agreed to in the "Uruguay Round" of worldwide negotiations related to tariffs and international trade, which was concluded in 1993.

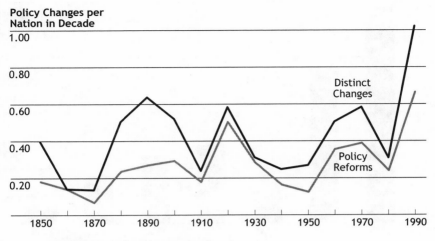

Policy Changes per Nation in Decade

Distinct Changes

Policy Reforms

Figure 3.1 Patent policy changes by decade.

The next two charts show that the changes that we highlighted above were not unique or peculiar episodes. Rather, these debates and policy changes are representative of the ways in which the patent system has changed more generally as we have moved into the modern age.

First, when we think back to the Parliamentary rebellion against Queen Elizabeth's patent grants at the beginning of the seventeenth century, the main concern was the degree of discretion the ruler had. Essentially, she had total freedom as to when and how many rights to grant. The evolution of a modern patent system required the institutionalization of limits on this executive discretion. The same process of limiting the freedom of the ruler—whether monarch, prime minister or president—has played itself out around the globe.

Figure 3.2 illustrates the historical process of reducing the discretion of rulers in granting patents. "Discretion" has many dimensions, but the general tendency can be seen by examining one critical dimension that can be measured and compared easily: the monarch's or executive's ability to extend the life of a patent beyond the stated grant period without obtaining any special permis-

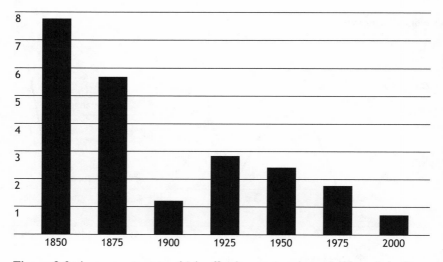

Figure 3.2 Average extent to which officials can extend patent life at their discretion in sixty nations.

sion from the legislature. Over time, the degree of discretion of this sort allowed to government officials has fallen sharply: the average extension that officials could offer has fallen from nearly eight years in 1850 to less than a year in 2000. We could also have looked at many other ways in which government officials have exercised discretion, such as the right to terminate or license the patent without the patentee's permission, the ability to vary the fee charged patentees, and the prerogative to review patent applications in different ways. These analyses all tell a similar story: the discretion of government officials has gradually but systematically been increasingly constrained by specific patent rules.

A prominent feature of both the early British patent controversy and the Dutch controversy was a desire to see that patents are granted only after some kind of systematic test to ensure that they go only to true inventors. Even after arbitrary royal favors were reined in, many countries evolved "registration" systems like that of the Dutch statute of 1817, in which the hard work of determining whether patents were really valid was pushed off onto the courts. The cost and disruption that suits over questionable patents entailed was a major concern.

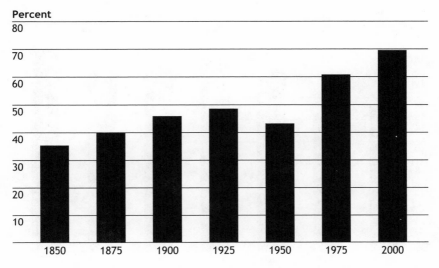

Figure 3.3 Share of patent systems in sixty largest nations with formal examination system.

Figure 3.3 displays that there has been a considerable movement from such registration systems to examination systems. Over time, the percentage of nations that examine patents prior to issuing them—rather than automatically granting patents to those who meet the basic requirements—has increased substantially. The share has climbed from 35 percent in 1850 to nearly 70 percent today. And the 70 percent with examination systems includes all of the major industrialized countries, in which the vast bulk of technological innovations originate.

The final figure shows one other theme, not developed at length in this section, but which will be important in the sections that follow. Patent protection has become stronger, which has led to more attention to the way in which these awards are made. Even if the quality of the way in which patents are examined had not changed—as we will argue, there are good reasons to be worried about this, at least within the United States—these awards are now far more important than they once were, so mistakes are more costly. While in the text that follows, we will emphasize the experience in the Untied States, the phenomenon is truly a global one.

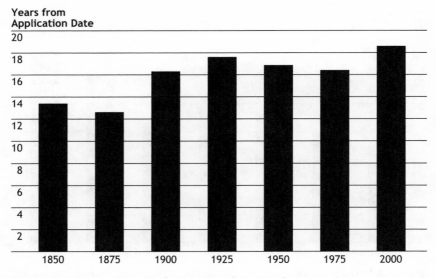

Figure 3.4 Average length of patent awards in sixty largest nations.

Figure 3.4 depicts one measure of patent protection: the length of time of the longest patent regularly granted, once again averaged across all active nations in our sample. While there have been some ebbs and flows in this measure—note the shortening of the average patent life during the anti-patent movement of the 1860s—the basic trend has been toward longer patent protection. The average patent today is nearly 40 percent longer than that in 1850. This increase in the degree of protection afforded patent-holders implies that assuring the validity of patents—an issue, which as we have seen, has long sparked passionate debate—is particularly critical today.

Lessons from History

As noted, the kinds of issues being debated today in the United States are not new ones. Disputes over the way that the patent system works have been commonplace for centuries. The same questions that are on the agenda today—for instance, the ability to reward inventors in a timely manner, the quality of the review provided by patent office procedures, and the risks and burdens created by litigation to enforce patents—have frequently been the subject of passionate debate.

Moreover, these episodes highlight the fact that no one right solution exists to many of these dilemmas. To be sure, we have seen some trends over time: as we highlighted above, patent office officials have gotten less discretion in how they make grants, patent awards have been scrutinized more intensively, and awards have gotten longer. But many different approaches to organizing patent systems have been tried, and many differences persist around the world. However the system is organized, there are likely to be people who think that patents are too easy or too hard to get, and to easy or too hard to enforce.

Finally, it is important to highlight the cyclical nature of historical patent controversies. The abuses of the Elizabethan era—where the ruler could make grants with the stroke of pen—led to reforms that by the eighteenth century were judged to have made it too expensive and too difficult to get patents in Great Britain. The 1817 Dutch law made it so easy to get patents, and made patents so powerful for their owners, that rising resentment then led to the outright abolition of patents in the Netherlands. This abolition led in turn to increasing complaints by inventors and the eventual reinstitution of the patent law. Far too often, fixes to patent law have created as many problems as they have solved. Patent policy is truly the kingdom of unintended consequences.

Chapter 4

The Silent Revolution

W e now home in from the broad sweep of history to
the shifts in the United States over the past two decades. These
years saw two changes that may initially appear trivial: a change in
the manner in which appeals of patent disputes were heard in the
federal courts, and some even subtler shifts in the financing of the
patent office. Yet, as we shall see, the shifts had profound effects.

Given the pendulum-like nature of historical patent policy illustrated in the previous chapter, it will not surprise the reader to learn
that the changes of the past two decades fit into a larger historical
pattern. In the late nineteenth and early twentieth centuries, patent
awardees were free to engage in virtually any activity, no matter
how seemingly anti-competitive. For instance, regulators could not
block multiple patent-holding firms from coming together to form
patent pools that were then used to collectively restrict output and
control prices. In 1902, the U.S. Supreme Court went so far as to
state "the general rule is absolute freedom in the use or sale of patent rights under the patent laws of the United States. The very
object of these laws is monopoly."[65]

From this high-water mark at the turn of the century, the power that patents conveyed to their owners began a long period of gradual decline. The permissive attitude towards restrictive practices by patent holders was eroded by a series of court decisions over the twentieth century. Indeed, by the 1970s, firms' use of patents to gain competitive advantage was highly constrained by the enforcement of laws governing competitive and anti-competitive behavior. The Department of Justice promulgated a list of "Nine No-Nos," which prohibited a wide range of seemingly innocuous strategic uses of patents. As overall economic performance deteriorated in the 1970s, and Japan in particular seemed to be "beating" the U.S. at the game of technological competition, there was increasing clamor for action to strengthen the U.S. innovation system.

On one level, therefore, the "pro-patent" policy changes of the 1980s and 1990s can be seen as the inevitable, perhaps even desirable, historical "backswing" after a long period of weakening patents. There is an element of truth in this perspective. But it does not capture the totality of what has occurred. If the only change in the late twentieth century had been to reinforce patent rights after a long period of decline, we probably would not be writing this book—though one still might want to ask whether the swing had been too extreme. As described in the Introduction, however, what has happened is the combination of a strengthening of patent rights with a weakening of the standards for the granting of patents. There are no natural or historical roots for this particular combination of changes. There is no evidence that anyone considered the likely effects of combining stronger patents with easier-to-get patents. When we then add in a final factor—that the changes manifested themselves most dramatically in technologically and economically crucial sectors such as software and biotech—we have the unusual combination of circumstances necessary for a "perfect storm," a complex and intensifying policy mess rather than a gently swinging pendulum.

While it is the combination of circumstances that is responsible for the mess, we need to understand each of the changes individually before we can understand their combined and mutually reinforcing effects. This chapter will address the restructuring of the courts; chapter 5 will consider the changing administrative status of the U.S. Patent and Trademark Office (PTO).

The Backdrop

Since the birth of the republic, almost all formal disputes involving patents have been tried in the federal judicial system.[66] Congress assigned patent litigation to the federal courts in light of the fact that patents are granted by the federal government and are inherently national rights. The initial litigation must occur in a federal "district" court. Once the case is decided at the district court level, one or more of the parties is likely to appeal the district court outcome; this appeal is heard by an "appellate" court. In October 1982, a new centralized appellate court for patents was established, which was named the Court of Appeals for the Federal Circuit. How did this shift come about? And why did it have such a dramatic impact on the patent system?

Before 1982, appeals of patent cases—like all other federal court cases—were heard in one of the twelve "circuit" courts of appeal, with each circuit corresponding to a geographic region; the First Circuit, for example, covers New England (and Puerto Rico). These distinct circuit courts differed considerably in their interpretation of patent law, with some of them more than twice as likely to uphold patent claims as others. The way in which the courts interpreted the requirement (discussed in the Introduction) that patents must not be obvious is a prime example. For instance, when interpreting design patents, some circuits required that the inventions would not be obvious to an "ordinary designer." Other circuits used the looser test that the design would not be obvious to an "ordinary intelligent man."[67] While the distinction may seem only semantic, the implications were frequently substantial, because an ordinary designer could be presumed more capable of creating new designs than a mere "intelligent man." Hence, many inventions that a court using an "ordinary designer" test might have considered trivial (that is, obvious to a hypothetical "ordinary designer") were deemed significant—and hence patentable—by other courts because an "ordinary intelligent man" would not have found them so obvious.

The persistent differences in patent litigation outcomes are illustrated in Figure 1, which depicts the fraction of cases won by the patent-holder in the different circuits between 1953 and 1977. To be sure, the selection of cases by district may not have been totally random: for instance, the First and Ninth Circuits may have had more appeals of cases involving high-technology firms because of the concentration of such companies in Massachusetts' Route 128 area and California's Silicon Valley. Furthermore, parties' willingness to appeal cases may have been affected by their perception of the likely outcome in the appellate court. But it is unlikely that such variations in the mixture of cases could explain the large disparities seen here. For instance, why should the patents litigated in the Eighth Circuit (covering the Great Plains states) have been almost seven times less likely to be valid than those adjudicated in the Tenth Circuit (Rocky Mountains) and four times less likely to be valid than in the Seventh Circuit (Illinois, Indiana, and Wisconsin)?[68]

Obviously, conflicting or inconsistent decisions in different federal circuit courts are not limited to patent law. Typically, when somebody loses a case in one circuit that they would have won under the legal standard used in a different circuit, they appeal to the U.S. Supreme Court, asking it to overturn the adverse circuit court ruling, and substitute the doctrine or approach adopted by a different circuit. Indeed, conflicting interpretations or policies in different circuits is one of the criteria that the Supreme Court uses when deciding whether to hear particular cases. When the Supreme Court rules in an area where the circuit courts have previously been in conflict, all circuits must then adopt the standard or approach specified by the Supreme Court. Thus, in principle, differences among the circuits are supposed to be temporary, lasting only until the Supreme Court gets a chance to weigh in and settle the disagreement.

In the case of patent law, however, important differences persisted because the Supreme Court rarely heard patent-related cases.[69] The justices were reluctant to devote their time to what they saw as banal commercial disputes. For instance, one of the few patent cases that was heard by the "Supremes" during the 1970s in-

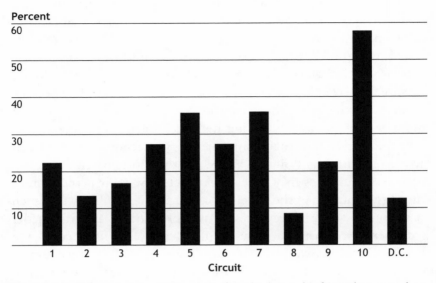

Figure 4.1 Share of cases where patents found value and infringed on appeal, by circuit, 1953–1977.

volved a dispute over a system to flush cow manure from the floor of dairy barns. Who would get the duty of writing the opinion for this "cow shit case" was a matter of considerable controversy—ultimately, it was assigned to Justice William Brennan because he had antagonized the Chief Justice with his acrid dissents in other cases.[70] Perhaps not surprisingly, the decision that resulted in this case was poorly reasoned and inconsistent with the Supreme Court's own earlier rulings.[71]

What was the result of divergent standards in different courts, not resolved by the Supreme Court? As described in the Introduction, the consequence was a "mad and undignified race."[72] Patent applicants and alleged infringers competed to have the cases heard in a circuit that would be sympathetic to their views.

In 1982, the U.S. Congress decided to tackle this chaos once and for all. It established a centralized appellate court for patent cases: the Court of Appeals for the Federal Circuit (CAFC).[73] In the congressional hearings that preceded the decision, lawmakers reassured constituents that the change would bring much-needed consistency to the volatile world of patent litigation. In addition, the new court—to be based in Washington, but to hear appeals from across the nation—was seen as alleviating the burden on existing appellate courts.

But from the very beginning of the push for this legislation, Washington insiders suspected that the new court would substantially boost patent-holders' rights. For instance, one of the key reports leading up to the congressional hearings was the Carter Administration's "Domestic Policy Review of Industrial Innovation." Frequent references were made to the competitive threat that the United States was facing from Japanese firms, the decline in venture capital financing and initial public offering activity over the course of the 1970s, and the mass lay-offs and retrenchments that were characterizing many industries at the time. The relevant subcommittee's report highlighted the ability of a strong patent system to allow firms to overcome the many competitive challenges at the time:

> Our Subcommittee concludes that the patent system is an essential element in our free enterprise system, has performed exceptionally well, and has made a significant contribution to the economic development of our country. This is so well accepted by the members of our Subcommittee, who have worked for many years directly with the patent system, that we tend to take it for granted . . . [T]he patent system, while fundamentally sound, could be strengthened so it does a better job in promoting decisions to commercialize innovations.[74]

Foremost among these steps, the Committee suggested, was the establishment of centralized appellate court for patent cases.

The subcommittee's confidence that a specialized court would lead to more patent protection has turned out to be justified. In part, the pro-patent outlook that the new court came to adopt may have been a consequence of the process by which the judges were selected. The danger that a specialized court might turn out too parochial was, in fact, recognized at the time. Reflecting the concerns of some members, the House had indicated that the court should feature a diverse range of backgrounds. As the congressional report summarizing the bill noted, "this [section] does not prohibit the President from appointing a patent lawyer to the CAFC . . . [but] does, however, clearly send a message to the President that he should avoid undue specialization."[75]

Despite these concerns, many of the new judges on the twelve-member CAFC had extensive experience with the patent system. Five of the initial judges were drawn from the Court of Customs and Patents Appeals, a specialized body that had heard appeals of disputes between patent applicants and the PTO (but not between private parties). The new court's chief judge, Howard T. Markey, was a patent lawyer who had previously chaired the old court. Judge Giles Rich, who until his death at age 95 in 1999 was an active member of the court, had been on the two-man committee that drafted the Patent Act of 1952 and was widely seen as the "dean of modern patent law."[76] Judges added in subsequent years—including Pauline Newman and Alan Lourie—had extensive experience with patent issues. Whether a consequence of their training and work experience or not, many of these judges proved to have a pro-patent outlook. Even when they were mixed with non-specialists, often the patent-savvy judges were asked—or volunteered—to take the lead in shaping and writing the decisions in patent cases.[77]

But the pro-patent orientation may have also been an almost inevitable consequence of the creation of a special court. The creation of a specialized court for patent cases was not a new idea—no less than thirty-two bills creating such a court had been introduced between 1887 and 1921 alone.[78] But these earlier efforts had failed, at least partly because many practitioners and academics had long argued that the creation of such a specialized patent court would have important negative consequences.

The first of the dangers that had previously been seen in the creation of a specialized patent court was the danger of "tunnel vision." Judges in such a specialized court might be unable to see the broader context in which firms operated. There were dire predictions as to what might happen if patent courts were isolated from other disciplines:

> The patent law does not live in the seclusion and silence of a Trappist
> monastery. . . . Once you segregate the patent law from the natural
> environment in which it now has its being, you contract the area of
> its exposure to the self-correcting forces of the law. In time, such a
> body of law, secluded from the rest, develops a jargon of its own,
> thought-patterns that are unique, internal policies . . . which are dif-
> ferent from and sometimes at odds with the policies pursued by the
> general law.[79]

In such a setting, critics feared, the patent judiciary and the lawyers
who practiced before them might turn inward, speaking in a private
language. They might begin to see the patent system as an end in
itself, without considering that it is one element of a broader economic system.

A manifestation of this same problem may be even more problematic: the judges may be swayed by a belief in the unique importance of the field. As Richard Posner has argued, judges in specialized courts may be particularly prone to identify with government
programs.[80] Put another way, they may be prone to be "captured"
by those who benefit from the programs.

The experience of the Commerce Court, a specialized court established in 1910 to regulate the railroads and utilities, was often
brought up as an example of this danger.[81] Before the establishment
of that court, appeals of decisions of the Interstate Commerce Commission had been heard by individual district courts. This process
led not only to delay, but also to inconsistency in the way that these
regulations were applied across the nation. The solution, many felt,
was a nationwide court. Even in the proposal stage, however, the
concept of the court aroused substantial hostility: many progres-
sives feared that allies of the railroads would be appointed to the
court, or, even if impartial judges were appointed, that frequent
contact with representatives of these corporations would lead to the
judges increasingly sympathizing with the railroads' view. Perhaps
reflecting this lack of consensus, the new court had a difficult bap-
tism. Immediately saddled with some of the most controversial
cases of the day, in its early decisions the court was perceived as
favoring the railroads and seeking to unduly rein in the Interstate

Commerce Commission. Less than three years after it was established, Congress abolished the new court.

An additional concern of the proposed court's critics related to job satisfaction. Most of us enjoy having a diverse array of challenges in our work life, and there is no reason why judges should differ. A skeptic might argue that many lawyers specialize in a given practice area. But a typical lawyer plays many roles, from arguing cases to negotiating transactions to providing informal guidance. An appellate judge just does one activity—hearing appeals. To further restrict the range of activity to cases in a single domain may reduce the attractiveness of the bench significantly.

Finally, some in 1982 worried about the possible manipulation of the appointment process. While it may be hard for a politician to anticipate the views of an appointee across a variety of disciplines, an appointee to a specialized court may be more easily vetted to ensure decisions of a particular type. This narrowing of focus might lead to the creation of highly ideological courts, reflecting the political preferences of the chief executive—or the special interests that gained a disproportionate control over the appointments process.

Despite these reservations, the Federal Courts Improvement Act established the CAFC in 1982. The arguments concerning the new court's greater efficiency and the benefits of consistency—as well as the desire of some to see a strengthened patent system—carried the day.

The Overall Impact

Over the next decade, in case after case, the court significantly broadened patent-holders' rights. A comparison of the CAFC's rulings with those of the previous courts illustrates the magnitude of the change. Perhaps the crudest way to see this is in the aggregate statistical tabulations. Whereas the circuit courts had affirmed 62 percent of district-court findings of patent infringement in the three decades before the creation of the CAFC, the CAFC in its first eight years affirmed 90 percent of such decisions. On the other hand, when the district court had found that a patent was invalid

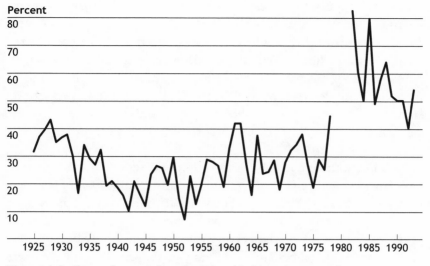

Figure 4.2 Share of patents found valid and infringed on appeal.

or not infringed—thereby denying the patentee enforcement of the patent—the circuits had reversed only 12 percent of the cases. In the first eight years of the Federal Circuit, 28 percent of these cases were reversed.[82]

The change is captured in figure 4.2, which shows the change in the number of cases where the appellate courts (whether the CAFC or the various circuit courts) found that a patent was valid and infringed from 1925 and 1993. This shows that during the pre-CAFC era, less than 30 percent of adjudicated patents were found to be valid and infringed. Once the CAFC was established, the share of patents found to be valid and infringed increased dramatically.[83]

Indeed, it is likely that the comparison in figure 4.2 substantially understates the swing at work. When we made it dramatically easier for a patent-holder to win in court, we might expect that many more cases would be brought, because the holder of a dubious patent who would not have sought to enforce it under the old regime may be tempted today to go to court. Even with the pro-patent court, such dubious cases are less likely to prevail, bringing down the overall percentage of cases won by patent holders. Over time, we would expect that this response by potential litigants to the changing standards would cause the observed difference between the new court and the old ones to narrow; indeed, this is exactly what we see in figure 4.2. But as the percentage of cases won by patent holders falls back towards the percentage that had previously prevailed, this does not mean that the CAFC is losing its pro-patent stance; it means that patent holders are winning as many or more cases as they did before, even though increasingly marginal patents are being asserted.

This likely change in the composition of cases brought is difficult to quantify, making it hard to interpret any comparison of the performance of the CAFC in recent years to the old performance of the distinct circuit courts. It is likely, however, that it took several years for the nature of cases brought to change, if only because the cases heard at the appellate level in any given year would have been initiated several years before. Thus, we can get a clear indication of the shift in orientation by looking at the short-run shift immediately after the creation of the CAFC. And this difference is dramatic. In the first four years of the CAFC's operation, the patent holder won 68 percent of patent cases. As can be seen from figure 4.1, this success rate is higher than the success rate that patentees enjoyed in the most pro-patent of the circuits (the Tenth Circuit) under the old regime. Thus, the CAFC did not merely standardize patent practice; it shifted patent practice to be more pro-patent than it had been anywhere in the previous decades.

With a sure inevitability, this change has affected the district courts where patents are first tried. (Remember, the CAFC is an appellate court, which hears appeals of cases that have already had an initial ruling at the district level.) After all, no judge enjoys seeing his findings reversed and criticized. The impact of the new direction is shown in figure 4.3.[84] Prior to the creation of the CAFC, about 30 percent of the patents were found to be valid and infringed at the district court level. After the creation of the CAFC, the percentage of awards upheld rose to over 55 percent.

Similarly, there is likely to be much more action "behind the scenes," that never makes it into the public view. Before filing suit, patent-holders will typically write to their rival, saying, "we

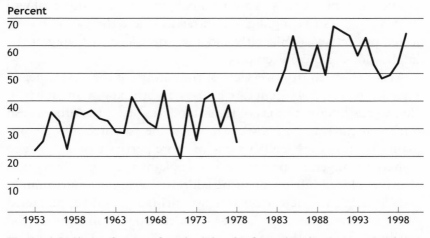

Figure 4.3 Share of patents found valid and infringed in district court trials.

think you are infringing our patent." In fact, in some instances, they send along a detailed legal complaint, ready for filing at the courthouse. In many cases, such communications lead to intense bargaining and a private settlement between the two sides. Such settlements never make it into the tabulations presented here or in the Introduction. But one would expect, and conversations with business people and their attorneys confirm, that the CAFC's pro-patent stance has had a profound impact on such negotiations and settlements, making patent-holders more eager to assert their claims, and accused infringers more inclined to pay up and settle rather than fight it out in court.

How Has the Federal Circuit Changed Things?

The statistical tabulations shown in the previous section show that something has happened. But more specifically, how has the court expanded patent-holders' rights? To fully capture the doctrinal shifts is a challenging task, which would take us deep into the arcane details of the patent system: for instance, the standard compilation of these decisions, *Patents and the Federal Circuit*, runs 1,200 pages, much of which is in a very small font. Instead, our goal will be more modest: to highlight a few areas where the CAFC has affected patent law significantly and a few decisions that suggest the implications of these decisions.

As a prelude to this overview of the rulings of the CAFC, let us review how a typical patent case evolves, and the key points at which the court's interpretations of legal standards affect the process. An infringement case typically starts when the patentee files a complaint, naming as defendants one or more parties that are alleged to have infringed its patents. The complaint will typically request that the alleged infringement be addressed via (1) a court injunction ordering the defendant to stop infringing, and (2) an award of money from the defendant to compensate for infringement up until such time as the infringement actually stops. The defendant will typically respond by saying (1) our products and processes do not infringe your patent(s); and (2) your patents are invalid anyway.

Most patentees ask that their cases be decided by a jury (more on this below); if there is no jury, the case is decided by a district court judge. Even in a jury case, the judge still plays an important role, deciding many legal issues before and during trial, and framing the exact wording of the question or questions put to the jury to decide.

While there will often be a host of subsidiary issues, the heart of most patent cases consists of determining whether or not the patent is indeed valid, and, if valid, whether the actions of the defendant do or do not infringe on the patent(s)'s claims. Because a patent is the result of a specified administrative process of the government, it is entitled as a matter of law to a presumption that it is valid. This means that the alleged infringer must bear a relatively heavy burden of proof in order to win a finding of invalidity: it must show by "clear and convincing evidence" that the patent is invalid. This standard is not as high as the "beyond a reasonable doubt" standard that applies in criminal cases, but if one visualizes a hypothetical scale on which the evidence on each side is balanced, proving invalidity requires something more than just a slight tipping in the direction of invalidity. By way of contrast, there is no legal presumption either way on the question of infringement. This means that, to prove infringement, the patentee needs to demonstrate that the "preponderance of the evidence" favors a finding of infringement; so long as the scale is tipped even the slightest bit towards infringement, infringement is to be found.

Once a complaint has been filed and responded to, the legal jousting proceeds under the supervision of the judge. Before the trial, there is a period of "discovery" during which each side gathers evidence it needs, including evidence that may be in the possession of the other party, but which must be provided if asked for. During this pre-trial period, the judge will make rulings that shape how the trial will proceed, including, importantly, a legal interpretation as to what the claims of the patent should be taken to mean. For example, if there are certain words used in the claims, and the parties dispute the meaning of these words in the context of the claims, the judge resolves this dispute before the jury is asked to decide if the claims have been infringed. In some cases, the judge may issue rulings that dispose of the case (one way or the other) without it ever actually getting to the jury. The losing party can appeal any such ruling to the CAFC.

Because of this pre-trial process, it is not unusual for months or even years to pass between the filing of a complaint and a decision at the district court level. Sometimes, the patentee will ask for a preliminary injunction, a court order halting the alleged infringing activity even before the trial has taken place. This request is acted on by the district court judge (though the judge's decision can be immediately appealed to the CAFC). The purpose of a preliminary injunction is to prevent irreversible harm that the patentee would suffer while the trial proceeds. For this reason, to win a preliminary injunction, the patentee must prove that it is very likely to prevail when the case eventually gets to trial, and that will suffer harm before the end of the trial that will be difficult to rectify after the fact.

Once the jury (or the judge, if there is no jury) has rendered decisions on the merits of the case, the judge makes the final decisions about the remedies (if any). The judge reviews any monetary award made by the jury to ensure its reasonableness, and the judge decides whether or not an injunction is to be issued precluding continued infringement. Once again, the final verdict can be appealed to the CAFC.

Like any other "game," the outcome of these contests is very sensitive to the rules under which they are played. And it is the CAFC who makes the rules. We turn now to see how the rules of this game have been systematically altered in favor of the patent holders.

1. Stronger Remedies

If a patent holder can prove infringement, he can request two kinds of remedies: damages for past infringement, and an injunction, which prohibits future infringement of the patent. The CAFC has boosted patent-holders' prerogatives in both these areas. We will first focus on the shifts in damages.

These damages can be computed in one of two ways. The more conservative approach is termed "reasonable royalties." Under this approach, the court considers a hypothetical world in which the two parties had willingly entered into a licensing negotiation at the time that the patent was awarded. The court then determines what royalty the two parties would have agreed to in this hypothetical negotiation, and orders a damage award equal to the amount of royalties that would have been due to the patentee under this hypothetical license agreement. The second approach, "lost profits," entails considering an alternative world in which the patent infringement simply did not occur. The profits that would have been earned by the patent-holder in this hypothetical realm are then compared to those actually earned by the firm. These differences might stem from lower profit margins—not having a monopoly, the patent-holder having had to sell the good at a lower price—or from fewer units sold. Patent-holders are free to make more speculative arguments as well, arguing that they would have successfully introduced a myriad of successful product extensions had they not had to focus on fighting the infringement.

The CAFC has enhanced the ability of patent-holders to gain substantial damages in these cases. First, with some encouragement from the Supreme Court, they have made it easier for awardees to increase their damages by interest.[85] Moreover, they have encouraged the use of lost profits, rather than the more modest reasonable royalties.[86] Some of these changes are entirely reasonable: for instance, few would dispute that infringed parties who need to wait for a long time to get a favorable judgment should be compensated for the long delay by receiving interest on the damage award. But in other cases, the moves to enhance patent-holders' damages may be problematic. For instance, in some cases, the CAFC has made it possible for patentees to receive the sum of the damages calculated from a reasonable royalty and lost profits calculations.[87]

Second, the court has strengthened the hand of patent-holders to seek more dramatic remedies against potential infringers. Even if these rights are not exercised in all cases, they can serve to empower the patentee at the bargaining table when negotiating settlements before, during, or after trial.

Perhaps the most dramatic way in which the CAFC has strengthened the remedies available to patentees is the availability of preliminary injunctive relief. As a general legal principle, a preliminary injunction—issued before a trial is held—is viewed as a relatively extreme action that is only justified to prevent irrevocable harm. Patent holders were long seen as not qualifying for this remedy, because the harm associated with infringement is merely commercial, and, hence, can always be remedied by later ordering the infringer to compensate the patent holder. In effect, when the consequences of actions are entirely monetary, they are never irreversible, because money can always be paid back. Thus, preliminary injunctions have always been available in cases where the action really could not be undone, such as releasing wolves into a national park, but were historically extremely rare in patent cases.

Breaking with long-established precedent, the CAFC has allowed preliminary injunctions in disputed patent cases.[88] The court enabled patentees to shut down a rival's business (through a preliminary injunction) even before a patent was proven valid, on the theory that the subsequent calculation or payment of damages was sufficiently uncertain as to render the harm due to infringement essentially irreversible. While some observers contend that the CAFC's sympathy for this draconian step has waned somewhat in recent years, the fact remains that a preliminary injunction, shutting down your business before there is even a trial, is now a real risk associated with fighting a claim of patent infringement. Even if the probability of this occurring is not large, it represents a significant shift in the relative bargaining power of patent holders and alleged infringers as they negotiate to settle their disputes.

This willingness to "tilt the table"—or change the relative power that patent-holders and alleged infringers bring to the bargaining table—has manifested itself in other ways as well. One of these is the issue of whether, if a trial does result in a finding of infringement, the patent holder will be granted a permanent injunction shutting down the infringing operation, or will instead be limited to receiving monetary compensation.

While it might seem that a patent holder ought to be entitled to shut down an operation that has been proven to infringe, the imposition of such an injunction is not mandatory, but rather is left to the discretion of the court. Historically, the patentee's right to exclusive use of the patented technology has been balanced against the major social costs that might be associated with shutting down a significant manufacturer of an established product. Given the long time period sometimes needed to resolve these cases, a company that built up an established product, believing in good faith that it was not infringing on others' patents, might have been allowed to pay a continuing royalty rather than being shut down when it is ultimately found to have infringed. But the CAFC has shown a greater willingness to allow patent-holders to permanently shut down infringers after trial, setting aside the concerns about the social harm caused by such moves.[89] Moreover, the types of parties that could obtain relief were expanded. Historically, courts routinely declined to shut down an infringing firm in cases where the patentee was not itself engaged in manufacturing the patented product, on the grounds that the social interest was not served by having no one selling the patented product. The CAFC has shown more flexibility in this regard, thereby handing individual inventors a powerful weapon.[90]

To understand the importance of these shifts, we will consider one seminal case: the bitterly fought battle between Eastman Kodak and Polaroid regarding the instant photography business.[91]

The origins of the dispute lay in the genius of the Polaroid Corporation's researchers. Under the leadership of its brilliant founder, Edwin Land, Polaroid had introduced the first instant camera in 1947. Rather than requiring film to be developed in a darkroom, as had been the case until then, the film was bundled with developer and photographic "fixer" that enabled a picture to be developed. The firm continued to push the technological frontier with the development of Polacolor in 1963, the unsuccessful Polavision (an instant color movie system), and the development of the paper-free SX-70 camera in 1972. Reflecting Land's strong belief about the necessity of developing a strong defensive position, the firm made frequent filings on its innovations: Land himself was the single largest patent-holder after Thomas Edison.

In 1969, Kodak—the much larger photographic filmmaker that collaborated in the past with Polaroid—made the fateful decision to enter the instant camera market itself. Working closely with their patent attorneys, they sought to develop a technological approach to instant photography that would not infringe Polaroid's patents. They entered the market with great fanfare in April 1976, and one week later, Polaroid sued, alleging that ten (later twelve) of its patents had been infringed.

What ensued was one of the costliest patent battles in history. The two parties spent five-and-a-half years in pre-trial discovery, generating thousands of exhibits and hundreds of depositions. The trial itself lasted seventy-five days; and another three-and-a-half years elapsed before Judge Rya Zobel rendered her decision. Ultimately, Kodak was found to have infringed seven of Polaroid's patents.

The changed legal environment was most starkly revealed in what followed. As the court considered whether to impose a permanent injunction, Kodak argued the social harm would be great:

- 16 million instant cameras already in the hands of consumers would be rendered useless.
- 800 full-time and 3,700 part-time employees would run the danger of losing their jobs.
- $200 million of investment in plant, property, and equipment would be made obsolete.

In addition, the firm would incur out-of-pocket costs of around $150 million in the form of rebates to consumers.

These potential costs did not sway Judge Zobel, who ordered the firm to exit the instant photography business. Kodak immediately appealed the decision, as well as the injunction, to the CAFC. In two swift decisions, the court refused to stay the injunction until the appeal was resolved—forcing Kodak to exit the instant photography business immediately—and then rejected the appeal. In late 1996, the Supreme Court refused to hear the appeal of this ruling.

And this was only the beginning of Kodak's pain. The final stage in the drama was a trial to determine damages for past infringement, which itself lasted ninety-six days. Polaroid argued that a "reasonable royalty" calculation would understate its losses, since it would not have licensed the patents to Kodak under any circumstances. The court agreed, and assigned damages of $454 million (which was divided almost equally between compensation for "lost profits" and "reasonable royalties"), along with interest of another $455 million. While far less than the $12 billion that Polaroid sought—in particular, the judge rejected the argument that Polaroid would have charged higher prices or altered its product introduction schedule had Kodak not been in the market—it was more than four times the largest damages in a patent case to date. While both parties appealed, ultimately the two firms settled the dispute for $925 million, close to the amount of the final judgment.

It is hard to state definitely whether these damages were too large or too small. But it is clear that the prospect of huge damages awards and the possibility of injunctive relief—especially in conjunction with the decline in patent quality that we will discuss in chapter 5—have led to great pressures on parties to settle disputes. Even if an alleged infringer is convinced that it is in the right, given the uncertainty of the litigation process and the possibility of a very costly punishment, it may choose to settle. The result may be that a truly innovative firm, trying to bring a valuable new product to market, ends up taking a license to an invalid patent in order to implement its own technology without the cost and distraction of litigation. Such a scenario is worrisome for several reasons:

- First, of course, the firm that pays royalties for an invalid patent suffers. On net, it receives less of the rewards for its own discovery than it deserves.
- Second, the firm's peers may be hurt: had the first firm chosen to fight the infringement suit, and the patent been struck down as invalid, then the patent-holder would be unable to pursue others in the industry. Put another way, a firm's decision to fight a patent generates a "public good," from which all the firms in the industry who are potential targets benefit. Worse still, the decision to settle can actually make it harder for others to challenge the asserted patent, because the patent-holder can use the fact that the first firm settled as evidence of the validity of the patent.

Ultimately, if paying this kind of protection money comes to be seen as a routine cost of introducing new products, the whole process of innovation becomes more expensive. As a result, there will be less innovation and society as a whole will be worse off.

2. Expanding the Number of Topics That Can Be Patented

The past several decades have seen an expansion of the number of areas where patent protection extends. The legal definition of what is "patentable," discussed in chapter 1, seems simple enough, but it has nonetheless launched many thousands of disputes.

The tendency towards expansion of the realm of patentability actually predates the CAFC. To cite one famous and important example, the Supreme Court—while considering the case of a new microorganism—noted in 1980 that "anything under the sun that is made by man" should be worthy of patent protection.[92] This change opened the floodgates to the patenting of bio-engineered products. The list of patentable biological products soon grew to include genetically altered yeast, genetic sequences from humans and other creatures, and even entire living creatures, such as oysters and mice.

But certainly the CAFC has played an important role in expanding the scope of what can be protected. Consider, for instance, the area of computer software. The Supreme Court had long been of two minds about the patenting of these programs. In one key decision, *Diamond v. Diehr*, they argued that on the one hand "a mathematical formula as such is not accorded the protection of our patent laws," but on the other hand, that "an application of a law of nature or mathematical formula to a known structure or process may well be."[93] In the *Diehr* decision, the court allowed a patent on a process for curing rubber where a computer program played an important role. The court noted that the formula behind the program was being used in a particular context—that is, there was no intention to seek protection beyond the particular application. The actual working of this distinction was quite arcane, and was the subject of many dozens of learned law review essays.

The CAFC has been much less ambivalent in expressing its enthusiasm for software patents. One illustration was the case *In re Alappat*.[94] The case involved a patent to treat data coming from a digital oscilloscope: before displaying the waves being generated on the scope, the program smoothed the data, eliminating any discontinuities. Unlike the rubber case, here the program ran on a general purpose computer rather than a specialized device. And the claims were broadly worded, so they could apply not just to data from oscilloscopes, but also to interfaces with computer monitors, laser printers, and televisions. Nonetheless, the CAFC reversed an earlier district court ruling and let the patent stand, opening the door to the widespread patenting of computer software.

But the clearest example of the CAFC's unwillingness to limit what can be patented relates to business method patents. Since the early days of the British patent system, there has been considerable ambiguity as to whether methods of doing business fell under the definition of patentable subject matter. As noted in the previous chapter, the seminal British case *Darcy v. Allin* held that any man "bringing a new trade into the realm; or any engine tending in furtherance of a trade that never was used before" could obtain a patent.[95] In subsequent decisions in the eighteenth and nineteenth centuries, however, British jurists specified that this definition extended only to tangible inventions. Outside the Anglo-American legal system—particularly in countries whose legal system evolved from the French code—this somewhat mushy, judicially created exclusion was made explicit in the form of a legislated prohibition on patents based on mathematical formulas and financial methods.

The treatment of business method patents in the United States had much of the same ambiguity as in England. A 1908 court decision, *Hotel Security Checking Co. v. Lorraine Co.*,[96] established that business methods were not patentable. Despite this ruling, patents on financial and other business methods have been issued by the PTO at least since 1971. For instance, the patents issued to Merrill Lynch in 1983 and 1986 for its cash management account (U.S. Patents No. 4,376,978, "Securities Brokerage-Cash Management System," and No. 4,597,046, "Securities Brokerage-Cash Management System Obviating Float Costs by Anticipatory Liquidation of Short Term Assets") were much discussed at the time they were awarded.

Nonetheless, there was a presumption by many practitioners that business methods did not fall into the four categories of patentable subject matter under U.S. law, namely "any new and useful process, machine, manufacture, or composition of matter,"[97] and, hence, that the patents were of questionable validity. Apparently, only two suits involving financial patents were filed prior to 1996 (involving the Merrill cash management system and College Savings Bank's CollegeSure certificate of deposit). Both cases were settled prior to trial, leaving the question of validity unresolved.

As a result of the skepticism about these patents, many financial institutions relied instead on trade secret protection. Under the legislation protecting trade secrets, firms can sue those parties who misappropriate their ideas (for instance, a former employee or a strategic partner). Unlike patents, which must be publicly disclosed to be effective, trade secrets can (and indeed must) be kept secret by the organization. Furthermore, trade secrets (such as the formula for Coca-Cola) remain in effect as long as the secrecy is maintained. U.S. patents, by way of contrast, expire twenty years after the original application date.

At the same time, trade secrecy has some significant limitations. Most importantly, trade secret protection does not block others who make the same discovery, whether independently or by "reverse engineering" the protected product (that is, using publicly available information to figure out the product's working). This feature is in contrast to patent protection, which allows the patentee to prosecute all infringers, even those who discovered the idea independently. Moreover, proving misappropriation can be very difficult, particularly in an environment such as Silicon Valley, where high employee turnover is the rule.

The critical change in regard to business method patents was the CAFC's July 1998 decision in *State Street Bank and Trust v. Signature Financial Group*. This case had originated with a software program used to fix closing prices of mutual funds for reporting purposes, on which Signature had obtained a patent in 1993 (U.S. Patent No. 5,193,056, "Data Processing System for Hub and Spoke Financial Services Configuration"). The patented system essentially allowed managers of fund complexes to efficiently adjust the reported value of portfolios, and to allocate expenses, taxes, and other costs. The patented method performs this calculation by multiplying a vector (the price of all the securities that the funds held) by a matrix (the holdings of each security in each fund).[98]

Signature then approached a number of mutual fund "custodians," the firms that handle the unglamorous task of managing the day-to-day operations of the funds. In a number of cases, Signature successfully negotiated licenses to its patent, collecting royalties from firms performing operations that it claimed were covered by the patent's claims. But licensing talks with State Street Bank (which serves as custodian for about 40 percent of U.S. mutual fund assets and is estimated to derive annual revenues of more than $3 billion for its services) were not fruitful in reaching an agreement. As a result, State Street Bank sued in 1996 to have the patent invalidated on the grounds that it covered a business method and was, hence, not patentable.

State Street's argument prevailed in the Federal District of Massachusetts, where the judge issued a "summary judgment" ruling that the case need not go to trial because the patent could not be found to be valid. Characterizing this area of the law as a "jurisprudential quagmire,"[99] Judge Patti Sarris ruled the patent was invalid both because of the "business method exception" to patentability and furthermore because it was just an electronic way of undertaking a process that had long been done with calculators or pencil-and-paper.

On appeal, however, the CAFC reversed the summary judgment. In its decision, the appellate court explicitly rejected the notion that there was a "business method exception." As the CAFC stated, "the [District] court relied on the judicially-created, so-called 'business method' exception to statutory subject matter. We take this opportunity to lay this ill-conceived exception to rest. Since its inception, the 'business method' exception has merely represented the application of some general, but no longer applicable legal principle."[100] The court underscored this shift by quoting from the dissenting opinion of CAFC Judge Pauline Newman in an earlier decision, in which she characterized the business method exception as "an unwarranted encumbrance to the definition of statutory matter [that should] be discarded as error-prone, redundant, and obsolete."[101] State Street's petition to the Supreme Court, asking them to review this appellate decision, was rejected without comment in January 1999. The CAFC's ruling did not prove the validity of the patent; they held only that a business method could be patented. Nonetheless, the two parties settled the dispute; State Street agreed to take out a license and dropped its attempt to prove the patent invalid.

Following the CAFC decision, and the Supreme Court's refusal to consider the case, numerous articles in journals geared toward finance and legal professionals interpreted *State Street* as unambiguously establishing the patentability of business methods. The authors urged financial organizations to reconsider their reliance on trade secret protection, and to aggressively seek to patent their discoveries.[102] Indeed, the number of business method patent applications has exploded, growing from 330 in 1995 (the year before the original ruling in the *State Street* case) to about 10,000 in 2001.[103]

3. Limiting Challenges to Patent Validity

As noted in the Introduction, one of the critical tests as to whether an invention is patentable relates to whether it is "obvious." The frequently invoked test is whether an individual who has "ordinary skill in the art"—thus, someone who is not Thomas Edison— would consider the discovery to be obvious. Numerous observers— whether friendly to or skeptical about the CAFC—have noted that the court has shown a willingness to see patents as non-obvious, even when there appears to be abundant prior art.[104]

The Supreme Court had ruled in 1966 that three considerations were of paramount importance in determining whether a discovery is obvious: the scope and content of the prior art, the differences between the prior art and the claims of the patent, and the amount of skill an average practitioner in the area under consideration possessed. Other more circumstantial considerations—such as whether the invention was commercially successful, whether others had tried and failed to undertake similar inventions, and whether the patented invention satisfied an unmet need—were deemed "secondary," though they "may be relevant."[105] The rationale for giving only secondary consideration to this kind of evidence was that commercial success could come about for many reasons, which may have little to do with the fundamental originality of the discovery. In the pre-CAFC era, the various circuit courts had differed in exactly how they interpreted these instructions, lending an element of uncertainty to the process by which obviousness was considered.

But the CAFC has placed much greater emphasis in its decisions on these supposedly "secondary" considerations. In fact, they have gone so far to state that such considerations are frequently "the most probative and cogent evidence in the record" and that these "must always when present be considered."[106] This has led to a variety of problematic—though predictable—consequences. For instance, firms, upon receiving patent awards, frequently will immediately approach their weakest rivals in the industry, demanding that they take out licenses. Firms that do not have the financial resources for a court battle, and whose modest sales may generate only small royalty obligations, can be expected to agree to a license even if they doubt the validity of the patent. The patent-holders then approach their more formidable competitors, those who might be more likely to challenge the validity of the patent in court, rather than acceding to license demands. But now, if it comes to a legal battle, the patentee can point to the fact that they have already successfully licensed the patent as evidence that it was non-obvious, on the basis of "commercial success." Indeed, an extension of the CAFC's logic—that commercial success demonstrates non-obviousness—would be that no patents should ever be struck down for obviousness, because the willingness of the patent-holder to go to the trouble and pay the legal fees for the application and the ensuing litigation is an indication that the award is of commercial importance.

Not surprisingly, creating new ways to demonstrate supposed non-obviousness has led to a declining ability of alleged infringers to prove that the patents that they are accused of violating are invalid due to obviousness. In 1975–76, for instance, in 45 percent of the appellate decisions where patent validity was decided upon, the grant was found to be invalid on grounds of obviousness. By 1994–95, the percentage had fallen to 5 percent.[107] Not only was the CAFC reluctant to strike down patents for any reason, but they were particularly loath to do so on grounds of invalidity.

An illustration of the difficulty of proving that an invention is obvious is the 2002 decision, *In re Lee*, which revolved around a technology at the very heart of the American way of life: the television remote control.[108] Sang-Su Lee, a researcher with Samsung Electronics in South Korea, applied for a patent for adjusting a video display device such as a television. Essentially, the patent outlined a process whereby a user choosing to enter into a "demonstration mode" would automatically be shown how to adjust a number of functions (for example, the brightness and contrast of the display).

The patent examiner had rejected this patent on the grounds of obviousness. In his decision, he cited two previous pieces of prior art. The first was a patent, awarded in 1984 to RCA, which called for the display of a menu of functions on a television, which the user could then adjust by pressing the associated key (for example, "Press 9 to adjust picture sharpness"). This patent did not, however, describe any demonstration of how to adjust the functions; perhaps RCA presumed that the average "couch potato" would be able to figure this out for him or herself. The second relevant bit of prior art was a video game, "Thunderchopper Helicopter Operations," which had a demonstration mode. Upon selecting this option, the user can learn how to play the game. The demonstration mode did not involve, it should be noted, any provisions to change the settings of the game. But the examiner concluded—and the PTO's appellate board concurred—that the combination of these two forms of art made Lee's patent application obvious assuming "common knowledge and common sense of a person of ordinary skill in the art."[109] As the examiner explained in his response, it was straightforward to add instructions on how to program a menu to an electronic tutorial.

The CAFC rejected this reasoning. In particular, the court concluded that the examiner had not justified why the combination of the earlier RCA function menu with the demonstration mode of the video game was an obvious step. The court noted that there was no reference in the examiner's writings or the Board's decision of a specific suggestion in the prior literature to combine the features of the two previous inventions. When rejecting a patent on grounds of obviousness, the court held, "all material facts . . . must be documented on the record, lest the 'haze of so-called expertise' acquire insulation from accountability."

Such decisions weakening the obviousness standard are hardly confined to high technology industries. Consider, for instance, *In re Dembiczak*, which upheld a patent on a trash bag made of orange plastic and decorated with lines and facial features, which when filled resembled a jack-o'-lantern.[110] The patent examiner, and the appellate officer, had rejected the patent, pointing to the many passages in children's books suggesting making stuffed bags decorated as Halloween pumpkins, as well as the well-developed prior art relating to plastic trash bags. Once again, the CAFC rejected this decision, arguing that the combination of these items was by no means obvious.

These decisions, and others with the same theme, set the bar very high for finding a patent to be obvious. Taken to their logical conclusion, these decisions suggest that any patent application that entails a common sense combination of two previously well-known ideas must be granted, unless there is an explicit pre-

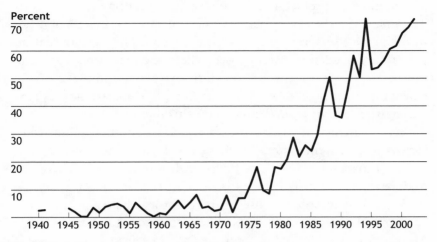

Figure 4.4 Share of patent cases tried before juries.

vious description of the particular combination that is described in the application. Since there are always going to be myriad combinations and recombinations of different approaches that no one finds time to, or bothers to, write down, the possibilities for patenting "new" combinations are virtually unlimited. Run out now, and get your patent on selling dog food on the Internet, navigating the Internet while riding one's bicycle, or playing the piano while feeding one's cat. Even lawyers generally sympathetic to the CAFC have expressed concern about the implications of this line of decisions.[111]

4. Increasing the Reliance on Juries

A fourth dramatic change that has occurred on the CAFC's watch is an increasing reliance on juries in patent trials. Figure 4.4 displays the trend over time. It reveals that, historically, the use of juries in patent cases was quite rare. Between 1940 and 1959, for instance, juries heard only 3 percent of the patent cases that went to trial.[112] The adjudication of these cases by judges was standard. Today, the use of juries in patent cases is standard.

The historical reluctance to employ juries reflected two factors. The first was judicial skepticism about the appropriateness of juries in such cases. In some cases, the courts went as far as state that no juries were needed in patent cases, where the technical, legal, and business issues at stake were frequently extremely complex.[113] As in other topics of patent law, however, a wide disparity had existed among the various federal circuits on this matter.

Second, many litigants expressed concern about the impact of juries on the patent system. In many cases, patent disputes involve complex disputes, which may be difficult for an average citizen to understand. (In fact, a lawyer for a patent-holder with a weak case is likely to be tempted to use his peremptory challenges to purge the jury of the members most likely to understand the issues.) Moreover, applying judicial review in cases heard by a jury is difficult: while a judge must lay out the reasoning behind his decision in a written opinion, the jury simply issues a verdict. Finally, many patent attorneys regard juries as excessively sympathetic to patent-holders, being too easily swayed by a beribboned patent document. As a result, the general attitude of the legal community—including judges—was that the request of a jury trial was a signal of a weak case.[114]

Far from sharing this skepticism, the CAFC has taken a relatively sympathetic view of juries. In a series of decisions, the court has stated that patentees have an absolute right to a jury trial on questions of patent validity, though judges can reserve for themselves the determination of how broad the individual claims in the patent are.[115] The CAFC has also been inclined to accept jury verdicts, even when serious questions have been raised about the reasoning behind the verdict.[116]

While the CAFC clearly believes in juries, it does not believe in them enough to allow them to hear all the evidence that attorneys might wish to bring before them. In particular, the CAFC has precluded the presentation to juries of information about the weaknesses and limitations of the patent examination process. (Anyone who confessed to having read this book would surely be prohibited from sitting on a jury in a patent case.) In decision after decision, the CAFC has reprimanded trial judges who have not clearly instructed jurors to presume the patent is valid.[117]

It might be thought that the increased reliance on juries is not disturbing. After all, why should the nature of the decision-maker affect the outcome of the case? But indeed, there does seem to be a discernable pattern: juries are much more sympathetic to patent-holders than judges. For instance, in an analysis of 299 litigated patents which were resolved between 1989 and 1996, Allison and Lemley find that juries found patents to be valid just over two-thirds of the time. When judges ruled—whether after bench trials or else before the trials (when we should see rulings only on especially strong cases)—the patent-holder was upheld less than 47 percent of the time.[118]

The sympathy of the jury is not the same for all patent holders. Kimberly Moore analyzes patent cases adjudicated in 1999 and 2000.[119] After eliminating cases resolved on summary judgment, she finds the disparity between juries and judges is even greater than that found in the earlier period analyzed by Allison and Lemely: juries were twice as likely to uphold patent-holders as were judges. Moreover, foreign patent-holders who are pursuing U.S. infringers are far less likely to win than others: in fact, they are only about one-quarter as successful. Meanwhile, patentees based in the same state as the venue where the case was tried are disproportionately likely to succeed.

Taking Stock of the Revolution

To be sure, not all decisions by the Federal Circuit have served to strengthen patent-holder rights. In an area as complex as patent law, there are always going to be decisions that go the other way. The prime example is the treatment of infringement through something called the "doctrine of equivalents."[120] But throughout, legal commentators—whether sympathetic to the court's rulings or not—collectively agree that the primary direction of the changes has been in the direction of strengthening patent-holders' rights.[121]

As we have emphasized, patents serve an important social function, and some recalibration in the direction of stronger patent protection was probably due given the long twentieth century decline. But as the cases in chapter 2 and this chapter illustrate, the strengthening of patent rights has now gone beyond recalibration to reach troubling proportions. And whatever might be the implications of this strengthening of patent rights in an ideal world, in the real world, the interaction between the stronger protection and a poorer patent office has had a profound effect. This second change will be our focus in the next chapter.

The Slow Starvation

T he legislator rose on the Senate floor, waving a thick report that decried the state of the patent system.[122] The patent office was fundamentally broken; indeed in the recent words of a federal judge, it was "producing evils of great magnitude."[123] Far too many patents were being issued, with only minimal review; the patent office was not even pretending to ascertain the novelty or validity of the idea. Multiple patents were being awarded on the same discoveries, or—even worse—on inventions that had been made many decades previously.

As a result, the Senator declared: "The original and meritorious inventor sees his invention . . . pirated from him, and he must forego the reward which the law was intended to secure to him in the exclusive rights in grants, or he must become involved in numerous and expensive lawsuits in distant and various sections of the country." Unless Congress acted to change this system, he concluded, the value of patents would be so depreciated that they would provide little value to inventors.

In light of recent press accounts, one might think that this scene was from a few months ago. But in actuality, John Ruggles rose to speak to the U.S. Senate in 1836.

As the Congressmen pondered this report, they considered stories such as that of the "Winged Gudgeon."[124] Michael Withers had received a patent in 1827 for such a device, a metallic piece (typically made of cast iron) that served as a connection between a water wheel and the shaft that it drove. He did not claim to have invented the gudgeon, or even one with wings, a technology that had been known for many decades. Rather, he claimed to have invented the process of beveling the wings: that is, making the surface of the wings angled to some extent. As was standard in those days, the patent examiners made no attempt to verify the claims prior to issuing the patent: they just checked to make sure that the paperwork was complete.

Many mill owners were outraged, particularly as Withers began approaching them to license his patent. They pointed out that beveled gudgeons had been commonplace for years prior to this patent filing, and, in any case, the discovery was not sufficiently significant to merit a patent. They sought to have a judge declare the patent invalid, but apparently because Withers had not yet sued anyone, they were not able to prevail.

Emboldened, Withers went one step further, actually arranging to have infringing gudgeons cast and sold in stores. Only after the laborious process of assembling the water-wheel was complete would he approach the mill owner, and declare himself to be the owner of the patent behind the gudgeon. The mill owner would be faced with the choice of paying royalties or dissembling the multi-ton finely engineered device. Few had the resources to pursue a court battle. But, if a mill owner looked likely to fight rather than to pay, Withers would move on to another target.

Ultimately, William Thornton, the nation's first Superintendent of Patents and a champion of the patent system, grew concerned about this behavior. His actions ranged from writing anonymous letters to newspapers denouncing the winged gudgeon patent and its owner, to refusing to issue authenticated copies of the patent documents to Withers' agents. As the patent's expiration neared,

Withers sued Thornton for slander over the statement that the patent was being used to defraud the American public. The messy dispute roiled Washington, with the Attorney General, Congress, and even the President drawn into the controversy. Ultimately, the suit was unsuccessful and the patent expired, but Withers retired a rich man.

The 1836 debate led to a fundamental shift in the U.S. patent system—indeed, we might argue, the last fundamental alteration to the system. No longer would patent applicants be able to automatically receive awards after making an application, as had been the case since 1793. Instead, they would need to file a detailed specification, outlining what they had discovered and why it was original and useful. Patent examiners would now examine all applications and seek to validate the newness of the claims before granting the patent. Because of the much greater scrutiny undertaken before the patent was awarded, abuses by illegitimate patent-holders like Michael Withers would be dramatically curbed.

But 169 years later, we are in many ways in 1835 once again, with a patent system that is profoundly broken. How has this situation come about? As we will argue below, the patent office has periodically come under great strains over the course of American history. Many of the same problems have reappeared in different guises over the decades. But during the past two decades, the pressures have been extraordinary.

In particular, three profound challenges have affected the effectiveness with which the patent examiners can do their job: Congress's willingness, even eagerness, to view the patent office as a governmental profit center, the lack of appropriate incentives within the patent office in an era of skyrocketing private sector compensation, and management miscues, particularly in the critical area of information technology. These factors have led to a situation where the examination process is under critical stress. The characterization of the patent examination system by the Democratic Leadership Council as "little more than a defacto registration system, with patent disputes more typically being resolved in the courts"[125] is not far-fetched. We have created a system where any patent application can ultimately issue, as long as the applicant is persistent enough. And the resulting problems of patent quality are

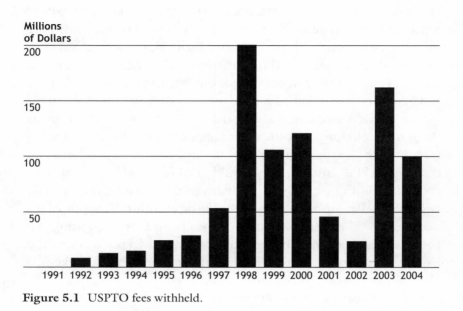

Figure 5.1 USPTO fees withheld.

particularly severe in the economically critical emerging industries of biotechnology, electronics, and software.

Budgetary Woes

At first glance, the reader might find it hard to accept the characterization of the patent office as impoverished. After all, it has become a significant contributor of capital to the overall federal budget. Figure 5.1 shows the office's annual "surplus": the amount of revenues in excess of expenses that Congress uses each year for general operating purposes. This amount has increased substantially over the years, reaching $200 million in 1998. While this amount declined somewhat in recent years, due at least in part to eased fiscal pressures as the government ran a surplus, the PTO anticipates that these transfers will increase again in upcoming years as the U.S. budget moves once again "into the red."[126]

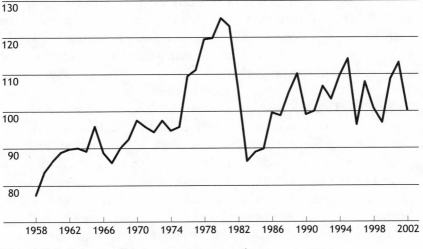

Figure 5.2 Patent application per patent examiner.

But these transfers are not a symptom of success; rather they are a cause of the problem with patent quality. It is hard to make a case that the PTO has an embarrassment of riches. Figure 5.2 shows the patent applications per patent examiner.[127] This chart tells a sad story: the number of applications that each examiner must handle has grown steadily. Between 1958 and 1975, for instance, there were never more than 100 applications received for each examiner. In nine out of eleven years since 1992, the applications per examiner have exceeded this threshold. Given everything we know about the greater value of technology in today's economy, and the greater stakes involved in patent disputes, we might have anticipated growth in the resources devoted to examining each patent, but just the opposite has held.

The level of resources is not only low relative to those enjoyed historically by the patent office, but also to that in other countries. For instance, in 2001, the European Patent Office had nearly the same number of examiners (5,069 *vs.* 5,362 in the United States), but received 54 percent fewer patent applications, making available roughly twice the manpower to examine each application.[128]

Why, it is natural to ask, does Congress persist in "robbing the till"?[129] Much of this has to do with the arcane way in which the federal budget process works. The process that sets the fees charged by the patent office (hence determining its revenue) is separate and distinct from the process that establishes the budget for its operation. And the budgeting process is essentially undertaken twice: first, when Congress passes a joint resolution that stipulates the overall levels of government revenues and expenditures, and then again when it passes the thirteen separate appropriation bills that allocate the actual funds that the government will spend in each area. The House and Senate Appropriations Committees are organized into thirteen subcommittees that are each responsible for reporting one of these measures.

Each subcommittee is given an amount of funds that it can spend. It is within these subcommittees where the competition for funds becomes most intense. For instance, within its subcommittee, PTO representatives will be jockeying for funds against Federal Bureau of Investigation officials arguing for a new computer system and State Department leaders seeking enhanced funding for embassy security. The fact that the amount allocated to the PTO ends up being much less than the amount taken in as revenue (based on fees set by a different committee) rarely figures into the fevered negotiations.[130]

The financial pressures are likely to increase in the years to come. In June 2002, the PTO promulgated its "21st Century Strategic Plan," billed as a major new initiative to improve the quality of PTO decision-making and to make it more productive.[131] The plan called for both an increase in fee levels and a restructuring of those fees: for instance, a separate fee would be charged for requesting that a patent be examined and for patents with multiple claims.[132]

The PTO Plan met with much comment, as well as considerable skepticism that revenues from the proposed fee increases would be used to improve PTO operations, rather than being once again skimmed off for general revenues.[133] After discussions with a number of groups, the PTO modified its proposals in the spring of 2003, and its modified fee proposals received the qualified support of patent owners and their attorneys.[134]

As part of the context of the Strategic Plan, President Bush's 2004 Budget proposal would reduce the projected rate of fee diversion to about $100 million for FY 2004, about half the amount that has been diverted in recent years. Nonetheless, the patent office's "customers" are still sufficiently wary about the prospects for fee diversion that they have asked Congress to build a "sunset" provision into the new fee increases that would make the fees revert to the old levels in three years unless Congress acts specifically to extend the increases.[135] This sun-setting appears to be designed to pressure both the PTO and the Congressional committees, which set its budget, to make sure that the new revenues are really used to improve PTO operations. The Bush administration opposed the sunset provision.[136] In the current and foreseeable budgetary environment, it is hard to be sanguine about the PTO getting the resources necessary to really do its job.

Incentive Issues

Partially as a consequence of these financial woes, the patent office has found it difficult to recruit and retain the best examiners. In some sense, this is not news; patent offices have long struggled to recruit and retain skilled examiners:

- Shortly after taking office in 1829, the third superintendent of the patent office, John Craig, aggressively complained about the extent to which the patent office's fee income was used by Congress to cover general government expenses. He noted angrily that such transfers were having a harmful effect on his ability to hold onto his modest staff of professionals: "At present the Patent Office is a source of revenue; which, it is presumed, the framers of its laws never intended; and the compensation received by those connected with it is far less, in proportion to their labor and responsibility than in any other office of the Government within the District [of Columbia]."[137]
- Between 1855 and 1857, Commissioner Charles Mason strove to address his inability to retain his staff, which consisted of twelve

patent examiners and twelve assistant examiners.[138] Over $14,000 of back pay was owed the examiners (equal to ten full years of salaries). This shortfall had arisen because of an additional Congress mandate: the legislators had instructed the patent office to distribute the seeds of promising new crops to farmers in addition to their traditional duties. While the legislators were amenable to remedying this problem, an error was introduced during the hurried conference committee finalizing the federal budget. Instead, all of the increased funds intended for the patent office were sent to the chaplains of the federal penitentiary system. (Meanwhile, whenever the patent commissioner would leave town, his boss, the tradition-minded Secretary of the Interior, would dismiss any female employees from the patent office staff.)

- In 1912, the President's Commission on Economy and Efficiency noted, after detailing many complaints from inventors, that "it is apparent that the specific complaints against the patent office just enumerated are in the main correct. The work is in arrears and many patents are proved invalid."[139] The report detailed the lure that the private sector held for young employees, and the disruption that the ensuing defections caused. To address this problem, the Commission suggested several remedies: increasing the number of senior examiners, boosting pay, and exploring new incentive schemes to boost retention.

- A special study of the Patent Office Society highlighted the plight of examiners in 1933.[140] Salary cuts, forced furloughs, and a lack of resources had sapped the morale of the examiner corps. It was noted that the typical patent examiner made under $2,000 per year. (To put this number in perspective, Congress in 1848 had mandated that examiners be paid $2,400 per year.[141]) As the *Journal of the Patent Office Society* pointed out, the carpenters building the shelving on which the patent examination files were stored made two-to-three times that amount: not a very attractive return for the seven years of college and post-graduate study that the typical examiner had. The result was predictable: incessant turnover. While the annual turnover rates were somewhat below the 25 percent and higher rates seen in the heady days of the late 1920s, even in the midst of the Great Depression, examiners were leaving their positions in droves.

- Vannevar Bush, one of the pioneers of post-war American science policy, reviewed the patent system for the Senate Judiciary Committee in 1956. He noted how the increase in the volume and complexity of scientific activity was placing severe strains on patent examiners. Neither the numbers nor the skill level of the examiners were up to par, he argued, and Congress had to make additional appropriations.[142]

Thus, this is far from a new issue. But as intellectual property has become so much more important, the stakes regarding the recruitment and retention of examiners have risen. Perhaps the best way to see this is through an illustration. First consider a new examiner, beginning at the initial step of the relatively senior grade of GS-11.[143] To qualify for such a position, our new candidate would have to have earned a bachelor's degree in his specialty area (typically biology, chemistry, engineering, or physics), and have either three years' professional experience or graduate study, or else a doctoral degree. Under an enhanced salary scale effective January 2002, these candidates would start at $53,000 per year. After twenty years at the organization, having achieved "primary examiner" status, they might expect to be making $100,000. (The average examiner, however, makes approximately $60,000.)

This may be contrasted with the opportunities in the private sector for comparably qualified individuals. Examiners departing the patent office have routinely doubled their salaries when joining law firms and corporate patent departments. Many employees without legal degrees have been hired, with the law firms financing their legal education while they undertake support work.[144] Fresh law school graduates specializing in patent matters have commanded offers as high as $150,000—plus, in some cases, generous signing bonuses.

The consequences of such a compensation differential are predictable. The PTO has had difficulty retaining patent examiners, particularly those skilled in examining the latest technologies. Many examiners see the patent office as an entry point for a corporate position: as soon as they have developed enough skills to be truly valuable examiners, they depart for positions at corporate legal departments or law firms.

Employers have snapped up these individuals, eager to take advantage of their knowledge of PTO procedures. As a result, by 2001, 55 percent of the examiners had been at the office for two years or less.[145] Defenders of the status quo might argue that this turnover is an inevitable consequence of running a government agency, but this rate is more than six times as high as that in the European Patent Office.[146]

Even beyond the level of compensation, the way in which the compensation of individual examiners is decided is also problematic.[147] Bonuses and promotions of patent office employees are based on their productivity, as measured in a very specific way. Patent examiners are given one point when they complete an initial review of a patent and another point when the application is ultimately allowed or rejected. (Various adjustment factors control for the seniority of the examiner and the complexity of the underlying technology.) But applicants can modify and appeal patents that are initially rejected, thereby postponing the earning of the second productivity point. Thus, a rejected patent will typically consume much more of an examiner's time than one that is allowed after the initial application. This scheme creates an obvious incentive for examiners to "go easy" on applicants and allow their patents to be granted. Moreover, it is clear that this incentive scheme achieves its ostensible objective: to get examiners to work very quickly. The examiner processing the typical patent spends only sixteen to twenty hours with each patent.[148]

In other cases, the pressures are even less subtle: examiners have been criticized by supervisors for undertaking too many reviews of patents prior to issue, and encouraged to issue more "first action" patents—those that are granted without an initial rejection and subsequent reformulation by the patent applicant.[149] Meanwhile, institutional mechanisms to protect patent quality have been weakened. Beginning in 1993, the PTO began cutting the staff of the Office of Patent Quality Review, the watchdog group that assesses the quality of issued patents. Over the succeeding years, the office's staff and activities fell by nearly half. While ultimately the PTO established a successor to this group, the impact on quality was detrimental.[150]

The pervasiveness of the incentives to get patents out the door can be seen in other ways as well. Over much of the past decade, the PTO's patents group had the following forthright "mission" statement: "The Patent Business is one of the PTO's three core businesses. The primary mission of the Patent Business is to help customers get patents."[151] This is a far cry from the office's traditional credo, which had been to "issue valid patents."[152] After the "mission" statement had received widespread criticism, the PTO began featuring a new set of objectives. In the 2002 PTO Business Plan, the announced goals were to "enhance the quality of our products and services" and to "minimize patent application processing time."[153] While this is less objectionable than making the issuance of patents to "customers" the office's mission, it is clear that, overall, the office remains oriented towards satisfying applicants, rather than ensuring the validity of the patents that are issued.

It might well be thought that this orientation to issuing patents would demoralize examiners committed to patent quality. And indeed, from the plaintive on-line postings by patent examiners, this is exactly what has happened. To cite a few examples:[154]

> When I first started here, I was told "when in doubt reject" and to try to reject. Now I am told, "when in doubt allow" and try to find a reason to allow.
>
> Hey, management pays you for good patents or bad, right? Why should you fight with management? Why reject?
>
> We have a cultural goal now. If some examiner is not issuing enough, his SPE (Supervisory Patent Examiner) will complain and make her or him feel like s/he's a weirdo anal retentive tight butt. . . . The examiner wonders why s/he is working so hard. The examiner wonders why s/he draws complaints from the boss, and bitter fusillades from attorneys that are used to slam dunks, not rejection.

A skeptic might argue that this is a generic problem, associated with many government agencies. In this sense, the PTO might not be much different from the Securities and Exchange Commission or the Justice Department, where young lawyers go to get some seasoning before heading off into private practice. Such employee turnover might be seen as a healthy thing, as it allows government agencies to recruit top-flight individuals who would not consider the government for a permanent career.

A substantial difference, we believe, characterizes the patent system, which makes the "revolving door" phenomenon more troubling in this context. In many senses, the provision of quality control in other governmental agencies is relatively straightforward, because the actions and decisions of "junior" staff are merely individual steps in a longer administrative process. There are well-defined break-points associated with decisions such as whether to proceed with a preliminary investigation, seek an indictment, and settle a case, and the decisions at these points are typically reviewed at multiple levels. For instance, staff members at the Federal Trade Commission must go before the five commissioners for approval before filing a complaint against a company for unsavory practices. By way of contrast, ensuring quality control over the patent examination process is much harder. Each patent application requires a distinct administrative decision, and involves a much smaller block of time than typical administrative decisions at other agencies. It is simply not possible to have every patent decision reviewed at a higher level. As a result, inexperienced, underpaid, and overworked patent examiners are making decisions on final administrative actions in a way that their equally junior counterparts at other agencies are not. Furthermore, since each patent application is unique (almost by definition), the examination process is unlikely to be routine even after an examiner has gained the experience of processing a large number of applications.

Investing Resources Wisely

The final aspect of this tale of woe relates to the management of the office itself. Even though the PTO has severely limited resources, as we have highlighted above, the wisdom with which these resources have been used has frequently raised questions.

We will focus on one example: the management of the information necessary for examiners to evaluate the "prior art" against which the novelty of patent applications is considered. Examiners' ability to manage and access this information is crucial to the validity of the patent approval process. We have already discussed a number of examples where a great deal of prior art existed, yet the patent examiners were unable to locate it and consequently issued a dubious patent.

Moreover, the effective searching of prior art by examiners is critical because of the incentives in the patent system itself. The applicant is obliged to disclose to the examiner any prior art of which he or she is aware. But what the applicant does not know about, the applicant cannot be required to disclose. Further, applicants face a clear disincentive to explore the prior art thoroughly. In particular, a major fear of corporations is "willful infringement." If they are found to have knowingly infringed a patent, they can be liable for three times the damages that they would otherwise need to pay, so a company does not necessarily want to make sure it finds out about all of the patents related to a technology it is pursuing. This rule has created incentives for firms to be scanty in their searches.[155] Thus, it is all the more essential that the PTO itself conduct thorough searches.

Yet this vital task has been addressed in a desultory manner within the patent office. As early as 1954, an advisory group noted the difficulty that the patent office was having in managing the flood of new technical knowledge that had emerged after World War II. It argued that the power of computers could make patent searching much more reliable than the traditional "shoe boxes" (paper files) that patent examiners used.[156] The patent searching process would be greatly facilitated by fast, flexible information technology, which could draw lessons from earlier patent searches and readily accommodate new fields of knowledge as they emerge.

The response in the decades that followed was always the same: to begin research and development projects.[157] In each case, the project was abandoned after a few years, with the claim that implementation would cost far too much. For instance, in the late 1960s, the office announced "Project POTOMAC" (Patent Office Techniques Of Mechanized Access and Classification). This automated system would enable patent examiners to rapidly search the prior art. After the expenditure of tens of millions of dollars, the effort was abandoned as a complete failure in 1972. An alphabet soup of other projects—HAYSTAQ (Have You Stored Answers To Questions), ILAS (Interrelated Logic Accumulating Scanner), RAMP (Random Access Mechanization of Phosphorus Compounds), CAMP (Card Mechanization of Phosphorus), and SECIR (Semiautomatic Encoding of Chemistry for Information Retrieval)—came to similarly ignominious ends.

By end of the 1970s, the failures of the patent office were becoming increasingly visible. With the prodding of President Carter, Congress enacted Public Law 96–517, which required the office to develop an automation plan within two years, with the expectation that it would be implemented soon thereafter. Almost immediately, however, the implementation plan—which called for the initiation of complete electronic searching by December 1987—began encountering difficulties.[158]

As congressional staff investigated, they found plenty of blame to go around:

- The patent office neglected to undertake a critical study of the space for the computers for several years, despite repeated reminders. Once a preliminary study was completed, it was determined that the original idea of clustering large workstations was not viable, because the building's air conditioning system could not handle the load. As a result, the entire system's architecture needed to be re-engineered.

- The Department of Commerce (under whose sway the PTO falls) did not follow accepted procurement policies for large computer systems, awarding a "cost-plus" award to develop the system. Rather than getting the private firm to commit to a set price, the Department agreed to reimburse all the costs plus an additional fee. Federal rules strongly discourage such contracts for the development of new computer systems, because it creates a situation ripe for abuse.

- The contractor appeared to fail to follow standard accounting rules and good management practices. Exacerbating this problem, the government officials failed to exercise their right to place officials in the contractor's office to oversee the activities.

Not surprisingly, the result was delays and cost overruns. By 1984, two years after the original estimate had been prepared, the projected cost had risen from $289 million to $448 million. By 1992 (several years after the original targeted completion date), this latter sum had been spent already on the project, but the effort was still far from complete. Neither foreign patent documents nor non-patent literature could be searched. The system was not anticipated to be completed until 1997, and the patent office acknowledged the total cost would reach $1 billion (expressing the total in the same 1984 dollars in which the previous estimate had been prepared).[159]

Moreover, there have been problems with the systems that have been implemented.[160] In 1994, the patent office decided to replace the interim system to search U.S. patents—which had been leased from a private firm—with its own system. After numerous delays, the patent office in 1999 introduced two new search engines, dubbed EAST and WEST. Only days after rolling out the new system, the managers pulled the plug on the existing automated system. The result was widespread chaos, as inadequately trained examiners struggled with the balky systems. While many of the problems were eventually addressed, the Department of Commerce concluded that the process by which the new systems had been implemented taught many lessons about how such implementations should be improved in the future.

While the automation efforts were floundering, the Office's traditional search resources have suffered. Patent examiners reported numerous frustrations, as they struggled to get the library to buy technical volumes and periodicals. In many cases, they became frustrated enough while waiting for approvals that did not arrive that they bought these volumes with their own money. Paper copies of foreign patents ceased being purchased in 1993, while the electronic versions of these documents did not become available until 2000. Meanwhile, the librarians were busy discarding the hard copies of scientific journals and replacing them with microfilm, which the harried examiners found much harder to quickly search and copy.[161]

The Consequences

While there is a formal process of patent examination, in practice the system seems more akin to a registration system: in many cases it appears that a determined patentee can get almost any award he seeks. The granted claims may not be as broad as desired, but a patent is likely to issue. This is the predictable result when underpaid, inexperienced, and overworked examiners are pushed to resolve cases as quickly as possible, and are given flawed and obsolete tools for finding and searching the prior art.

Cecil Quillen and his associates find evidence in support of this characterization of the situation in two recent studies.[162] They point out that while the rejection rates for U.S. patents appear impressive at first glance, these numbers are illusive. The false impression arises from the fact that when patent applications refile their proposals in response to an initial rejection by the PTO, in many cases this is counted as a fresh application. Fully one-quarter of the seemingly new applications are actually refiled rejected filings (more technically known as continuations), which means that the success rate is considerably higher. Because of ambiguities about the exact circumstances surrounding these additional filings, it is difficult to sort out exactly what is going on.[163] But putting aside the details behind the precise calculations, it seems clear that a very large fraction of applications are ultimately issuing.

Besides grant rates, there is another form of evidence for declining U.S. patent quality that can be derived from international comparisons. Dominique Guellec and his colleagues at the Organisation for Economic Cooperation and Development (OECD) in Paris have been integrating data on patents granted by the U.S. PTO, the European Patent Office and the Japanese Patent Office. Patents filed overseas are identified by a priority number that links the foreign patent application to a corresponding application in the inventor's home country. By tracing these linkages, OECD researchers have identified what they call "families" of patents that correspond to the same underlying invention. An invention that is successfully patented in all three of the world's major patent-granting jurisdictions is a relatively important one, both because its owner valued it enough to seek protection in all three, and because the examination systems in all three judged it sufficiently novel to merit patenting. This means that the number of such patent families originating in a given country in a given year provides a measure of the number of relatively important inventions produced in that country in that year. Further, because the measure is based on the actions of all three agencies, this measure is less subject than the raw patent counts to fluctuation due to changing practices in any one agency.

The OECD calculations indicate that the number of important inventions originating in the United States increased by 51 percent between 1987 and 1998 (the longest and most recent time period for which these calculations can be made). By comparison, the number of successful applications to the U.S. PTO by U.S. inventors increased 105 percent over the same period.[164] If the examination standards in the United States were not changing, we might expect successful applications in the United States by U.S. inventors to grow at about the same rate as our measure of internationally important inventions originating in the United States. Actually, we would probably expect families to grow somewhat faster than successful U.S. applications, as the process of globalization gradually induces more and more successful U.S. applicants to seek protection around the globe. The fact that the growth in successful PTO applications was, instead, twice as large as the growth of international families is hard to explain in any manner other than declining standards in the U.S. PTO, producing an ever-growing proportion of U.S. patents the patent-holders themselves did not think merited patenting elsewhere.

Moreover, the number of cases where important prior art is not cited by patent examiners is alarmingly high. We could run through examples in many industries until the readers' eyes would glaze over. Rather, we will just provide one particularly embarrassing example: a patent on the drafting of patent applications. After all, this seems like a subject where the patent office might be presumed to be true experts.

Consider Patent No. 6,049,811, which is for a "Machine for Drafting a Patent Application and Process for Doing So." This patent, granted in 2000 to two individual inventors in Texas, describes a computer that poses a series of questions to a potential patentee, asking him to describe his invention. The computer then drafts the various sections of a patent application. The application for this patent (which may or may not have been prepared using its own method) cited as relevant prior art just one other patent and two published articles.

As Greg Aharonian points out, a line of research at Hitachi anticipated this event by many years.[165] The giant corporation was awarded at least four Japanese patents for these discoveries. While Hitachi did not apply for protection in the United States, these patents were nonetheless part of the "prior art" that should have been considered. Consider, for instance, the description of Japanese Patent No. 3,292,562, "Control Systems for On-Line Presenting Document," which was applied for almost seven years before the U.S. patent: "To effectively produce a patent application form by inputting the items to be written into the application form to a patent control database. . . At application those items to be written into the application form are taken out of the database for production of an application file . . . . Thus, a patent application form is produced with great efficiency." Perhaps the reader will attribute the U.S. patent examiner's failure to find this bit of prior art to the limited access patent examiners have had to foreign patent documents. Indeed, had U.S. examiners been able to readily search foreign patent databases electronically, such an embarrassing miscue could perhaps have been avoided.

But as a matter of fact, there was abundant evidence as to what Hitachi was up to in another location: the official publication of the society of PTO staff and other intellectual property professionals. Indeed, in 1992, the *Journal of the Patent and Trademark Office Society* published an article by two of the managers of Hitachi's Intellectual Property Division, describing in detail their development of a new system to automate the patent application process.[166] Apparently the examiner also missed this publication in his search of the prior art.

The Special Problem of Emerging Industries

The overlooking of important and obvious prior art is a particularly severe problem in emerging industries. In the early days of new industries such as biotechnology, the Internet, and nanotechnology, there are likely to be few patents already issued but a considerable stockpile of knowledge in scientific journals and in the form of informal know-how. The patent office has search tools that allow it to efficiently search U.S. patents for prior art. But when little of the knowledge is in the form of patents, the quality of the searches is likely to suffer.

This is particularly true in areas such as software and business methods, where the non-patent prior art comes in many diverse and diffuse forms: not just published scientific articles, but also conference papers, business and other non-technical journals, users' manuals, and computer programs. In many cases, the patent examiners have lacked the training and the experience to ascertain where to find the relevant prior art.

The story of Vergil Daughtery III illustrates the inadequacy of the PTO in addressing new technologies. As an undergraduate and master's student at Georgia Tech's management school, Daughtery developed an interest in financial derivatives—financial products whose value is "derived" from some other, underlying, financial instrument. His finance class spent several weeks discussing option pricing. An option is a financial product that allows an investor to buy or sell at a set price (or some range of prices) at some future date. For instance, a call option may give the right to purchase a share of stock in a specified company at the price of $10 anytime in the coming year.

As would have been the case at any decent school, Daugherty's finance class studied the Black-Scholes option-pricing model, published in 1972 and recognized with a Nobel Prize in 1997. This model lets an investor determine the value of an option by entering a few simple measures into a calculator or spreadsheet. All the investor needs is the current price of the stock, the price at which the option can be exercised, the interest rate, a measure of how variable the stock price is, and the time until the option expires.

As Daughtery explained, "We were studying [this], and I just couldn't understand why there always had to be a time component in the model."[167] So he decided to put his idea into action. Soon after completing his master's degree, Daughtery began working for a non-profit agency that sets up group homes for disabled people. During his spare time, he undertook a series of filings for patent protection on his options-valuing idea. In particular, he claimed in his filings to have made an important financial innovation: figuring out how to price an "expirationless" option. Unlike the Black-Scholes formula, which generated values only for options that last a finite period of time, Daughtery's discovery would let investors price options that last forever.

By 2004, Daughtery had received two patent awards grants on his idea, and had a number of applications pending. The patents gave him broad rights to expirationless options. To commercialize this idea, he established a new company, Economic Inventions, and began encouraging investment banks and securities firms to take licenses to his patents. Daughtery is today continuing his licensing efforts, recently initiutiny negotiations with the Chicago Board of Trade.

At first blush, this account reads like an all-American success story. Patents have enabled a young, ambitious inventor to "get on the playing field." Without his patents, Daughtery would almost certainly not been able to enter into negotiations with giant financial corporations. As one commentator noted, "Not only can you invent a new way of doing business and effectively control that new way from a lakeside in North Carolina, you don't have to be some snobby Harvard or Stanford Ph.D. to do it."[168]

There is just one problem: Infinitely lived options are not a new idea. In fact, it is considerably easier to value infinitely lived options than to value those with a distinct life span, which is why a Nobel prize was awarded for solving the finite-lived option pricing problem. Economist Paul Samuelson (both alone and with Bob Merton) had solved the pricing of perpetual options in the mid-1960s, well before Fischer Black, Myron Scholes, and Merton analyzed the pricing of finite-lived options. To be sure, most introductory MBA finance classes do not get around to discussing the pricing of perpetual options because they are not as ubiquitous as finite-lived options. Nonetheless, the subject has been dissected in literally dozens of articles, many written by Nobel Laureates such as Merton and Samuelson.

It is not surprising that Daughtery did not realize his discovery had already been made many years before. But why did the patent office examiners not figure out that his solution wasn't novel? While Allen MacDonald, the examiner who approved Daughtery's initial application, did search earlier works, his hunt was astonishingly inadequate. For instance, he spent much of his time reviewing earlier patent applications. But because few earlier patent awards existed for financial methods, this quest revealed little. Certainly, it had not occurred to Bob Merton or Paul Samuelson to patent their pioneering work on infinitely lived options in the 1960s, and no one had filed for a patent on such options prior to Daughtery. The examiner also searched various literature databases for the phrase that had been employed by Daughtery: "expirationless options." This turned up nothing because the finance literature used the phrase "perpetual options" instead.

This kind of problem stems in large part from the organization of the PTO itself. Before 1998, the PTO handled few financial patent applications, because few observers believed that such awards could be enforced in the courts. Chronically strained for resources, the office assigned just a handful of patent examiners to evaluate financial patent applications. Then, in the 1998 *State Street* decision discussed in chapter 4, the CAFC opened the door to financial patents, indicating that financial discoveries and other business methods could be patented just like any other discovery. Soon the examiners were flooded with new applications.

Given the PTO's scarce resources, it is not surprising that they did not have the kind of staff experts in financial economics who knew of or could have identified the existing literature on perpetual options. Yet one can only imagine the befuddlement of the pinstriped investment bankers upon receiving Daughtery's letter to "cease and desist" using a technique that has been widely understood since the 1960s.

Whether Daughtery will succeed in profiting from his discovery remains an open question. But it is clear that others are profiting from business method patents, often of questionable validity. One example is Ronald Katz, who owns several dozen patents dealing with the interaction between computers and telephones. When you use a phone to check a bank balance, respond to a personal ad in the newspaper, or even participate in a teleconference, you may be infringing Katz's patents. Katz neither invented the telephone, the computer, nor even protocols such as caller ID. But his tall stockpile of complex patents has allowed him to successfully approach many financial institutions and software firms for royalties: he anticipates ultimately garnering $2 billion from his holdings.[169]

A more sanguine observer might point out that this is a short-run problem: eventually, this situation is likely to be resolved. As the PTO issues more and more patents relating to business methods, and other emerging areas such as nanotechnology, its examiners will become more expert in assessing what prior art is really out there. Over time, problematic patents such as Daughtery's should become much less common.

Three concerns make us reluctant to embrace completely this comforting perspective:

1. The earliest days of an industry are critical in affecting how an industry evolves. Students of business strategy have highlighted the importance of the advantage the early movers have in an emerging industry. New opportunities—whether auto tires in the 1910s or the Internet in the 1990s—are frequently characterized by the entry of dozens (or even hundreds) of new firms. Companies that can get a head start in such an emerging industry frequently are in the best position to survive the industry shakeout that almost inevitably follows, when many of these new firms are driven out of the industry. Such a competitive edge can be derived from many sources: customer familiarity with one's brand and the cost advantages associated with having more production experience than others are examples. But a strong patent position

is a particularly attractive advantage. Thus, if the patent office is rewarding the wrong firms during the critical early days of an industry, the distortions brought about by such miscues may be long-lived.

2. All patents are not created equal. Every study of the question has suggested that there is a very wide distribution of the value of awards, with a very small fraction of patents accounting for the bulk of the value in all patents.[170] These super-valuable patents are likely to be found disproportionately among breakthrough technologies and emerging industries. Thus, even if the problematic patents represent a small percentage of all awards by number, their value-weighted share may be much larger.

3. While the failure to find relevant prior art is clearly most acute, and perhaps has the most severe adverse consequences, in these new areas, the PB&J and other "low-tech" patents demonstrate amply that the PTO's failure to identify important prior art is systemic. Without more fundamental changes, experience will ameliorate, but will not solve, the problem of dubious software and business method patents.

The Pauperization of the System

Thus, we have seen that the patent office has been turned into a pauper. The ongoing transfers of resources from the patent office to general government coffers, the widening gap between compensation for examiners in the private and public sectors, the drive for "productivity" of a dubious sort, and the poor investments made by the PTO have combined to create a crisis in the quality of issued patents.

Taken alone, this change might have been simply worrisome. But conflated with the strengthening of the legal rights that patents convey, it has had a true multiplier effect, undermining and inhibiting the innovation system in manifold subtle and not-so-subtle ways. The fact that these effects have manifested themselves in crucial economic sectors, and have developed at a time when intellectual property has generally increased in economic significance, elevates this set of issues to the level of a potential economic crisis.

Thus, the seemingly endless stream of goofy patents we have talked about—and those we have not even mentioned, as the accessory kit for a snowman including lumps of coal, a carrot, and a corncob pipe, or the use of a tape measure to determine the appropriate bra size[171]—are not the benignly comic documents that they first appear. Rather, they are symptoms of a dysfunctional patent system, which, as we have highlighted in chapter 2, has affected the behavior of established firms and new entrants alike. In the next chapter, we turn to the examination of some of the efforts that have been undertaken to try to get the patent "train" back onto the tracks.

The Patent Reform Quagmire

or over seven decades, patent policy reformers had pushed for the creation of a patent opposition system. Task forces and commissions—consisting of seasoned patent lawyers, veteran policymakers, and learned professors—had urged the adoption of such a system. Finally, in 1997, the time appeared ripe for the adoption of this reform. And yet the effort to change the system failed.

Were the key actors in this reversal of fortune leading patent lawyers or academics who developed second thoughts? No, the key leaders in scuttling these reform efforts were a checkered cast of characters with little experience related to the patent system, ranging from G. Gordon Liddy, the rogue FBI agent who helped plan the Watergate break-in, to Oliver North, the key actor in the Iran-Contra scandal.

The rationale for a patent opposition system lies in the many examples we have seen in earlier chapters where patentees have received patents that appear to be illegitimate. Some have been due to gaming on the part of the applicant (for example, the use of continuation and divisional applications to modify patent claims while retaining an old priority date), others to poor reviews by harried and under-trained patent examiners. However, even when an opposing firm knows that an in-process or recently issued patent is invalid, it finds it very difficult to challenge a patent in the patent office. Instead, patents must be challenged in court, typically after the patentee has brought a charge of patent infringement against the firm.

Why should it matter, the reader may ask, whether the validity of the patent is disputed in the patent office or in court? The key reason is that the "playing field" in trials is very uneven. We have already referred to the "presumption of validity" that patent-holders enjoy, or, put another way, the high standards that alleged infringers must overcome to prove an issued patent is invalid. It is also important that defendants cannot raise many of the concerns about the quality of the patent examination process that we discussed in chapter 5; the CAFC has expressly ruled that the presumption of validity precludes introduction of evidence intended to call into question the integrity of government decision-making.

The disadvantageous position of the alleged infringer extends as well to the cost of litigation. The patentee must simply show that the defendant infringed his patent. While proof of infringement may turn on complex legal arguments about the meaning of the patent claims, it rarely involves a need to collect or sift through large volumes of physical evidence because the characteristics and function of the alleged infringing products are easy to see. The costs of such a case are frequently modest, and lawyers today are increasingly willing to handle these cases on a "contingency" basis: the plaintiff bears no cost, only sharing some of the up-side if the lawsuit is successful. In contrast, mounting a successful challenge to an issued patent frequently obliges the defendant to prove that the patent was invalid, an effort that entails extensive research into the prior art. (Much of the prior art, such as evidence that products incorporating the patented technology were being sold well before the patent application was filed, may, in fact, only be accessible to the patentee.) According to a 2001 survey, the cost of defending the typical infringement action with significant stakes (that is, with more than $25 million of economic value in dispute) was about $3 million. The cost of adjudicating a patent case had increased 25 percent in just two years.[172]

Many students of the U.S. system have seen pre-grant review as a way to address the difficulty of invalidating issued patents in court. For instance, the 1966 Commission on the Patent System had called for the publication of patent applications between eighteen and twenty-four months after filing, even though most patents will not have been reviewed at that point. The primary rationale for such publication was that this would reduce the number of errors associated with the patent issuance process. Individuals and firms could suggest "prior art" that the examiner should consider before deciding whether to issue a patent or not. No matter how talented the examiner, these individuals are unlikely to be the leading expert in each and every topic about which they review patents. Much as scientific journals recognize that the editor is unlikely to be able to effectively evaluate each paper alone, and, hence, recruit leading experts to provide "peer reviews," so too the judgment of the patent examiner could helpfully be supplemented by outside perspectives.

At least eight different bills calling for the introduction of patent reviews were introduced in the decade-and-a-half that followed the 1966 report.[173] Ultimately, a "re-examination" procedure was put into place in 1980. President Carter hailed this step as "the most significant improvement in our patent laws in more than a century."[174] But for several reasons the new procedure was a far cry from the process as originally envisioned by the Commission:

- *The timing of the procedure.* Rather than taking place before the patents issue, re-examinations occur after the award date. Both legal and psychological factors may make it harder to undo a patent award than not to grant one in the first place.
- *The extremely limited role in the dispute for the party who initiates a complaint.* This role was typically confined to filing an initial written statement that accompanies the "prior art" that is submitted for the patent examiner to consider. Moreover, the statement must be confined to a discussion of the applicability of that prior art and not the more general question of patentability. (In some cases, it may be possible to make a short written rebuttal to the patent-holder's claims as well.) The third party cannot present any oral arguments, or appeal any interim or final findings of the re-examination.

- *The narrow range of issues and evidence that can be considered in the proceeding.* The disputes can only focus on the extent to which patents and publications not previously considered by the patent examiner shed light on the extent to which the invention is novel and not obvious. For instance, a third party cannot challenge a patent on the grounds that the invention does not satisfy the utility, or usefulness, requirement. (Think, for instance, of the genome awards, where patents have been obtained on long stretches of genetic sequences whose function remains unclear.) Furthermore, prior art other than patents and other formal publications cannot be considered. In many new technologies, much crucial evidence falls into other categories—for example, software code critical to many disputes has neither been previously patented nor formally published. The restriction to "published" prior art severely handicaps third parties in precisely the areas where re-examinations would be most helpful.
- *The parties involved in hearing the re-examination request.* In some patent examiner groups, the same patent examiner who held the original hearing will conduct a re-examination hearing. In other cases, another examiner may be used. Often, a colleague down the hall from the original examiner does the re-examination. It is not implausible that even a fresh examiner will be reluctant to overturn the finding of one of his close peers.

Recognizing the limitations of these reforms, the 1992 Advisory Commission on Patent Law Reform called for a more effective form of re-examination. They called for, among other changes, more active involvement of third parties in these examinations and the inclusion of a broader range of challenges in re-examinations. The Commission seemed to model the ideal opposition system after that employed in Germany, where there are vigorous oppositions in the months after the patent issues involving a broad range of evidence.

In 1999, these suggestions were partially enacted in the American Inventor's Protection Act. While the act was hailed as fundamentally changing the re-examination system, the actual changes were modest. As Mark Janis noted: "The new inter parties re-examination system is, quite unfortunately, burdened with the same [features] that so thoroughly compromised the effectiveness of the original procedures."[175] The limited range of issues that can be covered, the ambiguities surrounding the litigation process, and the prominent role given the patent examiners in reviewing their own actions all continued to be problems. Moreover, Congress imposed a very high price for participation in this procedure: following an unsuccessful re-examination, the ability of the parties requesting the re-examination to challenge the patent in court would be greatly restricted.

The disappointing nature of these reforms is best illustrated in figure 6.1, which shows the number of patents that are re-examined each year. The re-examinations are divided by type: the traditional re-examination requested by a third party, those requested by the PTO Commissioner, and finally the new inter-party procedure.[176] The figure highlights the modest number of re-examinations: well under one-tenth of 1 percent of all patents issued in the United States result in re-examination requests. The contrast with Europe is striking, where the rate of opposition is nearly 7 percent, or about 100 times greater than in the United States.[177] And remember, European examiners are devoting something like twice as much time to the review of each application, and are rejecting a much higher proportion, so one would think that there would be less demand for re-examination in Europe, rather than more. The European procedure is also three times more likely to lead to revocation of the patent in question than in the United States. There is no evidence that the recent reforms have made patentees more willing to request re-examinations. In fact, the number of re-examination requests has been dropping, even as the number of patent awards has skyrocketed. The new "inter-parties" re-examination procedure is almost completely unutilized, with only six re-examinations of this type in the first three years it has been available.

Given the apparent need for a workable mechanism to weed out dubious patents, why is there so much controversy attached to publication of patent applications, so as to allow third parties to give notice of relevant prior art, and the development of a workable opposition procedure so validity battles do not have to be fought in

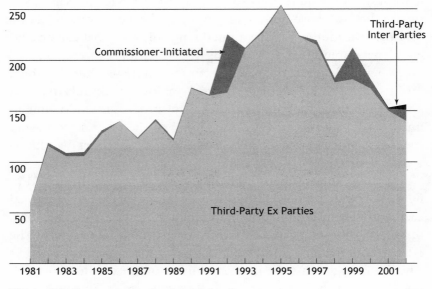

Figure 6.1 Patent re-examination initiated.

federal court? Many of the arguments revolve around the putative harm that such changes would have on small inventors. The presumption is that the publication of applications and allowing meaningful opposition would harm small firms in two ways:

- If patent applications are kept secret, then in the (increasingly rare) case where a patent application fails, the firm may be able to fall back on protecting the invention through trade secrecy. On the other hand, if patent applications are published (and they have to be published if outside parties are to have a chance to bring in relevant prior art or otherwise oppose them), then in cases where the patent is rejected, the firm's ability to get trade secret protection will have been lost. Denouncing what he called the "Steal American Technology Bill," for instance, Representative Dana Rohrabacher claimed that publication of patent applications would primarily benefit the Chinese Liberation Army and the Mitsubishi Corporation, who would eagerly appropriate ideas of small U.S. firms.[178]

- Large firms might be able to harass their smaller rivals by frequently opposing their patents. This strategy might make it harder for small firms to effectively build up their patent portfolios, as each stop along the way they are forced to make substantial expenditures for defensive purposes.

These arguments may appear initially compelling. But once again, they do not hold up to the light of day:

- As noted above, firms and individuals already seek patent protection for important discoveries outside the United States. In other major nations, today it is standard to publish applications eighteen months after the original filing date. Large multinational firms—such as Japanese trading companies and Chinese state-owned enterprises—recognize that these publications are valuable sources of information, and carefully scrutinize these applications. Meanwhile, individual inventors often are unaware of these publications, and cannot afford the costs of getting copies of these documents in a timely manner.[179]
- As we discussed in chapter 2, established firms already have many mechanisms for harassing smaller firms using traditional infringement suits. Given the substantial cost differential between a full-fledged trial and an opposition, it seems hard to argue that such an additional step will have that harmful an effect on smaller firms and individual inventors.
- Studies of the opposition system in Europe, which many have suggested as a model for the United States, provide little support for these claims. Awards by small entities are no more likely to be opposed than those of larger firms.[180]
- Small firms have as much, or more, to lose when invalid patents are wielded as litigation weapons as do large firms.[181] Conversely, given the high cost of litigation, they have at least as much to gain by the creation of a cost-effective and workable procedure for weeding out bad patents as do large firms.

Despite the limitations of these arguments, their advocates have been vehement in arguing about the harmful effect of oppositions. Among the voices that were most effective in swaying Congress were talk-radio commentators such as Oliver North and Gordon Liddy, who asserted that the move would harm small inventors.[182] Phyllis Schlafly, for instance, advanced the view that Japanese conspirators were driving the policy change:

> The Japanese, who don't invent anything but are mighty clever copy-cats, have been trying for years to break our system. They have been demanding that all the details of every invention be made public 18 months after the application is filed, regardless of whether or not a patent is ever issued. The American and Japanese systems are very different. Japan's economy is based on a partnership between government and the big corporations, and the Japanese patent system operates to make sure that industry controls and uses new innovations. The U.S. system, on the other hand, favors private property, individual innovation and ingenuity, and an open door of opportunity for entrepreneurs.[183]

Meanwhile, the voices of industry leaders, who would have the most to gain from a functioning patent system, have been strangely silent. In short, the situation reminds us of Yeats's immortal lines:

> The best lack all conviction, while the worst
> Are full of passionate intensity.[184]

Sad to say, even some of the leaders of the economics profession have climbed on the small-inventor bandwagon. A petition drive organized by MIT's Franco Modigliani protested the effort to reform the patent system, which included adding an opposition system. While the late Modigliani had contributed to human knowledge and prosperity in many ways—including explaining how savings changed over the human life-cycle and pioneering the modern theory of corporate finance—he had not done any research related to the economics of innovation or intellectual property. (But he has been awarded Patent No. 5,206,803, which covers a system that enables individuals to write checks against their pension fund, 401(k) account, or other retirement savings. This patent is remarkable for citing no non-patent prior art, even though at the time the patent issued, nearly 20 percent of the 401(k) plans offered a wide variety of borrowing plans.[185]) While the Nobel Laureates whom

Modigliani recruited, ranging across the ideological spectrum from Milton Friedman to Paul Samuelson, probably agree on little else, they loudly protested against the proposed patent policy reform:

> A delicate structure such as the patent system with all its ramifications should not be subject to frequent modifications. We believe that S. 507 could result in lasting harm to the United States and the world. [I]t will prove damaging to American small inventors and thereby discourage the flow of new inventions that have contributed so much to America's superior performance in the advancement of Science and Technology. It will do so by curtailing the protection they obtain thorough patents relative to the large multi-national corporations.[186]

As we have seen above, this argument is largely disconnected from the reality of how the patent system and patent litigation work (or do not work) today. While many luminaries in the profession joined in, the petition signers did not include the economists most known for research and writing on the economics of innovation, such as Kenneth Arrow, the Nobel Laureate in Economics who has thought most deeply on intellectual property issues. Though the distinguished petition signers surely meant well, it is certainly a sad day for the profession when several of its leading lights associate themselves with the same fallacies that enraptured Ollie North and Phyllis Schlafly. We do not have a good explanation for this state of affairs, unless maybe Gordon Liddy coerced them all into signing the statement.

Barriers to Patent Reform

We have already discussed the dramatic patent reforms enacted by the U.S. Congress in 1836, which led to the creation of the examination system. What is remarkable, though, is how few changes there have been since then in the United States. To be sure, there have been some shifts: for instance, in 1952, Congress did away with the "flash of creative genius" test as a precondition for a patent to issue.[187]

But overall, the U.S. system has been extremely stable, with features persisting long after the rest of the world has abandoned them. Put another way, even when the system has been shown to be fundamentally flawed, reform of the U.S. patent code has been exceedingly difficult to bring about.

Why is reform of the patent system so hard? An extensive body of work, often described as "political economy," provides an answer to this question, at least at a broad-brush level. These writings have emphasized the danger of "capture" of government programs.[188] Any program that assigns subsidies or assigns property rights is prone to the distortions that may result as interest groups or politicians seek to direct the public programs in a manner that benefits them. The theory of regulatory capture suggests that groups who have three shared characteristics will capture and control programs that create economic benefits:

- They stand to gain substantial benefits.
- Their collective political activity is not too difficult to arrange.
- The parties who are most affected by their actions are highly dispersed and find it difficult to organize.

To illustrate the basic idea, think of cosmeticians who push states to require extensive training and experience before granting licenses. Such barriers keep many aspiring entrepreneurs out of the business, which benefits the small, cohesive, easily organized group of incumbent cosmeticians. While everyone suffers slightly as a result, consumers are unlikely to be sufficiently annoyed on account of paying a little more for their permanents and buzz-cuts to march to their state capital in protest. Hence the regulatory process is likely to be captured, and reform that is in the broad (but diffuse) public interest is likely to languish.

While we might like to think that inventors and patent lawyers are different from hair stylists, the patent system has many features that make the problem of capture likely. The most important of these relates to the complexity of these laws. The set of lawyers who understand these issues is unlikely to be large. While probably few are inclined to intentionally perpetuate an inefficient system, the substantial gains that they enjoy from the current system's complexity—for example, lengthy and lucrative assignments—is likely to have a subtle effect on many practitioners' reactions to proposals for radical change.

Moreover, the negative effects of bad patent policy are very diffuse, and very difficult to see and understand. Consumers are unlikely to get excited about the extent to which subtle shifts in abstract judicial doctrine will affect the amount they pay for new products. Even CEOs are not apt to give these arcane issues the same kind of attention as something like tax policy—which affects a corporation's bottom line in a direct and transparent way.

Contributing to the constraints on policy debate created by the capture phenomenon is the bugaboo that the "small inventor" represents in the lore of patent policy. Analysis of the source of the political power of this invocation is beyond the scope of these authors, but there is no denying its potency. Despite the reality that the overwhelming bulk of technological innovation comes today from the organized laboratories of commercial firms, the mystique of the lonely, misunderstood, and ignored inventor, toiling away in his garage (yes, in the myth it is always a "he"), ranks with social security, the family farm, and home ownership among potent American political icons. It does not matter who you are, if you are fighting for the small inventor, you are likely to get a serious hearing.

A final source of inadequate public debate on the merits of patent policy issues is the lack of a common language among scholars and practitioners for thinking about these problems. In other fields where law and economics interact, such as tax policy and anti-trust, there has been a long tradition of lawyers and economists talking to each other about these issues. These dialogs have helped lawyers in many cases think more systematically about the problems, while enabling economists to better understand the real world challenges that policymakers face.

But this communication has not happened in the intellectual property field, at least not until the past few years. Far too often, intellectual property has had a second-class status within law schools, taught by practitioners in private practice rather than by prestigious legal scholars. While these individuals are often superb and highly dedicated teachers, their time outside the classroom is devoted largely to their professional activities. In short, they do not have a lot of time for writing pieces on the patent system, much less the kinds of informal interactions—for example, attending seminars and commenting on colleagues' papers—that is so important to the transmission of academic ideas.

Meanwhile, research by economists into the patent system has been quite modest. While many economists (present company included) used patents as data, measuring knowledge flows for example by looking at citations from one patent to another, relatively few looked at the workings of patent system itself. Most of the published economic work on the patent system has been highly theoretical, necessarily abstracting dramatically from the myriad details of how law and practice work. There is, for example, a significant economic literature that analyzes the pros and cons of "strong" patent protection, where "strong" has the abstract meaning that a large inventive step is needed before a patent will be issued, so that once a patent is granted the patentee controls a large portion of the technological terrain. But this kind of analysis is not very helpful in understanding the mess we find ourselves in today, where the office issuing patents has effectively lowered examination standards at the same time that the courts are making it harder to win a case proving that an issued patent is invalid.

These limitations in the scholarly analysis of patent policy do not really explain why the field should come to be dominated by the Phyllis Schlaflys of the world. But they do explain in part why the response to ill-founded policy arguments has not been as clear as one might hope.

An Illustration: The Patent Priority Debate

This description of the sources of patent policy problems is dry and abstract. But many examples can be offered of reforms that promise almost surely to boost national welfare that have been blocked by various special interests. In the preamble to this chapter, we discussed the case of patent oppositions; let us now turn to the question of patent priority.

The difficulties that federal officials have faced in reforming the patent system are well illustrated by the efforts to change U.S. policy so that a patent goes to the "first to file" a patent application on a given invention, rather than to the "first to invent." While this policy reform is not directly linked to the patent quality and patent litigation problems that we have highlighted, it is nonetheless interesting, because the case for changing U.S. policy seems so straightforward. Every other nation in the world awards patents to the applicant that is the "first-to-file" for patent protection.[189] The primary reason for the preference for "first-to-file" elsewhere is straightforward: while determining the party who is first to conceptualize an idea is often exceedingly difficult, it is easy to determine the filing date.

The United States, however, has clung to the first-to-invent system. In the United States, a patent is awarded to the party who can demonstrate (through laboratory notebooks and other evidence) that he was the initial discoverer of a new invention, even if he did not file for patent protection until after others did (within certain limits). The American patent system turned its back on the way the rest of the world operates in the very earliest days of the nation's history. The reason for this divergence from the rest of the world is shrouded with mystery today.[190] Perhaps the most compelling explanation for this decision lies in historical accident: at the time the Patent Act of 1793 was enacted, two dueling inventors, James Rumsey and John Fitch, were locked in a battle over the ownership of riverboat engine technology. Each had made several patent applications, but the orders of application and invention differed. So the particular design of the patent system would have an enormous influence on their individual fortunes. Not surprisingly, the men— and their financial backers, who had included both George Washington and Benjamin Franklin—exerted heavy influence to try to shape the system for their benefits. Whatever its origins, and despite the arguments for shifting away from "first-to-invent," this system has persisted for more than two centuries.

Over the years, a number of blue-ribbon commissions examining the workings of the U.S. patent system have recommended switching to a "first-to-file" system. For instance, this was the first and central recommendation of President Johnson's Commission on the Patent System. As they noted, replacing the first-to-invent system would have multiple advantages: "A first to file system will: encourage prompt disclosure of newly discovered technology; substitute for the delays and expense of interference proceedings a fair and inexpensive means by which an inventor can establish priority; and bring U.S. practice into harmony with that prevailing in almost all industrial nations."[191]

Much of the discussion in the Commission report (and in the supporting measures) highlighted the weakness of the system for resolving priority disputes in the "first-to-file" world. Unlike relying on a filing dates—which can be objectively and unambiguously determined—the process of determining which party is first to invent a discovery is far from trivial. Disputes over priority of invention are resolved through an "interference" proceeding before the PTO's Board of Patent Appeals and Interferences. In contested cases, the Board holds a hearing to determine which inventor first made the discovery.

The interference process has been characterized as "an archaic procedure, replete with traps for the unwary."[192] These procedures operate under their own rules, which are sufficiently complex that even the Court of Appeals for the Federal Circuit has misunderstood the process.[193] Deadlines and rules are characterized by "very strict and unforgiving enforcement,"[194] which means that hiring one of the relatively few (but very expensive) lawyers specializing in this area is truly essential. Moreover, the process can be quite protracted. For instance, the party with the first-issued patent in the dispute can impose considerable delays by asking that its patent be re-issued before the proceeding begins, a process that can take many months.[195] Reflecting these difficulties, in only about sixty cases annually has the party that was second-to-file been determined to have been the first-to-invent.[196] Thus, the United States persists in this complex, costly, and idiosyncratic system in order to reverse the priority of 0.03 percent of the patent applications filed each year. Moreover, as figure 6.2 shows, the frequency of such interferences in recent years has fallen sharply from historical levels, probably reflecting the lack of time that overworked examiners have had to examine the ever-growing queue of pending patents.[197]

Figure 6.2 Number of patent inferences declared.

By way of contrast, under a "first-to-file" system, disputes could be much more expeditiously resolved: the filing date can be readily determined by the patent office. Moreover, a "first-to-file" system would encourage inventors to file and hence disclose inventions in a timely manner. Despite these powerful arguments and the Johnson administration's backing, the legislation embodying the 1966 Commission's recommendations languished in Congress.

The next major effort to fix this mess began in 1992, when the Secretary of Commerce's Advisory Commission on Patent Law Reform made the abolition of the first-to-invent system its top priority.[198] The report highlighted that the persistence of this feature of the U.S. system was a major barrier to the harmonization of the patent systems around the globe. In particular, in 1985, the World Intellectual Property Organization (also known as WIPO, this Geneva-based international organization is responsible for administering the Paris Convention and subsequent treaties), began an effort to hammer out a draft treaty that set up a model patent law that, it was hoped, all nations could accept and adopt.

The 1992 Commission highlighted the fact that the United States had much to gain from the harmonization of the global patent system, since this nation is a net "exporter" of intellectual property. Worldwide harmonization would generally enhance the value of patents worldwide; as the world's greatest producer of inventions, we would be the greatest beneficiary of such enhancement. For instance, the draft WIPO accord called for the worldwide adoption of the "doctrine of equivalents," which allows a patentholder to claim a broader swath of technology than that in his original award.[199] This provision has been a longstanding part of American patent doctrine, but had been only rarely adopted elsewhere. The Commission noted that it was unlikely that other nations would agree to change aspects of their systems in ways desirable to us, unless the United States were willing to abandon an archaic practice in which it stands alone among the nations of the world.

Legislation embodying the 1992 Commission recommendation on changing to first-to-file—like that motivated by the 1966 report before it—soon encountered intense opposition. A frequently invoked argument for the first-to-invent system is that this provides protection for—you guessed it—small inventors, who supposedly take longer to translate a discovery into a completed patent application. If small inventors take longer to prepare patent applications, then they might lose out to better-financed rivals in a first-to-file world. Advocates have gone so far as to describe proposals to abolish the first-to-invent criterion—though without presenting evidence to support their claim other than a few well-worn anecdotes—as "the death knell of independent inventors."[200]

This argument appears to be specious for several reasons:

1. There are already strong pressures to file first. Economically important discoveries are typically the subject of patent filings in a number of countries: only relatively unimportant discoveries will be filed in the United States alone. Since virtually all nations outside the United States employ a first-to-file system, there is already an enormous pressure for inventors of all sizes to file quickly. Moreover, as noted above, in the vast majority of disputed cases under the U.S. system, the party who filed first still wins. At least in large part, this pattern reflects the features of the interference system that makes it easier for the party who is first to file to prove his case.[201]

2. Another recent reform of the U.S. system, adopted in the wake of the 1992 Commission report (and other contemporaneous reform efforts), created new provisional patent applications, which are simpler to file than full-fledged applications. Thus, obtaining a priority date is no longer a matter of completing a complex filing. As long as the applicant completes a full patent application by the first-year anniversary of the preliminary filing, he preserves the original filing date.

3. Furthermore, small entities, in fact, are frequently the loser in interference proceedings under the current system. In many cases, they lack the resources or the management wherewithal to keep the kind of detailed records that are needed to prove that they were the original inventor.[202] Moreover, the cost of this litigation—which can run into the hundreds of thousands of dollars— is frequently prohibitive to small private firms without "deep pockets" or ready access to the capital markets.

4. Finally, it is questionable how much weight should be assigned to the arguments of independent inventors, even if it were true that they benefit from the current system. As Bruce Lehman, PTO Commissioner at the time, noted, many of the most vocal independent inventors opposing the adoption of first-to-file are "weekend hobbyists . . . [rather than representatives of] knowledge-based industries."[203]

Once again, a legislative effort to adopt the recommendations fizzled: in January 1994, Commerce Secretary Ron Brown announced the administration would abandon the effort to convert the American system to first-to-file. Not surprisingly, this decision to renege on the part of the Clinton Administration led to an abandonment of the WIPO treaty process. Worldwide patent harmonization remains a distant and elusive goal of U.S. policy.[204]

While the voices raised in protest over the reform initiative in the 1990s—as those opposing earlier reform attempts—were led by advocates for small inventors, it is difficult not to conclude that the greatest beneficiary from the first-to-invent system is not small inventors, or any subset of inventors. It is rather the small subset of patent attorneys that specializes in interferences. Perhaps it is not surprising that the recommendation that appears to have been most influential in the Clinton Administration's decision to abandon this goal was a negative recommendation by the American Bar Association's House of Delegates.[205] In fact, some first-to-invent supporters have gone so far as to drop the thin cloak of language about "fairness" that surrounds their arguments, and acknowledged the substantial financial stake that the patent bar has in the current system.[206] While the overall expenditures on interferences per active patent lawyer may be modest, a few hundred attorneys handle the bulk of the interferences.[207] These individuals have a considerable stake in the survival of the current system, and will fight vigorously to preserve it.

Why Is Reform So Hard?

As these case studies suggest, the failure of federal efforts to reform the patent system is due to several factors:

1. The issues are complex, and sometimes difficult to understand. Simplistic claims frequently cloud these discussions. For instance, because firms use patents to protect innovations, it is frequently argued that "stronger" patents are beneficial for innovation, and virtually any change to the status quo is characterized as "weakening" or "threatening" the patent system. The lack of ready dialogue between economists and lawyers about these issues has limited the extent to which the discussion can be raised to the more appropriate—but harder to convey—level of how to maximize the patent system's effectiveness in encouraging innovation.
2. The people with the greatest economic stake in retaining a litigious and complex patent system—the patent bar—have proven to be a very powerful lobby. The efforts of the highly specialized interference bar to retain first-to-invent is a prime example.[208]
3. The top executives of technology-intensive firms have not mounted an effective campaign around these issues. The reason may be that many of the companies that are most adversely affected are small, capital-constrained firms that do not have time

for major lobbying efforts. And even for larger firms, the adverse consequences of a malfunctioning patent system are diffuse and indirect, which works strongly against the emergence of a consistent voice on this subject from the business world.

4. The ultimate harm of sand in the gears of the innovation system is borne by consumers themselves, for whom the adverse consequences are even more indirect and hard to detect. No one sees that products are more expensive because of the cost of litigation and patent royalties, and no one knows about products whose introductions were delayed or cancelled because of patent woes. Educated consumers can be forgiven for assuming that a debate in which Ollie North and Franco Modigliani are on the same side is one that can be safely ignored.

These problems may not be unique to patent policy. One can think of a variety of public policy areas where the Washington-based discussion has been frequently muddled, and the resulting decisions have been poor. Nonetheless, when there is a lot at stake, it is important to keep trying to keep the analysis of what is best for the greater good as part of the discussion.

Chapter 7

Innovation and Its Discontents

So the freight train is out of control, even if it has not yet jumped the tracks. While the patent system plays a vital role in creating and maintaining incentives for innovation, it is becoming more and more expensive to operate (and fight about). Worse, its pathologies increase the uncertainty associated with investment in innovation, and thereby undermine the very incentives it is designed to create.

We saw in chapter 3 that crises in which patents are accused of stifling rather than encouraging innovation have been a recurrent feature of the industrialized world. Unlike the nineteenth century Dutch crisis, there does not seem to be wide support this time around for abolishing the patent system. But it is time to recognize that the accidental combination of strengthening the legal value of patents while reducing the rigor of patent examination has damaged the system. It is time for a recalibration. Since the source of the mess is the combination of easier success in the courts and at the PTO, our proposed recalibration addresses both of these venues.

There is an old story that President Harry Truman once quipped that he would like to find a one-handed economist, because he was tired of getting advice from economists that always was in the form "on the one hand, it might make sense to do thus and such, but on the other hand it might not." We are not going to be able, in this chapter, to escape the occupational hazard of seeing potential costs and problems associated with all proposed solutions. We will, however, outline the most promising directions for reform to take.

Goals and Objectives

Before getting to recommendations, it is important to be clear about what it is that any reform of the patent system ought to be trying to accomplish. While different analysts of the patent landscape have emphasized different aspects of the patent policy problems, there is general agreement on broad goals for reform of the system:

IMPROVE PATENT QUALITY. "Patent quality" is, to some extent, in the eye of the beholder. Certainly, as illustrated by examples discussed above, people are getting patents for inventions that are not new and/or are obvious. One way to solve this, of course, would be to make it much harder to get a patent on anything. If we did that, the few patents that did issue would be of very high quality, in the sense of being very deserved by the applicant. But the objective of patent quality has to be more than just making sure bad patents *do not* issue. It has to include also making sure that inventors do get patents when they have a truly novel, non-obvious invention, that such patents are processed relatively quickly and reliably, and that once granted they provide an adequate property right to protect subsequent investment in the invention.

REDUCE UNCERTAINTY. The primary objective of reform should be to reduce the uncertainty that now pervades many aspects of the patent system. (Ironically, the only aspect of the patent process that has become more certain is the application process itself, as the ultimate granting of some patent from each original application has become almost a sure thing.) The sand in the gears of the innovation machine is that companies and individuals must constantly fear that their research and product development may come to naught, because someone is going to assert an as-yet unknown or untested patent against them. Further, when such an assertion of patent infringement is made, the uncertainty about the ability to defend against that assertion often leads either to abandonment of the allegedly infringing technology, or to an agreement to pay possibly unnecessary royalties.

KEEP COSTS UNDER CONTROL. The PTO currently spends roughly $1 billion/year for its operations. Patent applicants spend several times that amount, and patent litigants billions more. These resources might be well spent, if they achieved a reasonably smoothly functioning system. But the system is not working well, and it is reasonable to wonder whether we need to invest more of society's resources in the patent process. Ideally, we might argue, the PTO's finances should be decoupled from the amount that it raises in the form of fees: rather, it should spend whatever it takes to ensure high-quality applications. Realistically, however, it is unlikely that dramatically increased resources are going to be available, particularly for the operation of the PTO itself. So we need to look for solutions that go beyond throwing money at the problem.

Some Simple Truths

The next step towards reform is to understand some basic realities about the innovation process.

Mistakes Will Always Be with Us

Patent examination is never going to be perfect. Examiners are human. More important, there is an essentially irreducible aspect of judgment in determining if an invention is truly new. After all, even young Albert Einstein faced challenges while assessing applications as a "Patent Examiner-Third Class" in the Swiss Patent Office.[209] Therefore, we cannot hope to have a system in which no "bad" patents ever issue. What is important is to have a system with fewer bad patents. And, since there will always be mistakes, it is important to have a system that functions reasonably well despite the issuance of some bad patents.

Better examination will require more resources. At current application rates, it would be very expensive to give all patent applications an examination sufficiently thorough to reduce significantly the problems with bad patents being issued. Now, the patent system is important, so it is possible that spending several billion additional dollars on the PTO would be worthwhile for society. But this kind of dramatic increase in PTO resources does not seem very realistic in the current fiscal environment. Fortunately, it is also not necessary to expend the resources necessary to provide very reliable examination for all patent applications.

Much More Chaff Than Wheat

The first step to understanding why greatly increasing the resources for examination is not the best solution to the problem is to understand that most patents are, and always will be, worthless and unimportant. This is not a feature of the patent office; it is a feature of the innovation process. It is partly due to the human tendency for us each to think that our ideas are better than other people think they are. But it also reflects a deeper attribute of the process of technological development: the significance of a new idea usually cannot be known when it is first developed, because that significance depends on subsequent developments, both technological and economic. Many, many, "good" ideas are patented that never actually turn out to be worth anything. It is not that they should not have been patented to begin with. It is just that for every invention with lasting technological or economic significance, there will always be dozens or hundreds of ideas that seemed potentially worthwhile, but which eventually proved to be valueless.

The fact that almost all patents are ultimately worthless has an important implication for the "patent quality" problem. If most patents are doomed to be consigned to the dustbin of technological history, it cannot make sense to spend a lot of resources to make sure that they all receive very high quality examination before issuing. The legions of inventors and patent attorneys may not like to think about this, but for the vast majority of patent applications, it will simply never matter—either to the inventor, her employer, or competitors—whether the patent is allowed to issue or not.

Day in and day out, most of what patent examiners do is like what the officials do in the last minute of a football game where one team is already winning by thirty points. They go through the motions of making rulings, because rulings have to be made, but they do not matter to the outcome of the game. The key difference is that in the patent game, much of the time no one knows whether this particular case is going to matter or not. It is as if nobody—the officials, the players, and the coaches—have any idea of the score of the game, or if the game even matters. But they all take it seriously because there is some chance that the particular "game" they are playing will turn out (months or years later) to be important. For the ones that do turn out to be important, it will matter a lot if patents are granted that should have been. But for the others, there will never be important technological or economic consequences. And these "others" are the vast majority of all applications in the system.

"Rational Ignorance"

If careful examination is expensive, and the vast majority of patents will never matter to anyone, then it would be inefficient to expend society's resources on careful examination of all patent applications. In the colorful phrase of Mark Lemley, we can think of the poor quality of patent examination as representing "Rational Ignorance," by which he means that society is rationally choosing to remain ignorant about which patents really should be granted by the PTO.[210] Lemley argues that it is, in fact, reasonably efficient to simply accept that PTO examination will be of poor quality, and that the cases that really matter will have to be sorted out in the courts. Court cases are expensive, but because only the small fraction of patents that matter will ever get litigated, Lemley argues that the cost of litigation is, overall, efficient.

We agree with Lemley that it would be inefficient to provide thorough examination for all applications at the current rate of patent application. We disagree, however, that the current situation is acceptably efficient. First, while the out-of-pocket cost of litigation may be tolerable, the intangible cost of a system with pervasive low-quality patents is much higher than just the cost of paying lawyers to file and defend patent cases. The uncertainty that the current system creates for all parties regarding who can legally use what technologies is a cost that is very hard to quantify, but is surely significant. Talk to anyone involved in trying to commercialize new technologies, and you are likely to hear complaints about the headaches and uncertainty created by overlapping patent claims. Further, this uncertainty undermines everyone's incentives to invest in new technology. From the perspective of society as a whole, the loss of new products and processes that never make it to market, or that gain a toehold and are then abandoned after a threatened patent fight, is much larger than the visible costs of patent litigation. And, fortunately, there are changes that could be made in the system that would improve patent quality without requiring dramatic increases in the resources used in the examination process.

Inventors Respond to How the Patent Office Behaves

The key to more efficient patent examination is to go beyond thinking about what patent examiners do, to consider how the nature of the examination process affects the behavior of inventors and firms. To put it crudely, if the patent office allows bad patents to issue, this encourages people with bad applications to show up. While the increase in the rate of patent applications over the last two decades is driven by many factors, one important factor is the simple fact that it has gotten so much easier to get a patent, so applications that never would have been submitted before now look like they are worth a try. Conversely, if the PTO pretty consistently rejected applications for bad patents, people would understand that bad applications are a waste of time and money. While some people would still try—either because they are not smart enough to know they have a bad application, or because they are willing to take a roll of the dice—the number of applications would likely be considerably fewer than it has been in recent years.

Consider, just to illustrate the idea, the following thought experiment. Suppose that the PTO could dramatically reduce the issuance of patents on obvious or non-novel inventions by doubling the amount of time that the examiner spends on the average application. If the rate of application were unaffected by this change, it would require an approximate doubling of the PTO budget, as twice as many examiners would be needed to handle the flow of applications in a reasonable period of time. But it is unlikely that the rate of application would be unaffected by a dramatic change in examination standards. It is hard to know how much the flow of applications would be affected. But if the number of applications made each year were cut in half, then this doubling of examiner effort per patent could be brought about with no increase in the overall PTO budget.

This hypothetical is not intended to suggest that the problem is that easy; it is only meant to illustrate how the incentives faced by inventors and firms affect the efficiency of the system. As the quality of patent examination has deteriorated, the incentive for submitting marginal patent applications increased. A vicious cycle has emerged in which bad examination increases the application rate, which in turn overwhelms the examiners, reducing examination quality further and feeding on itself. If tools could be found to improve patent quality, this feedback would operate in the other direction, reducing the application rate and freeing up resources to further improve quality.

Potential Litigants Respond to How the Courts Behave

When the CAFC issues rulings that increase the chance of the patentee prevailing in an infringement suit, the consequences of this change are not limited to possible changes in the outcome of specific cases. Such a change in perceived success probabilities changes what disputes are, in fact, litigated. Conversations with attorneys involved in patent disputes make clear that the CAFC's strengthening of the offensive and defensive weapons of the patentee has significantly increased patentees' willingness to bring suit. Similarly, the change has significantly decreased the willingness of accused infringers to fight, even when they believe that the patents being used to threaten them are not valid. Constraining the growth in litigation, and the uncertainty created for all innovators by the risk of suit, will require a change in these incentives.

Get Information to Flow into the PTO

Another important aspect of incentives has to do with information: who has it, and what do they do with it? Much of the information needed to decide if a given patent application should issue—particularly information about what related technologies already exist—is in the hands of competitors of the applicant, rather than in the hands of the PTO. And there are strong incentives for firms to share this information. If a competitor has filed a patent application, the last thing we want to see is for them to be issued a patent on an application that would have been rejected if the PTO had known about our technology. We would thus have a strong incentive to provide this information, if only the PTO would give us an opportunity for input, and if taking advantage of such an opportunity does not create strategic disadvantages for us down the road. So creating opportunities of this sort is another way that the system could exploit the incentives of private parties in order to increase efficiency.

But lest we get overly excited about the beauty of incentives, it is important to recognize that private parties' reactions to the incentives they face can also gum up the works. In particular, any opportunity that we create for outsiders to provide the PTO with information that is adverse to their competitors' patent applications will be exploited opportunistically. That is, even in the case of "good" applications, if we can easily throw some kind of speed bump in our competitor's path, we will probably be happy to do so. This means that any change in procedures that makes it easier for competitors to intervene will, to some extent, increase the cost, uncertainty and delay for valid patent applications.

Ultimately, attention to incentives can mitigate, but not eliminate, the tradeoffs that must be made among the cost of the system, its reliability in terms of screening out bad applications, and the speed and certainty with which good applications are processed into issued patents. We could have a system that made very few mistakes, and issued valid patents quickly, but it would be a very expensive system to run, because it would require a lot of time by very experienced examiners. We could have a system that put so many hurdles in the path of an application that bad patents almost never issued, but without a lot of resources such a system would inevitably slow down or deny many valid applications. Or we can have the existing system, in which we make it so easy to get a patent that a lot of stuff gets through that should not.

What we cannot do is to weed out the trash without killing any good stuff, and accomplish this greatly improved sorting without expending more resources. But perfection need not be the enemy of the good. If we pay attention to the incentives that different reforms create for desirable and undesirable behavior, we can recalibrate the system to get a better balance between rapid approval of good applications and reliable rejection of bad ones, and do it without dramatically increased resources.

Building Blocks of Reform

There are three key conceptual pieces to our plan for patent policy reform:

1. Create incentives and opportunities for parties that have information about the novelty of inventions to bring that information to the PTO when it is considering a patent grant.
2. Provide the possibility for multiple levels of review of patent applications, with the time and effort expended escalating as an application proceeds to higher levels, so that money is not wasted on unimportant patents, but sufficient care is taken to avoid mistakes where the stakes are high.
3. Replace juries with judges and special masters in ruling on claims of patent invalidity based on the existence of prior art, so that parties threatened by invalid patents have a reasonable opportunity to make their case.

The first two of these proposals are aimed at making the PTO more effective at reasonable cost. The third proposal addresses the reality that the best of all possible PTOs will still make mistakes, and so we need a court system that is capable of rectifying those mistakes. The next section of this chapter explains the implementation of the changes at the PTO.

The Quest for Quality at the PTO

At a conceptual level, ensuring the quality of the PTO examination process has two key building blocks. First, Congress and the courts must provide the PTO with an appropriate definition of the standard for issuing a patent, particularly a definition of non-obviousness that separates the wheat from the chaff. Second, the PTO must have the appropriate procedures to implement that standard.

As discussed in chapter 4, decisions of the CAFC seem to have made it harder to use identified prior art to render an application obvious and thereby deny the patent grant. Some observers have suggested that revision of this CAFC doctrine is a necessary precondition to getting better patents out of the PTO.[211] In our view, it is very difficult to know how much difference these changes in legal doctrine are making, in a world in which patents issue for which it is clear that the PTO has simply missed the prior art. Hence, we propose beginning with improving the PTO and its processes. It is possible that these reforms will be inadequate. The revamped PTO may feel constrained by CAFC rulings to issue patents despite the existence of important prior art, or a reinvigorated PTO may find its decisions to deny patents repeatedly overturned by the court. If that happens, then the issue of the judicial or statutory changes necessary to recalibrate the non-obviousness standard will have to be joined, but at least it would then be possible to do that without the confusion and distraction of the tide of decisions that are bad by any standard.

Our proposed revamping of PTO procedures rests on the concept that the most efficient balancing of the need to bring in outside information against the reality that most patents are unimportant is brought about by a process with multiple potential levels of review. Examination would begin as it does now, with the review of an application by an examiner, and no participation by other parties. If, however, the examiner makes a determination that a patent should be allowed to issue, there would then be an opportunity for "pre-grant opposition." A public notice of the intention to issue a patent would be followed by a brief period of time in which other parties could submit to the examiner evidence, if it exists, of "prior art" that they believe should be the basis for a finding that the invention is not novel or is obvious and, hence, should not issue. This pre-grant opposition would not give outside parties any opportunity to argue their case, and they would not have access to legal discovery processes to produce additional evidence of prior art. It would simply be an opportunity for parties that have information in their possession to put this information before the examiner.

If this option had been in place when Vergil Daughtery was pursuing his patent on the "expirationless option" (see chapter 4), it would have been a simple matter for an investment bank, or an annoyed academic, to send the patent examiner the 1960s-vintage papers on the subject by Paul Samuelson. While the articles themselves are somewhat technical, one only needs to read their abstracts to realize that an infinite-lived option is not a new idea. With these papers in his possession, the examiner would have known that the Daughtery application was not novel, and presumably would have rejected it.

If, after reviewing any evidence that arises in this manner, the examiner decides to issue the patent, there would be a final opportunity for review in the form of a request for re-examination. This request would have to include a stated basis for a case that the patent is invalid, and the PTO could decline to grant the re-examination request if no such basis exists. But if re-examination does commence, it would be a complete review of the initial decision, undertaken by an independent examiner, and with opportunity for the parties requesting re-examination to argue their case.

The logic of re-examination—as distinct from pre-grant opposition—can be seen in the case of the Amazon "one click" patent (see chapter 2). Unlike the infinite-lived option, there is no pre-existing published scientific paper that unambiguously demonstrates the existence of prior art rendering the one-click patent non-novel or obvious. Rather, the case for its obviousness lies in the broad pattern of software practices in use over time. Making the case that this pattern rendered the Amazon application obvious would probably require argument and explanation, perhaps including testimony by expert witnesses. By design, the pre-grant opposition procedure does not permit this, because it must be kept quick and simple so as not to delay the bulk of valid patent grants. But a tremendous amount was clearly at stake in this dispute. If a viable re-examination option had existed, barnesandnoble.com and other parties would have had the incentive and opportunity to demonstrate the invalidity of the Amazon patent, resolving the dispute without the need to involve the courts.

The logic of this escalating series of examinations is that most patents would never receive anything other than the most basic examinations. But for those applications that really matter, parties would have an incentive and opportunities to bring information in their possession before the PTO, and the PTO would have the opportunity to make sure it makes the right decision in the cases that really matter. Let us now consider each of these steps in some detail.

Pre-grant Opposition

The history of efforts to institute pre-grant opposition at the U.S. PTO was discussed in the previous chapter. The logic of allowing limited opposition prior to grant is inescapable. The PTO cannot know everything there is to know, and the applicant does not have appropriate incentives to bring in information that undermines validity. Other parties are likely to have information that bears on validity, and they have an incentive to provide it. They have not historically been given any opportunity to provide it, partially because patent applications have been secret up until the time that a patent is granted. But now that applications are published eighteen months after application, there is really no reason not to allow parties that have information that they believe bears on the validity of a patent application to bring that information to the examiner's attention. At this stage, only the examiner will decide whether the information is relevant, and what consequences, if any, it has for the application. Therefore, there need not be any significant delay or increased expense.

Under current procedures, outside parties do have certain opportunities to insert information about prior art into the PTO process, but these opportunities are structured in such a way as to minimize both the incentive to use them, and the possibility that they will actually affect the outcome. For example, in the case of continuation and divisional applications (discussed in chapter 2), it is possible to learn from the PTO Web site that such an application has been filed, even before the application is legally "published." Under PTO rules, one can file a "protest" of such a pending application, arguing that the application should not be granted, on any grounds related to patentability, including obviousness. But the catch—which has no apparent purpose other than making it hard to get outside information into the process—is that such a protest has to be filed before the application is legally published.[212] Since legal publication occurs eighteen months after filing, this puts the would-be protester in the odd position of watching for new applications to pop up in the list of divisional/continutation applications, and getting in the protest before the application is technically "published." Go figure.

The other existing mechanism for adding information to the PTO record (short of requesting re-examination, discussed further below) is to simply dump citations of pre-existing patents or other publications into the patent file after the patent has issued.[213] Of course, this is too late for the information to have the desired beneficial effect of getting the examiner to make the right decision before it is too late.

The appropriate time period to allow outsiders to provide information about prior art is, of course, after publication—when the world is officially on notice that the PTO is considering granting a patent—but before the patent is granted, so that the information can be considered by the examiner before making that decision. As we have emphasized, creating such an opportunity need not unduly gum up the process, because outside parties would not be afforded the opportunity to argue their case or otherwise participate in the proceeding—only to provide information.

Given this limited participation, it is important that the legal treatment of information so provided not destroy anyone's incentive to provide it. In particular, if the patent issues despite the purported prior art submitted by an outside party, there should be no legal presumption regarding the validity of the patent over the art that was provided by the outside party. Otherwise, someone considering giving the examiner information would have to worry about "wasting" good stuff on an examiner who might not understand it, thereby destroying or seriously weakening its value in some future forum.

To make this concrete, suppose this procedure had been in place while the Daugherty patent was being examined, and someone had sent in the Samuelson articles, but for whatever reason the examiner still issued the patent. If there is ever litigation over this patent, parties would want to challenge the validity of the patent on the grounds that Daughtery's invention was not novel, given the previously published paper. If these papers had indeed been put in front of the examiner, standard legal practice would be to presume that they did not invalidate the patent, since the examiner saw them and issued the patent anyway. This presumption would make it more difficult to invalidate the patent on these grounds. If the party supplying these papers had had an appropriate opportunity to explain their significance to the examiner, it would be appropriate to presume that an examiner that nonetheless ignored them had good basis for doing so, and to put a heavy burden on anyone who later wants to argue their relevance. But the proposed procedure does not give the provider of such information any opportunity to explain its significance, so there is no reason to create a presumption that the information has been appropriately considered. Hence, it is both appropriate, and important in terms of maintaining good incentives, to allow people to submit such information but also to use it later, if necessary, without any adverse presumption.

Post-grant Re-examination

It is important that any opposition that occurs prior to the patent grant be of the limited form described above, so that it cannot be used strategically by competitors to delay or obstruct the granting of a valid patent. But because of this limited nature, pre-grant opposition is not likely to be sufficient to ensure that invalid patents are not issued. Thus, it is appropriate that the next step in the escalating intensity of examination be an opportunity for formal re-examination of issued patents. Compared to pre-grant opposition, re-examination should afford parties challenging a patent more opportunity to make their case. But precisely because of this greater opportunity, it is important that there be barriers in place that limit firms' ability to use re-examination strategically or frivolously.

The use of re-examination to eliminate bad patents exploits two of the important Simple Truths. First, it focuses additional examination resources not on all patents, but on the relatively small fraction of patents that are important enough to care about. It thereby offers hope to improve examination standards in a cost-effective manner. Second, it creates an opportunity for outside parties that hold relevant information about patentability to bring that information to the PTO's attention. By creating an incentive for outsiders to bring the relevant information to the examiner's attention, the examiner can make a better decision while using fewer public resources than would be necessary if the examiner had to independently go out and find all relevant information.

A final benefit of workable pre-grant opposition and re-examination procedures is that they would assist the PTO in getting itself educated about new and rapidly evolving technologies. Giving outsiders the opportunity and incentive to bring important, relevant information into the process will not only improve decisions in the individual cases where it occurs, it will provide general education for examiners about how new, dynamic fields are evolving, and where the prior art tends to be found. This should result in better decisions across the board.

Some strengthening of the examination received by all patents should complement the institution of effective re-examination and pre-grant opposition. The Rational Ignorance principle means that it is not efficient to give all patents the kind of scrutiny that they get in litigation or even in a re-examination. But the current standard is so low that it is almost surely inefficient. If the PTO set as a goal to approximately double the average examiner time per granted patent—including whatever time is needed to review evidence submitted under pre-grant opposition—and combined this increased care with effective re-examination, it ought to be able to credibly commit to a significant reduction in the issuance of obvious and non-novel patents. This will set up the "virtuous cycle" by discouraging applications that are made today only because applicants know that they can get away with it.

Unfortunately, there is no way to know how large a reduction in applications would be brought about by a credible tightening of examination standards. But there is reason to believe it would be significant. Since 1990, when the PTO was converted to its current user-friendly structure, applications have increased from about 150,000 per year to about 350,000 per year. There are multiple factors at work in this increase, including the enhanced value of patent protection since the creation of the CAFC and the expansion of patentability to cover unambiguously the areas of biotechnology, software, and business methods. There is also some evidence that the increased rate of application represents a real, broad increase in the underlying innovation rate.[214] But it is unlikely that these factors explain a greater than 100 percent increase over a dozen years. It is likely that a transformation of the examination process such that applicants know that frivolous applications will be denied would reduce the application rate to the range of 250,000 per year, roughly a third less than the current rate, and the rate that prevailed as recently as 1998. This means that a doubling of examiner effort per application could be brought about with only about a one-third increase in examiner resources. (Devoting twice as much effort to 250,000 applications would be equivalent to maintaining the current effort level if there were 500,000 applications, which is about a third more than there are now.)

Whatever the numbers might turn out to be, the important principle is that the loosening of examination standards in the last decade has set up a vicious cycle that is not good for inventors or for the PTO. This cycle has to be reversed. It will take time, because potential applicants will not immediately change their behavior. But the PTO must undertake real reform in order to break the vicious cycle, and try to establish the virtuous cycle of more credibly discouraging frivolous applications, which in turn will make it easier to muster the resources to sustain credibility.

Devilish Details

As discussed in chapter 6, patent opposition and re-examination are not, in fact, new ideas. European countries have used patent oppositions for many years.[215] Congress first introduced re-examination into the U.S. patent system in 1980. This procedure did not, however, allow parties other than the PTO and the applicant to participate in the proceeding, thus missing the opportunity to take advantage of information in the hands of third parties. In 1992, the Advisory Commission on Patent Law Reform recommended that the re-examination procedure be expanded to allow for the participation of outside parties.[216] In 1999, Congress introduced such third-party participation as part of the American Inventors Protection Act (AIPA).

Re-examination under the AIPA has not been a success. As we show in figure 6.1 of chapter 6, only 156 patents were, in fact, re-examined in 2002. And of these, only five were re-examined under the new AIPA procedure that permits third parties to participate substantially in the re-examination. To date, no patent has been withdrawn as a result of third-party requested re-examination. Given that some amount of mistakes in initial examination is inevitable, even a PTO operating efficiently and appropriately would likely have generated more than 156 re-examinations from the approximately 150,000 patents currently granted per year. Given the general agreement that a lot of these grants are dubious, it is inconceivable that a re-examination procedure perceived to be fair and effective would have gotten so little business.

The reasons why the new procedure is not widely used are easy to understand: Congress ignored some key recommendations of the 1992 Commission when it created the rules for re-examination.

The tension in the design of this process derives from the incentives—good and bad—that it creates. We want a procedure that makes it feasible and attractive for outside parties to bring to bear real information that they possess about the validity of a given patent. But we do not want to create an opportunity for competitors to frivolously or maliciously try to shoot down valid patents. Given that validity and frivolity are always to some extent subjective, these two objectives are partially in conflict.

In passing the AIPA, Congress erred on the side of making sure that the re-examination could not be abused to hold up valid patents. But the protections that it built in for the patentee make the procedure very unattractive, even to a party that has a valid basis for challenging a patent:

- If the re-examination results in the patent grant being withdrawn, the applicant can then appeal this decision to the courts. But a decision not to withdraw the grant cannot be appealed by a challenging party. This makes the risks inherent in the process asymmetric.
- On top of this, if there is ever subsequent litigation over the patent—because, for example, the patentee sues the party that challenged the patent for patent infringement—the challenger is legally barred from making any argument regarding the validity of the patent that they could have made in the re-examination, even if that argument was never considered by the PTO.
- Finally, the kind of evidence that can be brought by third parties to try to prove invalidity has been limited in two important ways. First, the evidence must be in the form of patents and other printed publications. For many of the most controversial patents, particularly in the software and business methods area, the evidence regarding the existence of "prior art" that ought to invalidate the patent may not be in the form of patents or other printed publications. Second, until this portion of the law was changed in 2003, challengers were barred from presenting at the re-examination evidence that was considered by the examiner during the initial examination process. This means that the re-examination process was useless for the situation where an examiner saw a piece of prior art, but failed to grasp its significance.[217]

So suppose that your competitor has just gotten a patent that you think is bogus, but which you are worried could be claimed to cover one of your products. You can ask for re-examination, but if you do, your hands will be tied as to what evidence you can bring; if you win, the competitor can appeal, but if you lose you cannot; and if you lose and end up in litigation later, you will be barred from making any argument in the course of that lawsuit that the judge decides you could have brought in the re-examination. Nine times out of ten, asking for re-examination is not going to be an attractive bet. You are better off waiting and taking your chances in court.

To create the appropriate incentives for outside parties to come forward with information that they have regarding validity, the re-examination process should have the following features:[218]

1. Parties should be able to bring forward any relevant factual evidence.
2. If a patent survives re-examination, parties should be barred in subsequent litigation only from making arguments that were specifically made and rejected by the PTO in the re-examination.
3. Re-examinations should be conducted by a specialized group of "re-examiners." An examiner who is drawn from the same group as the original examiner cannot be expected to have an open mind about whether a mistake might have been made.
4. Both the patentee and the challenger should have the right to appeal the PTO's decision.

These changes would shift the balance between encouraging valid challenges and discouraging frivolous ones in favor of more challenges. These changes can be prevented from stimulating excessive challenges by appropriate countervailing incentives. The AIPA already requires that the PTO find that a substantial new question of patentability has been presented, or it does not initiate a proceeding. This provides for quick and inexpensive disposition of truly frivolous challenges. Finally, the incentives of both applicants and potential challengers to avoid wasteful proceedings would be improved by the appropriate use of fees and cost-shifting. There should be a non-trivial fee for initiating a re-examination proceeding, say $50,000, paid in the first instance by the party challenging the patent. If the challenge is successful, and the patent is revoked, then the original patent applicant should be required to pay this amount plus the challenger's legal fees, to the challenger. Conversely, if the challenge is unsuccessful, the challenger should reimburse the applicant's costs for defending the patent (as well as having paid the fee for initiating the proceeding).

For a potential challenger who truly believes that an invalid patent poses an important threat to her business, this fee, and the risk of paying both sides' costs, will not be a significant disincentive to bringing the challenge. But it will provide some deterrent to someone who hopes only to throw sand in the works—knowing that the patent will likely still be held valid in the end. Conversely, for applicants that know they have pulled the wool over the examiner's eyes, the prospect of paying the fee plus both sides' costs may seem like a high price to pay for merely delaying the likely withdrawal of the patent. They will therefore have an incentive to fold their tents and go away. Further, the knowledge that this expensive and unattractive prospect likely lies at the end of the road will discourage marginal applicants from filing patent applications in the first place.[219]

The other major aspect of reform that we have identified is increased rigor of initial examination of patents. As discussed in chapter 5, in June 2002 the PTO released with some fanfare a "21st Century Strategic Plan" intended to transform itself into a "highly productive, quality-focused organization." It contains a variety of proposals designed to improve the functioning of the examination process. It also proposed an increase in application fees, and called upon Congress to appropriate all of the fees collected for patent applications to the PTO, instead of funding the PTO at levels below the revenues collected, as has been the practice in recent years.

After discussions with the patent community, the plan has been changed somewhat, and aspects of it have been presented to Congress. One aspect is a PTO proposal to "outsource" the search of prior art to private companies, leaving examiners only with the final determinations regarding patentability, to be based on the prior art identified by private contractors. In the June 2002 version of the Plan, the PTO had proposed that the applicants be required to hire search firms to prepare a prior art review for the examiner. This fox-hiring-the-guard-for-the-chicken-coop approach was roundly criticized, leading the PTO to amend its proposal. Even with the PTO responsible for supervising the outside search firm, this proposal remains controversial. The organization that represents examiners opposes it, on the grounds that examiners cannot ultimately be responsible for the quality of the validity decision if they are not doing the prior art searching.[220]

Ultimately, the decision as to whether the PTO search function remains "in-house" or is moved to the "outhouse" (so to speak) is not going to determine whether patent quality is improved. Until the process is changed so that other parties that know something about the technology surrounding a given application have the opportunity and incentive to bring that knowledge forward, there will be no cost-effective way to fix the problem of low quality patents.

Many players in the patent community have endorsed the PTO proposal to allow it to, in effect, retain all of the fees that it collects and spend those resources on the examination process.[221] But neither the PTO nor its supporters have grappled fully with the interplay among the resources needed for examination, the level of the application fees, and the revenue collected. It is certainly the case that the PTO needs to spend more on the examination process, both to upgrade its technology and to hire more and more highly qualified examiners. And it is appropriate for the applicants, as users of the PTO, to shoulder the burden of paying for this increased spending. It is likely, however, that higher fees, coupled with a truly significant improvement in examination standards, will reduce the number of applications. As discussed above, this is a good thing, because it will allow the PTO to concentrate its resources more effectively on the applications it does get. But it also means that, if the plan is truly successful, the total revenue collected will not be as great as the PTO is anticipating. Indeed, revenues could easily fall below the level of expenditures. When that happens, the PTO may regret having insisted on the importance of the link between PTO revenues and PTO expenditures.

This discussion illustrates an important point that is not visible in the current debate about the PTO Strategic Plan. The debate over "revenue diversion" is fundamentally off the point. It presumes that the level of fees that the PTO collects ought to determine the amount of money that it gets to spend. But that is backwards. Congress should start by figuring out how much money the PTO needs to do its job right. Because of the need to train and retain more and better examiners, and to update its information systems, that amount is probably somewhat greater than the amount that the PTO is being allocated. This need—not the fact that appropriations are less than revenues—is the reason why PTO appropriations should increase. Now, it is not unreasonable for Congress to take the position that the cost of running the PTO ought to ultimately be borne by patentees. This implies that the increased appropriations should be matched by PTO revenues, at least eventually, but the link ought to run from needed appropriations toward the setting of revenue levels—not the other way round.

Of course, giving the PTO more money will not magically make it more effective. It must also solve the management failures that plagued all of its earlier efforts to modernize its operations. More fundamentally, it has to change the very concept of "productivity" that it pursues. While the 21st Century Plan makes the right noises about "quality" rather than just serving "customers," the fact remains that the PTO defines its management objectives in terms of reducing the time it takes to process patents, and continues to reward examiners based on measures of productivity that encourage granting patents rather than granting only valid patents. What you measure and what you reward is going to be what your employees deliver. If the PTO is serious about patent quality, it has to overhaul its compensation structure, so that examiners are rewarded for denying applications on non-novel inventions, and for making those denials stick. Otherwise, the vicious cycle will continue, no matter how much more money is spent.

Leveling the Judicial Playing Field

Breaking the vicious cycle of bad examination and bad patent applications is the key to reform of the process that produces patents. But as we have emphasized, there are always going to be mistakes, and so it is important that the court system operate as efficiently as possible to rectify those mistakes, while also permitting owners of valid patents to enforce the legal rights the patent conveys. As discussed in chapter 4, the CAFC has significantly tilted the legal playing field in favor of patentees. In this section we discuss how we believe that this tilt needs to be adjusted, to preserve the rights of holders of valid patents while improving the reliability with which bad patents are weeded out.

The Presumption of Validity

The problem of actual or threatened infringement suits based on dubious patents is greatly aggravated by the legal doctrine that a patent granted by the patent office is entitled to a legal presumption as to its validity. Because of this presumption of validity, anyone challenging an issued patent must prove by "clear and convincing evidence" that the patent is invalid. As discussed in chapter 4, the "clear and convincing evidence" standard is not as high as the "beyond a reasonable doubt" that must be proved in a criminal case, but it does tilt the legal playing field in a validity dispute in favor of patentees. (By way of contrast, to win its infringement claims the patentee must prove infringement only by a "preponderance of the evidence," meaning that the balance of the evidence is in its favor.) Given that issues of prior art and obviousness are inherently to some degree subjective, setting this high standard for proof makes it hard for anyone to be confident that they can invalidate a patent, even if they think they have pretty good evidence of, for example, having independently developed their technology before the patented invention.

Another aspect of the presumption of validity is that the kind of evidence that can be presented to prove invalidity is limited. If we are trying to convince a jury that a patent was granted that should not have been, we might want to try to show just how few hours the examiner worked on the application before granting it, or the number of other patents approved by this examiner that have subsequently been found to be invalid. But such evidence is typically not allowed, on the theory that an examiner working in an official governmental capacity has to be presumed to have done the job appropriately.

These legal rules go a long way to explaining why many firms, faced with a claim of infringement of a patent that they think is invalid, nonetheless will drop an infringing product or pay a royalty. It simply may not make sense to fight if some of your weapons are inoperable, and your opponent is protected by high walls.

The presumption of validity accorded patents has an explicit statutory basis,[222] but it is an example of a broader principle of administrative law: issues that have been appropriately vetted before a competent decision-making body should be presumed to have been decided correctly. From the local zoning board to the U.S. Environmental Protection Agency to the Federal Trade Commission, these decisions are typically made after some kind of open administrative process, in which all interested parties generally have a right to participate. There is an inherent logic to affording a degree of deference to decisions made in this manner.

But as we have seen, the process by which a patent is granted is fundamentally different from these other administrative decisions. All interested parties are most definitely not invited to participate in the examination process. There is, thus, fundamentally a much weaker logical case for the presumption of validity that the patent statute affords to issued patents.

Going beyond the conceptual framework, the current practice of the PTO is also clearly inconsistent with a presumption of validity. Outside of legal doctrine, reasonable people do not hold a presumption if everyday observation demonstrates that the presumption in question is often false. Further, because of the Rational Ignorance principle, there is a sense in which validity could never be a logically sensible presumption to make about all patents. So it might seem logical to drop the presumption of validity, allow evidence of examiner indifference or incompetence to be presented if it exists, and create a level playing field on which the jury simply decides whether the evidence, on balance, favors validity or invalidity of a challenged patent.

There is, however, an important reason to maintain the presumption of validity. Remember that the fundamental purpose of the patent system is to give inventors a basis for expecting that they will have an opportunity to recover investments that they make in developing and commercializing their invention. When a start-up firm goes out to raise money for this purpose, it is important that the patent or patents that are claimed as the basis for the protecting the firm's technology have the presumption of validity. If, instead, the validity issue were reduced to a legal coin flip, it would greatly increase uncertainty. Uncertainty is the enemy of investment, so patents of uncertain validity would be much less effective in providing a base for development of innovations.

Thus, instead of eliminating the presumption of validity, we would like to change the system so that it is, in fact, a reasonable presumption to hold. This is why a viable re-examination process is so important. Because of the Rational Ignorance principle, it would never be reasonable to assume that the output of the overall initial examinations process could be presumed to be valid. But if all parties have the opportunity to request re-examination on the basis of factual evidence in their possession, then the presumption becomes reasonable.

If re-examination was never requested on a given patent, it is indeed reasonable to presume that the patent is valid, because the parties most likely to hold evidence of its invalidity had an incentive and an opportunity to present that evidence. This is not to say that a patent for which re-examination was never requested is proven valid, but only that it is reasonable for there to be a presumption of validity, with all that implies regarding the standard of proof that must be met by a party that ultimately does wish to challenge such a patent. And if a patent is re-examined, and survives re-examination, the Rational Ignorance principle does not apply. A request for re-examination—which under our proposal is reasonably expensive—combined with a decision by the applicant not to withdraw in the face of such a request, tells the PTO that this is an important application. We should expect the patent office in a re-examination proceeding to devote sufficient resources to "get it right." Again, this procedure does not prove validity, but it is enough to form a basis for a presumption of validity.

Thus, the existence of a viable re-examination option serves the interests both of parties worried about invalid patents and parties who want the full economic benefit of their valid patents. It helps the former by providing a forum in which appropriate incentives are created for third parties to bring forth relevant facts, and for the PTO to devote the appropriate resources to sifting through those facts. Perhaps less obviously, it helps the holders of truly valid patents, because it can be the "dog that didn't bark." If an effective re-examination procedure exists, then the fact that it is not invoked in a given case provides a logical (as distinct from a legal) basis for overcoming the Rational Ignorance principle, and truly presuming that the patent is valid.

Trial by Jury

Another complaint of attorneys who defend infringement suits is that the right of jury trial stacks the deck in favor of patent holders. There seem to be several parts to this argument. First is the uncontroversial observation that the evidence in a patent case can be highly technical, and the average juror has little competence to understand and evaluate it. On the surface, the effect of juror incompetence would seem to be neutral as between an accused infringer and a patentee. Even if it is neutral, however, having decisions made by people who cannot really understand the evidence does increase the uncertainty surrounding the outcome. Such uncertainty is a major factor in accused infringers settling rather than fighting even when they think they have a pretty good case.

More subtly, jurors' inability to grasp technical evidence may interact with the presumption of validity in a way that helps patentees and hurts accused infringers. Where the standard of proof is that whichever party on balance presented better evidence wins, then perplexed jurors would not seem to favor one side over the other. And this is, indeed, the standard for proving infringement, which is what the patentee needs to prove to win. But when one side has to achieve a reasonably high level of proof, it seems plausible that jurors' inability to truly understand the evidence being presented is not neutral, but rather acts against the party that must achieve a high standard of proof. If, at the end of the trial, the jurors are simply befuddled by the evidence, the most likely outcome is that they will conclude that neither side has made a convincing case. Thus the "clear and convincing evidence" standard combined with decision-making by juries makes it likely that the patentee will win on validity questions. (This is why most patentees ask for a jury trial.) Put another way, it is very difficult to ever make the evidence "clear and convincing" to a group of people who do not have the necessary training and education to understand it.

Regardless of whom it benefits, to non-lawyers it does seem hard to argue that lay jurors are the best decision-makers in patent suits. Of course, the right to a jury of one's peers is a venerated concept in Anglo-American law. But there is not really any sense in which a patent jury is, in fact, a jury of peers. A jury of scientists and engineers—the actual peers of the inventor—probably would be a relatively competent decision-making group. But, of course, that is not what we get. If we left patent cases to judges rather than juries, we would still not have scientists. But judges spend their professional lives evaluating evidence in many different disciplines, and have to develop some ability to sort through it. Further, a judge always has the ability to appoint a "Master," an outside expert in the service of the court, who can rule on specific technical questions by the judge.

The CAFC has, in fact, put some limits on the role of juries in patent cases. In particular, it is the job of the judge, not the jury, to interpret the patent's claims.[223] Typically, judges receive written and oral arguments, and often the testimony of expert witnesses, and then issue detailed instructions to the jury regarding what the claims mean. Thus, when it comes to the question of infringement—on which the patentee needs to carry the burden of proof in order to win—the judge assists the jury by interpreting the technical language of the claims before putting the question of infringement to the jury. But when it comes to a lack of novelty or obviousness—which the accused infringer must prove in order to invalidate the patent, and must do so with clear and convincing evidence—the jury gets no such help. These decisions are inherently no less technical than those of claim construction, and there does not appear to be any logical or substantive argument as to why a lay jury is the appropriate decision-making body for these questions. It would be entirely feasible for the judge to "construe" the novelty and obviousness of the patented invention relative to some other invention, just as the judge "construes" the claims of the patents. The ultimate question of patent validity could still be left up to the jury. If, for example, the judge ruled that the patent at issue was obvious or non-novel relative to some other specified invention, there might still be a dispute as to whether that other invention was, in fact, part of the prior art at the time of patent filing. The jury could then appropriately decide that question, based on testimony and documentary evidence as to when the invention in question came to be known.

If the PTO were revamped so that a presumption of validity was appropriate, and if the burden of proving invalidity by "clear and convincing evidence" were made feasible by removing the technical determination of novelty and non-obviousness from the jury, then patent litigation would be the appropriate last resort when disputes over patent claims cannot be resolved any other way. There would still be patent suits, and they would still be expensive. In areas where technology is changing rapidly, and there are numerous competing and overlapping claims, there would still be considerable uncertainty about who has the rights to what technology. But the pervasive fear that almost any modern (or not so modern) product or process is continuously at risk of facing an infringement claim would be dramatically reduced. And when claims are made based on patents of questionable validity, accused infringers would negotiate from a position where both parties expect a reasonably competent determination as to novelty and non-obviousness. This should reduce (though not eliminate) the incentive to pay royalties and settle rather than undertake a challenge that is risky, no matter how questionable the validity of the asserted patent.

Software, Genes, and Other Alleged Patent Nightmares

We have seen the difficulties that have been created by bad patents in many different technologies and industries. And we have discussed the inherent difficulties that arise because granting patents restricts and inhibits cumulative and overlapping inventions. In our view, the changes described above offer the best hope of creating a patent system that encourages invention, though we have no illusion that any reform can create a perfect system, or one that somehow eliminates the inherent tradeoffs.

Other observers, grappling with the current dysfunction of the patent system with regard to particular technologies or industries, have concluded that the problems of encouraging invention in that particular setting require a patent policy that distinguishes among technologies. Software, business methods, and certain aspects of biotechnology such as genetic sequences are all technologies for which the courts have expanded the range of patentable subject matter beyond what was perceived to be patentable at the end of the 1970s. Each of these areas has subsequently been characterized by major controversies over patents that appear to be either invalid, overly broad, or both, leading to concern that the patent system is inhibiting rather than encouraging invention in these areas. As a result, there have been numerous suggestions that inventions in these areas should not be patentable, or, if patent protection is to remain available, that different rules and procedures are necessary to adapt the institution of patents to these technologies.

We believe that trying to tailor the patent system to different technologies would be a mistake. The major problems that are perceived in these areas are, in essence, manifestations of the broader problems of the system as a whole. Hence, the best solution is to fix the system as a whole. Furthermore, while theoretical arguments can be made in favor of "tuning" the attributes of patent protection in different technological areas to reflect the attributes of different technologies, opening the door to such tuning is likely to quickly lead to special pleading that will not serve the public interest. To understand these arguments, we consider in turn the three most important perceived problem areas: business methods, software, and biotechnology.

Funny Business over Business Methods

The CAFC's elimination of the long-perceived prohibition on patenting business methods was discussed in chapter 4. And we have discussed some of the sillier manifestations of this new art form, such as the Amazon one-click patent. The European Patent Office does not permit patents on business methods, and some have suggested that creating a new business method is not, fundamentally, an act of "invention," and, hence, should not be the basis for a patent. Following the controversy over the "one-click" patent, Jeff Bezos of Amazon.com proposed that the patent life for software and business method patents be reduced from the standard twenty years to only three to five years.

It is clear that the PTO has done a disastrously bad job in testing applications for business patents against the prior art. And this is not really surprising. The prior art that patent examiners find most easily is previously issued patents. Beyond old patents, they have some ability to search for and identify prior art that appears in other published forms, such as scholarly publications. But in the area of business methods, most of the prior art is not in patents; indeed, it cannot be, because until recently people thought that business methods were unpatentable. And the prior art is not usually in publications, at least not the ones that the PTO is used to looking at. The prior art of business methods is in the day-in-and-day-out practice of businesses large and small. That is hard for the PTO to find, and it has done a bad job of it.

But the solution to that problem is not to abolish business method patents, it is to change the structure of the examination process so that opportunities and incentives are created for the parties that do have knowledge of the relevant prior art to bring it forward. As noted above, it is unlikely that the one-click patent would have survived an appropriately designed re-examination process.

The argument that new business methods are not really inventions is, at best, an irrelevant semantic one, and, at worst, a kind of techno-snobbery that is inconsistent with how technology evolves in general. What is the substantive difference between a "tinkerer" who comes up with some new kind of machine and a business visionary who comes up with a new method of inventory management? In either case, the invention may be made with or without the benefit of "science" in any meaningful sense. To say that one is technological and one is not is pointless. The real question, from a policy perspective, is whether the incentive provided by patent protection is necessary to bring forth the invention, and/or to protect it sufficiently to justify the investment necessary to work the kinks out and develop the raw idea into a viable commercial product or process. One can come up with individual examples of new business methods that required little development investment, but the same is true of inventions in other areas. As a general proposition, important new business methods are not dissimilar from other forms of innovation: they often require major investments of time and money in development; there are methods other than patents (e.g., secrecy) that can sometimes be used to protect these investments, but there are also cases where, in the absence of patent protection, the risk of imitation would seriously undermine development incentives.

In summary, the problem with business patents is that many have been issued for inventions that were obvious, and, hence, should not have been granted. If you got rid of these invalid patents, there is no evident problem of business method patents inordinately restricting ongoing business innovation. With the right procedures, the number of patents on business methods would probably be small, because there is a lot of prior art out there against which one would have to prove novelty and non-obviousness. But there is no fundamental reason why an entrepreneur who really does come up with a novel and non-obvious method of doing business needs patent protection less than an entrepreneur trying to make a go of comfortable high-heeled shoes or a new way of using radio spectrum for cell phones.

Software: An Open and Shut Case for "Open Source"?

Closely related to the controversy over business method patents is tremendous unhappiness over the granting of patents on software. Like business methods, this is an area where much of the prior art is not in patents, and often not in published works, but rather in practice. Again, the PTO has done an awful job of making sure that applications for software patents are tested against this non-published prior art. The result has been a deluge of patents granted on software concepts that are not new.

Making things even worse, the PTO, with the apparent guidance of the CAFC, also seems to have reduced or eliminated the requirement that a patent application describe the new invention with sufficient detail to enable one skilled in the relevant art to reproduce the invention.[224] This drastic weakening of the "enablement" requirement seems to have led to a situation where patents can be attained on the idea that something could be performed with software, without the patent applicant having done much at all to implement the idea.[225] The result has been a flood of patent applications on myriad diverse software ideas; in principle the recipient of such a patent then has the right to exclude others from implementing the covered software idea, despite the fact that they have never implemented, or even described implementing, the idea themselves.

Once again, the solution to these problems does not seem to be software-specific. The PTO should grant patents only on novel, non-obvious software developments, and should require the applicant to describe the covered software in some detail, so that patents only go to people who have created something rather than to those who merely thought about creating something. The horror stories about ridiculous software patents would then go away along with the PB&J, one-click, and other disasters.[226]

There are some who would go further and argue that patents are fundamentally inapplicable to software.[227] This argument has two related pieces. The first is the straightforward observation that software innovation was flourishing before the 1980s, when the CAFC clarified and broadened the patentability of software. This seems to show that patents for software are not necessary. More fundamentally, it is argued that software development is, by its nature, so cumulative that it is impossible to parse out the contribution of one developer sufficiently to grant patent rights, and it is counterproductive to try to do so because subsequent development will be hampered. These ideas are embodied in what has come to be called the "open source" and "free software" movements, which oppose software patents. The more radical members of these movements argue that all software should be in the public domain, available for all to use or modify as they see fit.[228]

It is surely true that there was software innovation before software patents were widely used. As with all other technologies, it is unlikely that software development would grind to a halt without patent protection. And it is also true that software innovation is a highly cumulative process. But the reality is that virtually all innovation is a highly cumulative process, and the patent system has been struggling with the tradeoffs that implies for a long time.[229] The relevant question is: on balance, would a properly administered regime of software patents foster innovation, by allowing parties that make true breakthroughs a measure of protection to reduce the risks of commercializing that development? As with business methods, we have not had a test of such a system because the PTO has failed to implement the requirements of novelty, non-obviousness, and enablement.

If the overall patent system were reformed as we have proposed, the only software that would be patentable would be that which truly represents a non-obvious step forward, and the implementation of which is laid out in some detail. Granting patents of this sort would not stop others who wish to work within the open-source paradigm from doing so, and would not prevent open-source advocates from arguing their case and trying to convince computer users not to buy patented software. It may be that the advantages of open-source development are sufficient that many or most software developers would choose to forego patents and work within the open-source paradigm instead. If the PTO were doing its job properly, any software that is developed and published freely by open-source advocates or other programmers could never itself be patented, because no one could ever claim novelty in having created it. So a properly functioning patent system is not inconsistent with a vibrant open-source software movement. The real enemy of open-source software—and software innovation more generally—is the abysmal implementation of software patents, not the concept. The real question is whether a programmer who has a truly new software invention ought to have the option of patenting it rather than making it open-source. No one has put forth a convincing argument why that choice should not lie with the innovator, rather than being made for the entire industry as a matter of law or policy.

Should Mere Mortals Control the Human Genome?

The last important area in which the CAFC expanded patentability is biotechnology. And again, there has been much concern about the granting of patents that appear obvious in light of previous developments, and which grant broad rights that seem to cover with one patent many diverse possible uses. As with software and business methods, the solution lies in rigorous enforcement of the fundamental rules governing obviousness and novelty.

As mentioned in chapter 2, an additional concern in biotechnology is the patenting of research tools. It is feared that the need to pay royalties on multiple distinct research tools in order to market a given product is retarding or will soon retard the inventive process. But again, one must be careful to distinguish the problem of bad patents from an allegation that patents are bad. If patents are granted only on novel, non-obvious inventions, then researchers will have to pay royalties to others only for the use of research tools that were truly invented by the patent owner. Arguably, if the PTO is doing its job, a patented research tool will be one that might not have been available at all, if the researcher who secured the patent had not developed it. It does not seem unreasonable, in such a case, for a royalty to be paid.

Does One Patent "Size" Really Fit All?

Lurking in the background of the preceding paragraphs is the overarching question of whether we should have one set of patent rules that govern all inventions, or whether the system can be made more efficient by tailoring patent rules to the specific attributes of different technologies. In the world of theoretical patent analysis, it is easy to show that the attributes of patent protection should vary depending on the characteristics of the technology. Thus, there appears to be a fundamental theoretical case for differential patents, and perhaps even for permitting patenting of some technologies but not others. The problem with using this theory as a basis for policy, however, is that the technology characteristics that could provide the basis for differential patent treatment are typically abstract and difficult to quantify empirically. It is easy, for example, to talk about cumulative innovation as a theoretical phenomenon, but it is very difficult to say concretely whether invention is more or less cumulative in one sector versus another. So while there is a theoretical case for a system that is not uniform, there is no theoretical or empirical basis for saying specifically how patent treatment should differ across specific technologies.

There is also a strong practical argument against differential treatment. Simply put, differential treatment is hard to implement, because as soon as patentees in a particular category get treatment that is different from everyone else, there will be an inevitable tendency for people to position themselves to get the most favorable treatment. An example can be seen in the PTO's efforts to deal with the outrage over business method patents by instituting a special internal review of all business method patents, on the grounds that the prior art is difficult to identify.[230] In effect, patents that fall in a particular patent class are examined twice, to try to make sure that non-traditional prior art is not missed. The result has been a decline in applications in the targeted class, but a continued rise in applications related to business methods more broadly defined. This suggests strongly that applicants have been going out of their way to classify their patents outside of the class targeted for special (more rigorous) treatment. As a result, the PTO's efforts, however well intended, are not likely to solve the broader problem of invalid business method patents being granted.

By and large, the presumption today is that everyone gets the same patent treatment.[231] Without this presumption, there would be tremendous pressure by particular industries to get features in "their" patents that they found desirable. Of course, the arguments for these preferences would always be couched in public interest terms, but when an industry lobbyist starts talking about the public interest, we all know it is a good time to keep an eye on the consumer's wallet.

Even in the current system, where the general presumption is for uniformity, there are always pressures for special treatment. These pressures have been particularly acute in the pharmaceutical industry, where Congress opened the door for such gaming when it passed the Hatch-Waxman Act, which allowed the PTO to extend the length of patent coverage for drugs that had languished for an extended time in regulatory review process.[232] In recent years, bills have been introduced in Congress to provide extended patent life for specific drugs, such as the allergy drug Claritin.[233] In the fall of 2002, a provision protecting a vaccine made by pharmaceutical maker—and large donor to Republican campaigns—Eli Lilly was inserted at the last minute into President Bush's domestic security legislation. While Senate Majority Leader Bill Frist of Tennessee had pushed such a provision earlier, he has denied inserting it in the domestic security bill. The provision became law despite the fact that no one, either on Capital Hill or in the White House, is willing to admit putting it in the final version of the bill.[234] This kind of shenanigans would likely be much worse in a world in which it was broadly accepted that differential patents for different technologies were appropriate.

So there is grave danger in trying to "fix" the problems perceived to be associated with patents in particular areas by fooling with specific differential patent treatment for these technologies. And this danger is simply not justified by evidence that the problems in business methods, software, and biotechnology derive from the unique properties of these technologies. Rather, the relative inexperience of the PTO with these technologies, combined with their critical importance for the economy, has made the broader, more fundamental problems with the system most evident. It is vitally important to fix the problems with patenting in these areas—but the way to do that is to fix the problems with the patent system more generally.

A Less Kind, Less Gentle Patent System

So we do not want this crisis to go the way of the Dutch patent crisis. We cannot abolish patents—or even weaken the fundamental presumption of validity for appropriately issued patents. What we need to do is make sure that, before they can be used to restrict the commercial activities of competitors, patents have gotten the appropriate scrutiny to ensure their validity. At the same time, we need to accept that the PTO will still make mistakes, and create a judicial system that deals with those mistakes in a balanced way. Doing this without an infeasible increase in resources for the patent office will require that the system be significantly modified. The modifications should be carefully tuned to create incentives so that private parties have the incentive and opportunity to bring information to bear, but have limited incentive and opportunity to act simply to gum up the works.

The key aspects of our proposed re-organization are:

- Greater resources devoted by the patent office to the process of examination, and the efficient use of these resources to bring the day-to-day operations of the PTO into the 21st century;
- The institution of pre-grant opposition, whereby outside parties could provide information on prior art to the examiners before a patent issues;
- The institution of effective re-examinations of granted patents, with a true opportunity to prove invalidity before an open-mined re-examiner, combined with appropriate incentives to discourage frivolous requests for re-examination; and
- Enhanced scope for judges or specially appointed masters to decide technical issues of novelty and obviousness.

Taken as a package, these reforms harness the incentives of private parties to bring information to the table in an efficient way. And they respect the Rational Ignorance principle, by bringing to bear a sequence of more rigorous (and, hence, more expensive) investigation, as the stakes get higher. Most patents will continue to get a relatively cursory review and then be forgotten. More important ones will get a more rigorous review, and one can presume that fewer mistakes will be made in important cases as a result. For the few cases that really matter and the PTO still got wrong, the courts will provide a balanced and reasonably reliable final determination as to patent validity. As a result, the uncertainty and patent black-mail that increasingly threaten the whole innovation system should be reduced.

Economists have often been perceived as hostile to the patent system. We do not consider ourselves anti-patent. We are just anti-bad patents, and anti-blackmail made feasible by a court system stacked against those who challenge the bad patents. We want a patent system that can be presumed valid, because a valid patent system is vital to the continued health of innovation, and, hence, economic growth and prosperity.

Notes

1. "Smucker Protects Peanut Butter-Jelly Sandwich Patent," *Reuters News Service*, (January 25, 2001).

2. These tests are delineated in section 101 of Title 35 of the U.S. Code, with the exception of the last two items. These last two criteria relate to two special classes of patents, known as plant and design patents, which operate under their own special rules. These awards make up only a tiny fraction of the patents awarded each year, so we will not spend much time discussing them.

3. This process is complex, because applicants frequently withdraw an application, and make a "new" application that is really a continuation of the previous one. This makes it difficult to measure precisely the fraction of original applications that are ultimately granted. See Cecil Quillen, Ogden Webster, and Richard Eichmann, "Continuing Patent Applications and Performance of the U.S. Patent and Trademark Office—Extended," *Federal Circuit Bar Journal*, Vol. 12, No. 1 (2002), 35–55, and U.S. Patent and Trademark Office, "Comments on 'The Effects of Continuing Patent Applications,'" unpublished manuscript, 2003, for a discussion of these issues.

4. We will discuss this issue in more detail in chapter 7.

5. U.S. Patent No. 6,004,596, December 21, 1999.

6. Patent Nos. 5,443,036 and 6,368,227, respectively. The PTO has ordered the last patent re-examined after it attracted considerable press attention for having been awarded to a boy who was five years old at the time of the filing of the patent application. (His father was the patent attorney.)

7. This paragraph is based on, among other sources, a wide variety of press releases from Qualcomm's web site; its filings with the U.S. Securities and Exchange Commission; and press articles such as Peggy Albright, "Qualcomm Beats Patent Challenges," *Wireless Week*, (February 25, 2002), 14.

8. The information in this paragraph is from Biogen's filings with the U.S. Securities and Exchange Commission; a variety of analyst reports; historical material on the firm's Web site; and discussions with company executives.

9. Michael Kremer, "Creating Markets for New Vaccines: Part I, Rationale" and "Creating Markets for New Vaccines: Part II, Design Issues," *Innovation Policy and the Economy*, 1 (2000), 35–118.

10. The history of British prizes for invention is reviewed in depth in "Report and Minutes of Evidence Taken Before the Select Committee of the House of Lords Appointed to Consider of the Bills for the Amendment of the Law Touching Letters Patent for Inventions with Appendix and Index," *Parliamentary Papers* 1851 (486) XVIII, 1851.

11. Joseph A. DiMasi, Ronald W. Hansen, and Henry G. Grabowski, "The Price of Innovation: New Estimates of Drug Development Costs," *Journal of Health Economics*, 22 (2003), 151–185.

12. "PhRMA Industry Profile," Pharmaceutical Research and Manufacturers of America, http://www.phrma.org/publications/publications/profile02/ index.cfm (last visited January 2, 2004).

13. This account is taken from Ira Flatow, *They All Laughed . . . From Light Bulbs to Lasers: The Fascinating Stories Behind the Great Inventions that have Changed Our Lives*, New York: Harper Collins, 1992, chapter 11.

14. As discussed in chapter 3, the early 1970s was a time of maximal scrutiny by the governmental authorities that enforce laws regulating competition of business strategies that used patents to build broad positions of market dominance.

15. Windows is also protected through copyright, though this largely protects only the software code itself, and not the ideas behind the program.

16. A classic discussion of this phenomenon is in Richard Schmalensee, "Advertising and Entry Deterence: An Exploratory Model," *Journal of Political Economy*, 90 (1983), 636–653. In addition, "learning curve" effects may give the initial producer a substantial cost advantage. (The pioneering treatment of these issues was in Kenneth J. Arrow, "Economic Welfare and the Allocation of Research for Invention," in Richard R. Nelson, editor, *The Rate and Direction of Inventive Activity: Economic and Social Factors*, Princeton: Princeton University Press, 1962, 609–625.)

17. *Edison Elec. Light Co. v. United States Elec. Lighting Co.*, 47 F. 454 (C.C.S.D.N.Y. 1891).

18. See Arthur Bright, *The Electric-Lamp Industry: Technological Change and Economic Development from 1800 to 1947*, New York: Macmillan, 1949.

19. See *Wright Co. v. Herring-Curtiss Co.*, 204 F. 597, 614 (W.D.N.Y. 1913), as well as the discussion in George Bittlingmayer, "Property Rights, Progress, and the Aircraft Patent Agreement," *Journal of Law and Economics*, 31 (1988), 227–248.

20. These issues have been explored in a series of papers by Suzanne Scotchmer and her co-authors. For an overview, see Suzanne Scotchmer, "Standing on the

Shoulders of Giants: Cumulative Research and the Patent Law," *Journal of Economic Perspectives*, 5 (1991), 29–41.

21. For a comprehensive examination of patent litigation trends, see Jean O. Lanjouw and Mark Schankermann, "Enforcing Intellectual Property Rights," STICERD, LSE Economics of Industry Group Discussion Paper: EI/30, 2001.

22. See Federal Trade Commission, *Report of the U.S. Federal Trade Commission on the Radio Industry in Response to House Resolution 548*, Washington: Government Printing Office, 1924.

23. This section is based on interviews with the management of HBN Shoe and other industry observers.

24. The estimated royalties are from Kevin G. Rivette and David Kline, "Discovering New Value in Intellectual Property," *Harvard Business Review*, 78 (January-February 2000), 54–66. The calculation of TI's 1999 profits is based on Texas Instruments' March 2, 2000, proxy filing.

25. Kevin G. Rivette and David Kline, *Rembrandts in the Attic: Unlocking the Hidden Value of Patents*, Boston: Harvard Business School Press, 2000.

26. For accounts of this case, see *British Telecommunications PLC v. Prodigy Communications Corp.*, 189 F. Supp. 2d 101 (S.D.N.Y. 2002) and 217 F. Supp. 2d 399 (S.D.N.Y. 2002); Brenda Sandburg, "Closely Watched Hypertext Patent Case Dismissed," *Legal Intelligencer*, 226 (August 26, 2003), 4ff.; and many other press accounts.

27. *British Telecommunications PLC v. Prodigy Communications*, United States District Court, Southern District Court of New York, Memorandum and Order Granting Summary Judgment (August 22, 2002).

28. See Bronwyn Hall and Rosemarie H. Ziedonis, "The Patent Paradox Revisited: Determinants of Patenting in the US Semiconductor Industry," *Rand Journal of Economics*, 32 (2001), 101–128.

29. Standard-setting bodies often set guidelines for licensing (for example, requiring members to license relevant technologies on "reasonable and non-discriminatory terms"), but typically do not become involved in enforcing these rules. Instead, they will rely on antitrust authorities and private parties to enforce these provisions through litigation. For an introduction to the issues posed by intellectual property rights in standard setting organizations, see Mark A. Lemley, "Intellectual Property Rights and Standard-Setting Organizations," *California Law Review*, 90 (2002), 1889–1980.

30. See U.S. Federal Trade Commission, "Analysis of Proposed Consent Order to Aid Public Comment," http://www.ftc.gov/os/1998/9808/d09286ana.htm (last visited January 2, 2004).

31. *In the Matter of Summit Technology Inc. and VISX Inc.*, Complaint filed March 24, 1998, Docket No. 9286, U.S. Federal Trade Commission.

32. This discussion is based on *Sandisk Corp. v. Lexar Media, Inc.*, 91 F. Supp. 2d 1327 (S.D. Cal. 2000); *Lexar Media, Inc. v. Sandisk Corp*, U.S. District Court of Delaware, Docket No. 00-CV-817, especially "Complaint," September 7, 2000,

"Answer," September 27, 2000, and "Stipulated Dismissal with Prejudice," November 27, 2000; and a wide variety of press releases and news stories, including Steven Fyffe, "The Flash Menace: The Saga Continues," *Electronic News*, 46 (November 13, 2000), 44ff.

33. Rebecca Eisenberg, "Bargaining Over the Transfer of Proprietary Research Tools: Is This Market Failing or Emerging?," in Rochelle Dreyfus, Diane L. Zimmerman, and Harry First, editors, *Expanding the Boundaries of Intellectual Property: Innovation Policy for the Knowledge Society*, Oxford: Oxford University Press, 2001, 223–250. See also Kimberly Blanton, "Patent 5,693,473," *Boston Globe Magazine* (February 24, 2002), 10–15, 20–28.

34. *John M. J. Madey v. Duke University* No. 1:97CV1170, slip op. (M.D.N.C. June 15, 2001); 307 F.3d 1351 (Fed. Cir. 2002).

35. *Duke University v. Madey*, 123 S.Ct. 2639 (2003).

36. American Intellectual Property Law Association, *Report of Economic Survey 2001*, Arlington, Virginia, AIPLA, 2001. Based on 248 responses, the median cost estimate was $3 million; the twenty-fifth percentile response was $1.7 million, and the seventy-fifth percentile estimate was $4.5 million.

37. Ibid. For cases with less than $1 million at stake, the median cost estimate is $499,000, with a twenty-fifth percentile estimate of $301,000 and a seventy-fifth percentile estimate of $750,000, based on 242 responses.

38. *Rambus Inc., v. Infineon Technologies*, 318 F.3d 1081 (Fed. Cir. 2003); *Rambus, Inc. v. Infineon Technologies AG, et al.*, District Court for the Eastern District of Virginia, Memorandom Opinion of Judge Robert E. Payne on Infineon's Request for, Attorneys Fees and Costs.

39. *Rambus, Inc. v. Infineon Technologies AG, et al.*, District Court for the Eastern District of Virginia, Memorandum Opinion of Judge Robert E. Payne on Infineon's Request for Attorneys' Fees and Costs.

40. Dan Johnson and David Popp, "The Effects of the Timing of Patent Revelation on Innovation," Unpublished working paper, Wellesley College and Syracuse University, 2003.

41. See *Rambus, Inc. v. Infineon Technologies AG, et al.*, Memorandum Opinion of District Judge Payne, cited above, and also dissenting opinion of Judge Prost, United States Court of Appeals for the Federal Circuit, 01–1449, -1583, -1604, -1641, 02–1174, -1192, (January 29, 2003).

42. *Rambus Inc. v. Infineon Technologies AG, et al.*, No. 3:00CV524, slip op. (E.D. Va. May 2, 2001).

43. The judge concluded that Infineon had proved lawyer fees and related expenses of over $7.1 million, and expert fees of over $900,000.

44. *Rambus, Inc. v. Infineon Technologies AG, et al.*, 318 F.3J 1081 (Fed. Cir. 2003)..

45. Gretchen Hyman, "Industry Takes Sides in Rambus v. Infineon," www.internetnews.com/infra/article.php/2108831 (last visited January 2, 2004); *Infineon Technologies AG v. Rambus, Inc.*, 124 S. Ct. 227 (2003).

46. This account is based on a variety of sources. Most important were *Albie's Foods. Inc. v. Menusaver, Inc.*, 2001 U.S. Dist. LEXIS 21411 (E.D. Mich. 2001) and 170 F. Supp. 2d 736 (E.D. Mich. 2001); and the filings in this and in the companion Ohio case (*J. M. Smucker Co. v. Albie's Foods, Inc.*, Northern District of Ohio, Docket No. 5–01–01182-DAP).

47. *Amazon.com, Inc., v. barnesandnoble.com, Inc.*, 239 F.3d 1343 (Fed. Cir. 2001).

48. As we will discuss in chapter 7, when viewed in one narrow way—applications in U.S. Patent Class No. 705—the number of business method patent applications fell in 2002. As we note there, this is likely a consequence of "gaming" by applicants to avoid the extraordinary scrutiny and lengthy delays associated with the processing of patent applications in patents in this class.

49. The original quote was from J.E.T. Rogers, "On the Rationale and Working of the Patent Laws," *Journal of the Statistical Society of London*, 26 (1863), 127.

50. Fritz Machlup and Edith T. Penrose, "The Patent Controversy in the Nineteenth Century," *Journal of Economic History*, 10 (1950), 1–29.

51. See the discussion of these early codes in Erich Kaufer, *The Economics of the Patent System*, Fundamentals of Pure and Applied Economics, Vol. 30, Chur, Switzerland, New York: Harwood Academic Publishers, 1989, chapter 1; and Guicio Mandich, "Venetian Patents (1450–1550)," *Journal of the Patent Office Society*, 30 (1948), 166–223.

52. This account is based on, among other sources, Klaus Boehm and Aubrey Silberston, *The British Patent System: I. Administration*, Cambridge: Cambridge University Press, 1967; Harold Fox, *Patents and Monopolies*, Toronto: University of Toronto Press, 1947; and Christine MacLeod, *Inventing the Industrial Revolution: The English Patent System, 1660–1800*, Cambridge: Cambridge University Press, 1988.

53. *Darcy v. Allin*, 74 Eng. Rep. 1131, 1139 (1602).

54. 21 James I, ch. 3, § 6 (1623).

55. Ibid.

56. This account is based in large part on H. I. Dutton, *The Patent System and Inventive Activity During the Industrial Revolution, 1750–1852*, Manchester: Manchester University Press, 1984; Boehm and Silberston, note 52 above; and MacLeod, note 52 above.

57. The story of John Harrison is told in W. S. Laycock, *The Lost Science of John "Longitude" Harrison*, Ashford, United Kingdom: Brian Wright Associates, 1976; and Dava Sobel, *Longitude: The True Story of a Lone Genius who Solved the Greatest Scientific Problem of His Day*, New York: Penguin Books, 1995.

58. The general discussion of the anti-patent movement is based on Machlup and Penrose, note 50 above and Edith T. Penrose, *The Economics of the International Patent System*, Baltimore: Johns Hopkins University Press, 1951.

59. July 26, 1851, 812. This quote is taken from Machlup and Penrose, note 50 above, 19.

60. John Stuart Mill, *Principles of Political Economy*, London: Longsmans, Green & Co.,1909, book V, chapter x, 932 (first published, 1848).

61. G. Doorman, "Patent Law in the Netherlands," *Journal of the Patent Office Society*, 30 (1948), 225–241 and 258–271. The quote is on 238.

62. The account of the Dutch patent situation is based on Doorman, ibid.; and Eric Schiff, *Industrialization Without National Patents*, Princeton: Princeton University Press, 1971.

63. For a careful weighing of the evidence, see the discussion in Schiff, ibid.

64. These compilations are based on the data-set described in Josh Lerner, "150 Years of Patent Protection," *American Economic Review Papers and Proceedings*, 92 (May 2002), 221–225; and Josh Lerner, "150 Years of Patent Office Practice," National Bureau of Economic Research Working Paper No. 7478. The changes in patent policy examined are the presence of patent protection for important classes of technologies, the length of patent protection, the amount of time individuals have to put their patent into practice, and major changes in the cost of patent protection.

65. *E. Bement & Sons v. National Harrow Company*, 186 U.S. 70, 91 (1902).

66. This principle is enshrined in U.S. law at 28 U.S.C. § 1338(a).

67. Rochelle C. Dreyfus, "The Federal Circuit: A Case Study in Specialized Courts," *New York University Law Review*, 64 (1989), 1–77.

68. The source of this information is Gloria K. Koenig, *Patent Invalidity: A Statistical and Substantive Analysis*, New York: Clark Boardman, 1980. These comparisons are based on 1,447 cases, and the statistical margins of error are small relative to the observed differences. The differences across circuits also remained consistently wide over the different years examined.

69. For instance, in her careful compilation of patent cases at all levels of the federal judicial system between 1953 and 1978, Gloria Koenig is only able to identify four Supreme Court decisions on the question of patentability. See Koenig, note 68 above, 4–17.

70. Bob Woodward and Scott Armstrong, *The Brethren: Inside the Supreme Court*, New York: Simon and Schuster, 1979. The case in question was *Sakraida v. Ag Pro, Inc.*, 426 U.S. 955 (1976).

71. David E. Wigley, "Evolution of the Concept of Non-Obviousness of the Novel Invention: From a Flash of Genius to the Trilogy," *Arizona Law Review*, 42 (2000), 581–606. See the discussion on pages 596 and 597.

72. U.S. Congress, Committee on the Judiciary, Subcommittee on Improvements in Judicial Machinery, *Federal Courts Improvement Act of 1979: Hearings on S.677 and S.678*, Washington: Government Printing Office, 1979.

73. The court was also given responsibility over a variety of other matters, such as trademarks and cases where the United States was a defendant in regard to personnel matters and other claims.

74. Advisory Committee on Industrial Innovation, U.S. Department of Commerce, *Final Report*, Washington: U.S. Government Printing Office, 1979, 152.

75. See the discussion in Daniel J. Meador, "Origin of the Federal Circuit: A Personal Account," *American University Law Review*, 51 (1992), 581–620.

76. "Oldest Active Federal Judge Dies," *The Third Branch*, 31 (July 1999), http://www.uscourts.gov/ttb/jul99ttb/oldest.html (last visited December 24, 2003).

77. Helen W. Nies, "Celebrating the Tenth Anniversary of the United States Court of Appeals for the Federal Circuit," *George Mason University Law Review*, 14 (1992), 505–512.

78. Margaret M. Conway, *Single Court of Patent Appeals—A Legislative History*, Study No. 20, Subcommittee on Patents, Trademarks, and Copyrights, Committee on the Judiciary, U.S. Senate, 85th Congress, 2nd Session, Washington: U.S. Government Printing Office, 1959.

79. Simon Rifkin, "A Specialized Court for Patent Litigation? The Danger of a Specialized Judiciary," *American Bar Association Journal*, 37 (1951), 425–426. The quote is on page 425.

80. Richard Posner, "Will the Federal Court of Appeals Survive Until 1984? An Essay on Delegation and Specialization of the Judicial Function," *Southern California Law Review*, 56 (1983), 761–791.

81. Felix Frankfurter and James M. Landis, *The Business of the Supreme Court*, New York: Macmillan, 1928.

82. These statistics are gleaned from Koenig, note 68 above, and Robert P. Merges, *Patent Law and Policy: Cases and Materials*, Charlottesville, Virginia: Michie Company, 1992.

83. These data are compiled from P. J. Federico, "Adjudicated Patents, 1948–1954," *Journal of the Patent Office Society*, 38 (1956), 233–249; Koenig, note 68 above; and Donald R. Dunner, J. Michael Jakes, and Jeffrey D. Karceki, "A Statistical Look at the Federal Circuit's Patent Decisions: 1982–1994," *The Federal Circuit Bar Journal*, 5 (Summer 1995), 151–180. None of these studies examine the years 1979 through 1981.

84. Figure 4.3 is derived from Koenig, note 68 above, and information provided by Kimberly Moore. These data were originally published in her article, "Judges, Juries, and Patent Cases—An Empirical Peek Inside the Black Box," *Michigan Law Review*, 99 (2000), 365–408, and is based on her analysis of litigation files.

85. In particular, in decisions such as *Latria Corp. v. Cambridge Wire Cloth Co.*, 785 F.2d 292 (Fed. Cir. 1986), the CAFC has made clear that infringers are expected as a matter of course to pay interest on damages from the date of the infringement to the date the judgment is entered against the firm.

86. *Del Mar Avionics v. Quinton Instrument Co.*, 836 F.2d 1320 (Fed. Cir. 1987).

87. See, for instance, *State Industries, Inc. v. Mor-Flo Industries, Inc.*, 883 F.2d 1573 (Fed. Cir. 1989).

88. Previously, preliminary injunctions had been only granted in patent cases when the decision was "beyond question": for instance, when the patent had al-

ready been proved valid in court and been widely accepted in the industry. For the seminal CAFC decision in this matter, see *Atlas Powder Co. v. Ireco Chemicals*, 773 F.2d 1230 (Fed. Cir. 1985).

89. See the conclusion, for instance, in by Robert L. Harmon: "Injunctive relief against an infringer is the norm [in decisions by the CAFC]" (*Patents and the Federal Circuit*, 5th edition, Washington: Bureau of National Affairs, 2001, 767). Typically, the CAFC has left to the district courts the task of formulating the precise language of the injunctions.

90. For representative cases along these lines, see *Roche Products v. Bolar Pharmaceutical Co.*, 733 F.2d 858 (Fed. Cir. 1984); and *Fromson v. Western Litho Plate & Supply Co.*, 853 F.2d 1568 (Fed. Cir. 1988).

91. *Polaroid Corp. v. Eastman-Kodak Co.*, 641 F. Supp. 828 (D. Mass. 1985), 789 F.2d 1556 (Fed. Cir. 1986), 107 S. Ct. 178 (1986). This account is made on the judicial record, many press accounts, as well as Gerard Sobel, "The Court of Appeals for the Federal Circuit: A Fifth Anniversary Look at its Impact on Patent Law and Litigation," *American University Law Review*, 37 (1992), 1086–1139; and Fred Warshofsky, *The Patent Wars*, New York: John Wiley & Sons Inc., 1994.

92. *Diamond v. Chakrabarty*, 447 U.S. 303, 309 (1980). P. J. Federico, long-standing chief examiner of the PTO, had originally used this phrase at the time of the 1952 alteration to the patent laws.

93. *Diamond v. Diehr*, 450 U.S. 175 (1981) (the quotes are on 191 and 187, respectively).

94. *In re Alappat*, 33 F.3d 1526 (Fed. Cir. 1994).

95. *Darcy v. Allin*, 77 Eng. Rep. 1260 (K.B. 1602).

96. *Hotel Security Checking Co. v. Lorraine Co.*, 160 F. 467 (2d Cir. 1908). The case concerned a restaurant bookkeeping system.

97. 35 U.S.C. § 101.

98. A skeptic might note that principles of linear algebra have been well known since the work of Arthur Cayley and August Möbius in the mid-nineteenth century.

99. *State Street Bank and Trust v. Signature Financial Group*, 927 F. Supp. 502, 506 (D. Mass. 1996).

100. *State Street Bank and Trust v. Signature Financial Group*, 149 F.3d 1368, 1375 (Fed. Cir. 1998).

101. *In re Schrader*, 22 F.3d 290, 298 (Fed. Cir. 1994) (Newman, J., dissenting).

102. Examples include William T. Ellis and Aaron C. Chatterjee, " 'State Street' Sets Seismic Precedent," *National Law Journal*, 21 (September 21, 1998), B13 and B18; and Barry D. Rein, "A New World for Money Managers: Circuit Upholds Financial Patent," *New York Law Journal*, 220 (September 21, 1998), S1 and S8.

103. These figures are based on http://www.uspto.gov/web/menu/ pbmethod/applicationfiling.htm (last visited December 24, 2003) and Wynn

Coggins, "Business Methods Still Experiencing Substantial Growth—Report of Fiscal Year 2001 Statistics," *PTO Today*, 2 (November/December 2001), 12–13.

104. See, for instance, Martin J. Adelman, "The New World of Patents Created by the Court of Appeals for the Federal Circuit," *Journal of Law Reform*, 20 (1987), 979–1007; John Barton, "Reforming the Patent System," *Science* 287 (2000), 1933–1934; and Cecil D. Quillen, Jr., "Innovation and the United States Patent System Today," presented October 19, 1992, at "Antitrust and Intellectual Property: Practice and Policy Issues for the 1990s," a Continuing Legal Education Institute cosponsored by the ABA Antitrust and Patent Sections.

105. *Graham v. John Deere Co.*, 383 U.S. 1, 17–18 (1966).

106. *Stratoflex, Inc. v. Aeroquip Corp.*, 713 F.2d 1530, 1538 (Fed. Cir. 1983). The problems with the court's treatment of the CAFC's treatment of non-obviousness are discussed at length in Robert P. Merges, "Commercial Success and Patent Standards: Economic Perspectives on Innovation," *California Law Review*, 76 (1988), 802–876.

107. These statistics are based on those presented in Glynn S. Lunney, Jr., "E-Obviousness," *Michigan Telecommunications and Technology Law Review*, 7 (2001), 363–422.

108. *In re Lee*, 277 F.3d 1338 (Fed. Cir. 2002).

109. *Ex parte Lee*, No. 1994–1989 (Bd. Pat. App. & Int. Aug. 30, 1994; on reconsideration September 29, 1999).

110. *In re Dembiczak*, 175 F.3d 994 (Fed. Cir. 1999).

111. See for instance, Paul F. Morgan, "Personal Comments for the Joint FTC and DOJ Public Hearings on Intellectual Property Law," http://www.ftc.gov/os/comments/intelpropertycomments/morganpaulfattachment.pdf (last visited December 24, 2003).

112. Kimberly Moore generously provided us the data in Figure 4.4. It was originally published in her 2000 article cited at note 84 above and is based on data from the Administrative Office of the Federal Courts.

113. Gary M. Ropski, "Constitutional and Procedural Aspects of the Use of Juries in Patent Litigation," *Journal of the Patent Office Society*, 58 (1976), 609–646, 673–702.

114. See, for instance, the discussion in George Newitt and Jon Nelson, "The Patent Lawyer and Trial by Jury," *John Marshall Journal of Practice and Procedure*, 1 (1967), 59–73; and Robert L. Harmon, "Seven New Rules of Thumb: How the Federal Circuit Has Changed The Way Patent Lawyers Advise Clients," *George Mason University Law Review*, 14 (1992), 573–597.

115. See especially *In re Lockwood*, 50 F.3d 966 (Fed. Cir. 1995), and *Markman v. Westview Instruments, Inc.*, 52 F.3d 967 (Fed. Cir. 1995).

116. *Richardson v. Suzuki Motor Co.*, 868 F.2d 1226 (Fed. Cir. 1989).

117. Prior to the creation of the CAFC, a number of circuits—particularly the Second Circuit, which encompassed New York State and part of New England—had placed limits on the degree of special consideration patent-holders should re-

ceive, expressing skepticism about the quality of the patent examination process. (See, for instance, *Carter-Wallace, Inc. v. Davis-Edwards Pharmaceutical Corp.*, 443 F.2d 867 (2d Cir. 1971).) An illustration of the CAFC's attitude towards such practices is the derisive comments about "cynical judges" in *American Hoist and Derrick Co. v. Sowa and Sons, Inc.*, 725 F.2d 1350, 1359 (Fed. Cir. 1984). This opinion also emphasizes the importance of "the deference that is due to a qualified government agency presumed to have properly done its job."

118. John R. Allison and Mark A. Lemley, "Empirical Evidence on the Validity of Litigated Patents," *AIPLA Quarterly Journal*, 26 (1998), 185–276.

119. Kimberly A. Moore, "Xenophobia in American Courts," unpublished working paper, George Mason University.

120. The CAFC considerably narrowed the applicability of the doctrine in its decision in *Festo Corp. v. Shoketsu Kinzoku Kogyo Kabushiki Co.*, 172 F.3d 1361, 187 F.3d 1381 (Fed. Cir. 1999), but this decision was partially reversed by the Supreme Court in 2002. The general consensus today, however, is that patents are narrower than they were before this decision. See, for instance, Allen R. Jensen, "Festo Schmesto: Will the Federal Circuit Listen to the Supreme Court?," *Intellectual Property Today*, 10 (August 2002), 6 ff.

121. See, for instance, the Adelman, Barton, Dreyfus, and Quillen articles discussed at notes 67 and 104 above.

122. This account is based on P. J. Federico, editor, *Outline of the History of the United States Patent Office*, Washington: Patent Office Society, 1936; and Edward C. Walterscheid, *To Promote the Progress of Useful Arts: American Patent Law and Administration, 1798–1836*, Littleton, Col.: F. B. Rothman, 1998.

123. *Thompson v. Haight*, 23 Fed. Cas. 1040, 1041 (C.C.S.D.N.Y. 1826).

124. This account is based on Edward C. Walterscheid, "The Winged Gudgeon—An Early Patent Controversy," *Journal of the Patent and Trademark Office Society*, 79 (1997), 533–549; and *Withers v. Thornton*, 30 Fed. Cas. 402 (C.C.D.C. 1827).

125. Democratic Leadership Council, "Briefing: Reforming the Patent System," http://www.ndol.org/ndol_ci.cfm?contentid=611&kaid=140&subid=293 (last visited December 24, 2003).

126. The source of these data is http://www.ipo.org (last visited December 24, 2003), as compiled from PTO and U.S. Office of Management and Budget documents. The 2003 and 2004 data are taken from PTO's annual budget requests, and are the amount of diversion that they anticipate.

127. Figure 5.2 is based on the annual reports of the U.S. Patent and Trademark Office, as well as supplemental data from Bronwyn H. Hall, "Fishing Out or Crowding Out: An Analysis of the Recent Decline in U.S. Patenting," unpublished working paper, University of California at Berkeley and the Office of Public Affairs at the PTO.

128. The U.S. figures are from U.S. Patent and Trademark Office, *Performance and Accountability Report Fiscal Year 2001*, Washington: U.S. Patent and Trade-

mark Office, 2002; and U.S. Department of Commerce, *FY 2001 Corporate Plan for the U.S. Patent and Trademark Office*, Washington: U.S. Patent and Trademark Office, 2000. The European figures are from European Patent Office, *Facts and Figures 2002*, Munich: European Patent Office, 2002.

129. This section is based on Sandy Streeter, *The Congressional Appropriations Process: An Introduction*, Washington: Congressional Research Service, 1999; and interviews with practitioners.

130. At least in part, this reflects the failure of the PTO to clearly articulate how the added funds would lead to improvements in the office's operations. As Representative Howard Coble has stated, "the agency will be better positioned to acquire greater appropriations if it can do a better job of demonstrating how it is using available resources to meet clearly defined objectives" (Subcommittee on Courts, the Internet, and Intellectual Property, Committee on the Judiciary, U.S. House of Representatives, "Oversight Hearing On The U.S. Patent And Trademark Office: Operations And Fiscal Year 2003 Budget," April 11, 2002, http://www.house.gov/judiciary/coble041102.htm (last visited December 24, 2003).

131. Statement of James E. Rogan, Under Secretary of Commerce for Intellectual Property and Director of the United States Patent and Trademark Office, Before the Subcommittee on Courts, the Internet, and Intellectual Property, Committee on the Judiciary, U.S. House of Representatives, Hearing on the "United States Patent and Trademark Office Fee Modernization Act Of 2003," April 3, 2003, http://www.house.gov/judiciary/rogan040303.htm (last visited December 24, 2003).

132. U.S. Patent and Trademark Office, *21st Century Strategic Plan*, Washington: U.S. Government Printing Office, 2002.

133. Stephen B. Maebius and Harold C. Wegner, "Intellectual Property's 21st Century Trojan Horse: The Rogan Billion Dollar Patent Tax," unpublished working paper, George Washington University Law School and Foley & Lardner (quote is from the unnumbered executive summary).

134. See Statement of Michael K. Kirk, Executive Director, American Intellectual Property Law Association, before the Subcommittee On Courts, the Internet, and Intellectual Property, Committee on the Judiciary, U.S. House Of Representatives, Hearing on the "United States Patent and Trademark Office Fee Modernization Act Of 2003," April 3, 2003; Statement of the Intellectual Property Owners Association, Submitted to the Subcommittee On Courts, the Internet, and Intellectual Property, Committee on the Judiciary, U.S. House Of Representatives, Hearing on the "U.S. Patent and Trademark Fee Modernization Act Of 2003," April 3, 2003. (Both are archived at http://www.house.gov/judiciary/courts040303.htm (last visited December 24, 2003).

135. Statement of Intellectual Property Owners Association, ibid.

136. Statement of Director Rogan, note 131 above.

137. P. J. Federico, editor, *Outline of the History of the United States Patent Office*, Washington, Patent Office Society, 1936, 93–94.

138. This account is from Kenneth W. Dobyns, *A History of the Early Patent Offices: The Patent Office Pony*, Fredericksburg, Va.: Sergeant Kirkland's Museum and Historical Society, 1997.

139. U.S. House of Representatives, Committee on Patents, *Report of the Investigation of the United States Patent Office Made by the President's Commission on Economy and Efficiency*, Washington; Government Printing Office, 1912, 107.

140. These issues are discussed in "Editorial: Salary Reductions of Patent Examiners," *Journal of the Patent Office Society*, 15 (1933), 407–412; and in "Report of the Executive Committee of the Patent Office Society," *Journal of the Patent Office Society*, 15 (1933), 842–856.

141. "Debate on a Bill to Increase Force and Salaries in the Patent Office," *Journal of the Patent Office Society*, 1 (1919), 588–596.

142. Vannevar Bush, *Proposals for Improving the Patent System*, Study No. 1, Subcommittee on Patents, Trademarks and Copyrights, Committee on the Judiciary, U.S. Senate, 84th Congress, 2nd Session, Washington: Government Printing Office, 1956. See especially pages 29–30.

143. The following two paragraphs are based on material reported in http://www.uspto.gov/web/offices/ac/ahrpa/ohr/jobs/exam.htm and http://www3.uspto.gov/go/jars/sgs.html, as well as interviews with current and past employees of the PTO. (Both cites last visited December 24, 2003.)

144. "Patent Professionals: A Hot Commodity," *POPA News*, 01 (February 2001), http://www.popa.org/newsletters/feb01.shtml (last visited December 24, 2003).

145. "Prepared Statement of James F. Cottone, President, National Intellectual Property Researchers Association," *Patents: Improving Quality and Curing Defects*, Subcommittee on Courts, the Internet, and Intellectual Property, Committee on the Judiciary, U.S. House of Representatives, 107th Congress, 1st Session, Washington: U.S. Government Printing Office, 2001.

146. U.S. Patent and Trademark Office, "PTO Business Plan: February 2002," http://www.uspto.gov/web/menu/fin03presidbudg1.pdf. While the rate of turnover fell in 2001 to 9 percent from the 14-percent rate in 2000 (http://www.bizjournals.com/extraedge/washingtonbureau/archive/2001/06/18/bureau2.html (last visited December 24, 2003)), this may be due more to the economic slowdown than to any increase in employee satisfaction.

147. This paragraph is based on Brenda Sandburg, "Patent Applications Flow Freely," *Legal Times*, 21 (February 22, 1999), 12, 21, and on conversations with current and former employees of the PTO.

148. Statement by David E. Martin, *Patents: Improving Quality and Curing Defects*, note 145 above, 65.

149. "Agency Pushes to Cut Actions-Per-Disposal," *POPA News*, 98 (December 1998), http://www.popa.org/newsletters/dec98.shtml (last visited December 24, 2003).

150. U.S. Department of Commerce, Office of the Inspector General, Office of Audits, *United States Patent and Trademark Office: Patent Quality Controls Are Inadequate*, Report No. PTD-9977-7-0001, Washington: U.S. Department of Commerce, 1997.

151. U.S. Patent and Trademark Office, *PTO Business Plan*, Washington: U.S. Government Printing Office, 2000, 20.

152. "Political Group Decries 'Defacto Registration System' at PTO," *POPA News*, 98 (November 1998), http://www.popa.org/newsletters/nov98.shtml (last visited December 24, 2003).

153. U.S. Patent and Trademark Office, *PTO Business Plan: February 2002*, http://www.uspoto.gov/web/menu/fin03presidbudg1.pdf, p. 12 (last visited December 24, 2003).

154. These comments are taken from Gregory Aharonian, "A Few Patent Examiners Complain About Patent Quality," *PATNEWS*, (January 28, 1999).

155. For a discussion of the difficulties that thorough searching can cause firms, see Robert O. Bolan and William C. Rooklidge, "Imputing Knowledge to Determine Willful Patent Infringement," *AIPLA Quarterly Journal*, 24 (1996), 157–190.

156. U.S. Department of Commerce, Advisory Committee on Application of Machines to Patent Office Operations, *Report*, Washington: U.S. Department of Commerce, 1954.

157. The next paragraphs are based on U.S. General Accounting Office, *ADP Acquisitions: Patent Automation Encountering Major Planning and Procurement Problems*, Report No. GAO/IMTEC-86-19, Washington: U.S. General Accounting Office, 1986, and "Statement of Ronald J. Stern, President, Patent Office Professional Association," Subcommittee on Courts and Intellectual Property, Committee on the Judiciary, U.S. House of Representatives, March 19, 1998, http://www.house.gov/judiciary/41172.htm (last visited December 24, 2003).

158. The persistence of these problems, despite Carter's reform efforts, should not be surprising for those who have studied government agencies closely. As James Q. Wilson points out, government agencies form entrenched and well defined cultures, which can be very hard for appointed leaders or legislators to change. See the discussion in *Bureaucracy*, New York: Basic Books, 1989.

159. U.S. General Accounting Office, *Patent and Trademark Office: Key Processes for Managing Automated Patent System Development are Weak*, Report No. GAO/AIMD-93-15, Washington: U.S. General Accounting Office, 1993.

160. These accounts are based on Cindy Skrzycki, "System's Trademark: Have a Slow Day," *Washington Post*, (November 19, 1999), E1; "New Automated Tools a Mess for Patent Searches," *POPA News*, 99 (November 1999), http://www.popa.org/newsletters/mov99.shtml (last visited December 24, 2003); U.S. Department of Commerce, Office of the Inspector General, Office of Systems Evaluation, *United States Patent and Trademark Office: Search System Problems Being*

Addressed, but Improvements Needed for Future Systems, Report No. OSE-12679, Washington: U.S. Department of Commerce, 2001.

161. See the complaints, for instance, in Gregory Aharonian, "Fire PTO Librarian," *PATNEWS*, (June 1, 1999); "PTO Commissioner's On-Line Discussion with PTO Examiners," *PATNEWS*, (March 17, 2000); and Gregory Aharonian, "Problems at the PTO Library," *PATNEWS*, (May 28, 1999).

162. Cecil D. Quillen, Jr. and Ogden H. Webster, "Continuing Patent Applications and Performance of the U.S. Patent Office," *Federal Circuit Bar Journal*, 11 (August 2001), 1–21; and Cecil Quillen, Ogden Webster, and Richard Eichmann, "Continuing Patent Applications and Performance of the U.S. Patent and Trademark Office—Extended," *Federal Circuit Bar Journal*, 12 (August 2002), 35–55.

163. For critiques of Quillen's methodology, see George A. Clarke, "U.S. Continuity Law and Its Impact on the Comparative Patenting Rates of the U.S., Japan, and the European Patent Office," *Journal of the Patent and Trademark Office Society*, 85 (2003), 335–349; and U.S. Patent and Trademark Office, "Comments on 'The Effects of Continuing Patent Applications,' " unpublished manuscript, 2003.

164. Both growth rates were calculated by the authors using data provided by Dominique Guellec, Division of Science, Technology and Industry, Organization for Economic Cooperation and Development, Paris, April 2003.

165. Gregory Aharonian, "How Totally Technically Incompetent is the Patent Office?," *PATNEWS*, (April 14, 2000).

166. Yukihiko Takada and Kiyonobu Matsumoto, "Development of Advanced Hitachi Electronic Patent Application System Toward a New Patent Age of Improved Support for the Operation of an Intellectual Property Department," *Journal of the Patent and Trademark Office Society*, 74 (1992), 315–334.

167. Quoted in Robert X. Cringley, "There's No Tomorrow—How One Man is Trying to Take Time Out of Derivative Securities Trading," http://www.pbs.org /cringely/pulpit/pulpit20010726.html (last visited December 24, 2003). See also http://www.nextrade.org (last visited April 14, 2004).

168. Ibid.

169. Eric W. Pfeiffer, "Setting Patent Traps," *Forbes ASAP*, 169, (June 24, 2002), 65–73. This paragraph is also based on Teresa Riordan, "Stockpiling Technologies that Allow Telephones and Computers to Talk to Each Other," *New York Times*, (October 31, 1994), D2.

170. See, for example, Ariel S. Pakes, "Patents as Options: Some Estimates of the Value of Holding European Patent Stocks," *Econometrica*, 54 (1986), 755–784; and Dietmar Harhoff, et al., "Citation Frequency and the Value of Patented Inventions," *Review of Economics and Statistics*, 81 (1999), 511–515.

171. Patents 5,380,237, and 6,467,180, respectively.

172. American Intellectual Property Law Association, *Report of Economic Survey 2001*, Washington: AIPLA, 2001.

173. This paragraph is based on N. Thane Bauz, "U.S. Patent Examination: Recommendation for Change Based Upon a Comparative Study of German Law," *Creighton Law Review*, 27 (1994), 945–984; and Allan M. Soobert, "Breaking New Ground in Administrative Revocation of U.S. Patents: A Proposition for Opposition—and Beyond," *Santa Clara Computer and High Technology Law Journal*, 14 (1998), 63–187.

174. "Patent and Trademark System Reform," *Weekly Compilation of Presidential Documents*, 16 (December 12, 1980), 2803.

175. Mark D. Janis, "Inter Parties Patent Reexamination," *Fordham Intellectual Property, Media and Entertainment Law Journal*, 10 (2000), 481–499. The quote is on page 485.

176. The data is taken from the PTO's annual reports. The tabulation does not include re-examinations initiated by patent awardees, since the motivation for such requests is fundamentally different than the others.

177. Stuart J. H. Graham, Bronwyn H. Hall, Dietmar Harhoff, and David C. Mowery, "Post-Issue Patent 'Quality Control': A Comparative Study of U.S. Patent Re-examinations and European Patent Oppositions," in Wesley Cohen and Stephen Merrill, editors, *Intellectual Property in the Knowledge-Based Economy*, Washington: National Academies Press, 2003, 74–119.

178. *Congressional Record*, 143 (April 17, 1997), H1668.

179. In 1999, the U.S. Congress, recognizing this problem, allowed the PTO to begin publishing applications after eighteen months, assuming the same patent had been filed abroad as well.

180. Graham, et al., note 177 above.

181. Evidence in support of the claim that small firms suffer disproportionately from strategic patent behavior can be found in such analyses as Jean O. Lanjouw and Josh Lerner, "Tilting the Table? The Use of Preliminary Injunctions," *Journal of Law and Economics*, 44 (2001), 573–603; and Josh Lerner, "Patenting in the Shadow of Competitors," *Journal of Law and Economics*, 38 (1995), 563–595.

182. For the campaign against these reforms, see Teresa Riordan, "A Proposal to Overhaul Patent Law Has One Congressman Hopping Mad About the Changes," *New York Times*, (April 14, 1997), D7.

183. "The Ominous Attack on American Inventors," *The Phyllis Schlafly Report*, 38, (March 1998) (archived at http://www.eagleforum.org/psr/1998/mar98/psrmar98.html (last visited December 24, 2003)).

184. William B. Yeats, "The Second Coming," *Michael Robartes and The Dancer*, Dublin: Cuala Press, 1921.

185. Saul Hansell, "Spending It; A Card for Borrowing From Yourself," *New York Times*, (August 27, 1995), C6.

186. http://www.eagleforum.org/patent/nobel_letter.html (last visited December 24, 2003).

187. This test was widely seen as having been imposed by the Supreme Court in its decision in *Cuno Corp. v. Automatic Devices Corp.*, 314 U.S. 84 (1941). For

a history of this provision, see *Graham, et al. v. John Deere Co. of Kansas City, et al.*, 383 U.S. 1 (1966).

188. For classic expositions of these arguments, see George Stigler, "The Economic Theory of Regulation," *Bell Journal of Economics*, 2 (1971), 3–21; and Gary S. Becker, "A Theory of Competition Among Pressure Groups for Political Influence," *Quarterly Journal of Economics*, 98 (1983), 371–400.

189. Macedo exhaustively examined the policies in other nations in 1988, and determined that the Philippines was the only other nation with a "first-to-invent" system (Charles Macedo, "First-to-File: Is the American Adoption of the International Standard in Patent Law Worth the Price?," *Columbia Business Law Review*, 1988 (1988), 543–586). Since then, the Philippines has switched to a "first-to-file" system (The Intellectual Property Act of the Philippines, Republic Act No. 8293, Part II: The Law on Patents, chapter III, section 29).

190. Various explanations are reviewed in Sean T. Carnathan, "Patent Priority Disputes—A Proposed Re-Definition of 'First-to-Invent,' " *Alabama Law Review*, 49 (1998), 755–815. The account of the Rumsey-Fitch controversy is based on Edward C. Walterscheid, "Priority of Invention: How the U.S. Came to Have a 'First-to-Invent' System," *AIPLA Quarterly Journal*, 23 (1995), 263–319.

191. President's Commission on the Patent System, *"To Promote the Progress of ... Useful Arts" in an Age of Exploding Technology*, Washington: U.S. Government Printing Office, 1966, 6.

192. Ian A. Calvert, "An Overview of Interference Practice," *Journal of the Patent Office Society*, 62 (May 1980), 290–308.

193. The case in question was *Parks v. Fine*, 773 F.2d 1577 (Fed. Cir. 1985), a judgment that the court modified at 783 F.2d 1036 (Fed. Cir. 1986).

194. Paul F. Morgan, "So You Think You Want to Get Into an Interference? Some Things You should be Aware of First," *Journal of the Patent and Trademark Office Society*, 74 (1992), 303–314.

195. William Kingston, "Is the United States Right about 'First-to-Invent'?," *European Intellectual Property Review*, 7 (1992), 223–226.

196. These figures are somewhat dated, being based on the years 1992 to 1994. The last published compilation of these statistics is Ian A. Calvert and Michael Sofocleous, "Interference Statistics for Fiscal Years 1992 to 1994," *Journal of the Patent and Trademark Office Society*, 76 (1995), 417–422.

197. Figure 6.2 is based on the PTO's annual reports.

198. Advisory Commission on Patent Law Reform, *A Report to the Secretary of Commerce*, Washington: Government Printing Office, 1992.

199. World Intellectual Property Organization, "Draft Treaty Supplementing the Paris Convention for the Protection of Industrial Property as Far as Patents are Concerned," United Nations Document PLT/DC/3, Article 21.

200. John R. Emshwiller, "Patent-Law Proposals Irk Small Inventors," *Wall Street Journal*, (April 30, 1992), B1.

201. These features are discussed in George E. Frost, "The 1967 Patent Law Debate: First-to-Invent vs. First-to-File," *Duke Law Journal*, 1967 (1967), 923–942.

202. See the anecdotes related, for instance, in Bernarr R. Pravell, "Why the United States Should Adopt the First-to-File System for Patents," *St. Mary's Law Journal*, 22 (1991), 797–811.

203. Sabra Chartrand, "Facing High-Tech Issues, New Patents Chief is Reinventing a Staid Agency," *New York Times*, (July 14, 1995), A17.

204. For a chronology, see Robert W. Pritchard, "The Future is Now—The Case for Patent Harmonization," *North Carolina Journal of International Law and Commercial Regulation*, 20 (1995), 291–328.

205. Kim Taylor, "Patent Harmonization Treaty Negotiations on Hold: The 'First to File' Debate Continues," *Journal of Contemporary Law*, 20 (1994), 521–545 (see the discussion on pages 524 and 525).

206. Coe A. Bloomberg, "In Defense of the First-to-Invent Rule," *AIPLA Quarterly Journal*, 21 (1993), 255–263.

207. See, for instance, the representative calculations in Charles R. B. Macedo, "First-to-File: Is the American Adoption of the International Standard in Patent Law Worth the Price?," *Columbia Business Law Review*, 1988 (1988), 543–586.

208. This is not a new problem. For instance, in the 1850s, patent lawyers and lawyers led a concerted effort to encourage the patent office to be more permissive in granting patents. The arguments were largely articulated in *Scientific American* magazine, whose publishers also operated the largest patent agency in the world at the time. These efforts were successful: the rejection rate of patent applications fell by more than one-half over the decade. For a discussion, see Robert C. Post, " 'Liberalizers' versus 'Scientific Men' in the Antebellum Patent Office," *Technology and Culture*, 17 (1976), 24–54.

209. Ronald W. Clark, *Einstein: The Life and Times*, London: Hodder and Stoughton, 1973.

210. Mark Lemley, "Rational Ignorance at the Patent Office," Public Law and Legal Theory Working Paper No. 46, School of Law, University of California at Berkeley, 2001.

211. Dan Burk and Mark Lemley, "Is Patent Law Technology Specific?," Public Law and Legal Theory Research Paper No. 106, School of Law, University of California at Berkeley

212. 35 U.S.C. § 122(c); 37 C.F.R. § 1.291.

213. 35 U.S.C. § 301.

214. Samuel Kortum and Josh Lerner, "Stronger Protection or Technological Revolution: What is Behind the Recent Surge in Patenting?," *Carnegie-Rochester Conference Series on Public Policy*, 48 (1998), 247–304 and "Unraveling the Patent Paradox," unpublished working paper, University of Minnesota and Harvard University, 2003.

215. Graham, et al., note 177 above.

216. The Advisory Commission on Patent Law Reform, "A Report to the Secretary of Commerce," August 1992.

217. The prohibition on evidence previously considered by the examiner derived from a CAFC decision under the pre-AIPA procedure in which re-examination could be initiated by the PTO but excluded third parties (*In re Portola Packaging*, 110 F.3d 786 (Fed. Cir. 1997)). Congress could have overruled this decision in the AIPA, but chose not to. A law passed by Congress and signed by President Bush in 2003 finally overturned this decision.

218. These and other issues related to improving the re-examination process are discussed in "Patents: Improving Quality and Curing Defects," Hearing before the Subcommittee on Courts, the Internet and Intellectual Property, Committee on the Judiciary of the House of Representatives, May 10, 2001.

219. We should also note that as part of the AIPA, the U.S. Congress stipulated a two-month window in which others can submit prior art after patent applications are published. No one seems to do so, because (a) not all applications are published, (b) many parties are still unaware of this provision, and (c) people do not want to limit their ability to use prior art in subsequent litigation.

220. Statement of Ronald J. Stern, President, Patent Office Professional Association, Submitted to the Subcommittee on Courts, the Internet, and Intellectual Property, Committee on the Judiciary, U.S. House of Representatives, Hearing on "The U.S. Patent and Trademark Fee Modernization Act of 2003," April 3, 2003.

221. Statement of Michael K. Kirk, Executive Director, American Intellectual Property Law Association, before the Subcommittee On Courts, the Internet, and Intellectual Property, Committee on the Judiciary, U.S. House Of Representatives, Hearing on the "United States Patent and Trademark Office Fee Modernization Act Of 2003," April 3, 2003; Statement of the Intellectual Property Owners Association, Submitted to the Subcommittee On Courts, the Internet, and Intellectual Property, Committee on the Judiciary, U.S. House Of Representatives, Hearing on the "U.S. Patent and Trademark Fee Modernization Act Of 2003," April 3, 2003.

222. 35 U.S.C. § 282.

223. *Markman v. Westview Instruments, Inc.*, 52 F.3d 967 (Fed Cir. 1995).

224. Dan Burk and Mark Lemley, "Is Patent Law Technology Specific?," Public Law and Legal Theory Research Paper No. 106, School of Law, University of California at Berkeley.

225. James Bessen and Robert M. Hunt, "An Empirical Look at Software Patents," unpublished working paper, Research on Innovation and Federal Reserve Bank of Philadelphia, 2003.

226. Burk and Lemley argue that the very logic that allows the CAFC to judge a sketchy description of what software might do as satisfying the enablement requirement will, inevitably, lead the court to judge many of the software patents currently being granted by the PTO to be invalid on the grounds of obvious-

ness. Of course, it would be far preferable not to grant all those valid patents to begin with.

227. James Bessen and Eric Maskin, "Sequential Innovation, Patents, and Imitation," Working Paper No. 00–01, Department of Economics, Massachusetts Institute of Technology, 2001.

228. See, e.g., http://www.gnu.org/philosophy/savingeurope.html or http://www.free patents.org/ (both last visited January 2, 2004).

229. For a discussion of historical disputes over patenting in the auto, aircraft, semiconductor and computer industries that bear much resemblance to the current software and business methods controversies, see Robert P. Merges and Richard R. Nelson, "On the Complex Economics of Patent Scope," *Columbia Law Review*, 90 (1990), 839–916.

230. http://www.uspto.gov/web/offices/com/sol/actionplan.html (last visited January 2, 2004).

231. Burk and Lemley argue that this uniformity is something of an illusion, because the CAFC interprets the uniform rules differently in different industries.

232. The rationale for the act (more formally known as the Drug Price Competition and Patent Term Restoration Act of 1984) was to ensure that each new drug had a minimum period during which it was on the market and protected by patent coverage. While the act called for these extensions to be reviewed and granted in a formal process by the PTO, the introduction of special legislation geared towards particular drugs soon followed.

233. Charles Babcock, "Patent Fight Tests Drug Firm's Clout: Claritin Maker Goes All Out in Congress" *Washington Post*, (October 30, 1999), A1.

234. Sheryl Gay Stolberg, "A Capitol Hill Mystery: Who Aided Drug Maker?," *New York Times*, (November 29, 2002), A35.

Index

Page references followed by *fig* indicate an illustrated figure.